Purchasing Manager
Aide-Memoire

Purchasing Manager Aide-Memoire

Second edition

Ian Eglin

First published 2010
This edition published in 2011 by Egism. Baildon, UK.

Copyright © 2010, 2011 by Ian Eglin
British Library Cataloguing in Publication Data.
A catalogue record for this book is available from the British Library

ISBN 978-0-9566022-1-3

Typesetting and cover design by www.wordzworth.com

Also available in hardback.

For Henry & Madeleine
(more precisely, their college fees)

Aide-memoire are notes or memoranda taken and used to jog the memory at a later point in time. The term was used in the British diplomatic service and tactical aide-memoire (TAM) are still used by British armed forces, particularly by junior army officers who use them to remember sequences of orders.

Thanks to Mark Simpson MCIPS for his advice and support.

Contents

Preface

Do you ever read 400 page purchasing textbooks that seem to be exercises in writing lots of vague theoretical points but with very little practical content? If so, you're not alone. Hopefully, this book is different. It is written not as an academic work but as practical guide for people directly employed in purchasing and related roles.

The book covers most of the main subjects that you are likely to come across as a purchasing manager or buyer in general industry. Some of the topics raised will have a wider business application and may be of interest to managers of purchasing staff or from other business functions. It is predominantly UK focused, particularly the sections relating to the legal aspects of buying. Topic lengths are short and to the point. The aim is to provide you with a broad perspective of the subject and yet provide practical solutions and techniques for specific purchasing issues or problems.

Subject matter has been based for the most part on practical experience. The experience of someone who has read the books, studied the subject, but whose main knowledge comes from over 20 years working as a buyer and purchasing manager in British industry.

Hopefully, it will confirm many of the things you already knew or suspected but never had the time to research. Sometimes, it may bring to your attention styles and practices that you were either not aware of or had dismissed as irrelevant.

It is unashamedly written from the perspective of the purchaser. In general, it takes the standpoint of a manager, but sometimes it takes the perspective of the more junior member of staff. It contains a lot of facts and in parts it can be hard going. For that reason I have tried to drop in quirky quotes and opinion. Not all of the quotes or opinions are meant to be taken too seriously.

If you do find the book useful or otherwise, I would welcome your comments at eeglen@toucansurf.com

"Be careful in dealing with a man who cares nothing for comfort or promotion, but is simply determined to do what he believes to be right. He is a dangerous uncomfortable enemy, because his body, which you can always conquer, gives you little purchase upon his soul".
Gilbert Murray

Changing Purchasing in a Changing World

Globalisation

"Who moved my cheese" Dr Spencer Johnson

Globalisation, the integration of the world's economies through the free movement of people, capital and technology; has had a profound effect on the UK economy and how UK companies do business. During the last 20 years globalisation has almost certainly accelerated due to the wide adoption of liberal economic, political and social policies which have been in large part propagated by the information technology revolution and the growth of truly multinational corporations.

In addition to, or more likely as a result of globalisation, there have been two significant changes in the world economic order. First there was the disintegration of the Soviet bloc and secondly the marked shift in industrial and economic power to the developing countries of Asia.

In the Soviet Union, political and social change, summed up by the terms 'glasnost' (openness) and 'perestroika' (restructuring), ended the economic division of Europe. As a result the effective size of the European trading area increased by 300 million people but more significantly it opened up to trade a number of low labour cost countries in the heart of Europe. Secondly, and perhaps more significantly, the rapid industrial growth of developing countries, particularly China, shifted the industrial fulcrum of the world firmly toward the East. To put this into perspective, in 1973 China represented about 1% of world GDP by 2010 China represents about 10% of world GDP and is growing at a rate of about 10% per annum. China is now the world's largest exporter with 9.6% of total world trade in 2009 and is the world's second largest economy.

The principle effect of these changes has been to engage vast and previously untapped low cost labour into the global economy. According to the IMF, the global workforce has increased fourfold during the last 2 decades. Multinationals and even modest sized companies have rushed to move production from the UK and other western countries to places like China to take advantage of the lower labour costs.

Meanwhile governments in the developed world have taken a liberal economic attitude toward open trade, particularly with China. Markets in the west have been the source of China's export led growth, resulting in a trade surplus of about US$200 billion in 2009. At the same time, the UK and other developed countries have taken a very relaxed view of the decline in their own manufacturing industry. Indeed, it could be argued that industry has been wilfully neglected whilst government has spent most of its time pre-occupied with domestic welfare and rights issues.

What has this meant for the UK economy? Some historical comparisons put matters into context. In 1973, the UK accounted for 6% of world GDP and manufacturing represented 30% of the UK economy. In 2010, the UK accounted for less than 4% of world GDP and manufacturing only about 12% of the UK economy. Unsurprisingly in 2008 the UK had a trade deficit of £94 billion.

The main response of what remains of UK industry has been to consolidate and attempt to reduce costs. Companies have sought to do this by concentrating on their core business activities, using low cost sources of supply and employing new organizational methodologies. In practical terms it has led to policies such as: offshoring, outsourcing, low cost country sourcing and lean type manufacturing.

- Offshoring is the wholesale transfer of businesses to low costs countries. The most obvious example of this being the use of overseas call centres but increasingly UK manufacturing companies are moving production overseas to low cost countries. A prime example of this being Dyson moving to Malaysia in 2002. More recently we have seen companies moving manufacturing facilities from the UK to low labour cost EU countries, such as Kraft moving confectionary production from the UK to Poland and Slovakia.

- Outsourcing is the contracting out of business functions or operations to third party suppliers or providers. It has been of growing importance to companies seeking to concentrate on core business activities. Like offshoring, it is driven by the need to cut costs but unlike offshoring, it tends to derive its cost benefits from using specialists rather than simply low cost labour.
- Low cost country sourcing is the strategy of purchasing raw materials and components from countries with lower labour and production costs but continuing to assemble product in the home country. Generally the higher the labour-content of a component, the greater the potential savings.
- Organisational improvements. Companies have sought to reduce costs through improved organizational efficiency. To achieve this they have embraced various consultancy fads and introduced new manufacturing methods such as lean manufacturing, TQM, six sigma, and JIT amongst others. The success of these largely imported management theories has been mixed. Anecdotal evidence suggests that the most successful transplants of these methods into western industry have been by subsidiaries of Japanese companies. It seems that the presence of Japanese management is an important factor in their success.

So where does purchasing fit in? The answer is that the success of all of these policies relies to a large extent upon successful purchasing and materials control.

Unfortunately, many traditional purchasing departments have not always had the wider skill set needed to manage these new strategies and additional responsibilities. The wider skill set needed by purchasing professionals in these changed circumstances includes:

- The willingness to do much more overseas travel and be effective in dealing with overseas suppliers and logistics.
- The ability to play a more active role in the internal operations of the business and in particular the capability to lead multidisciplinary supply chain focused project teams.

The adoption of additional responsibilities has not always been an easy transition for either purchasing staff or for other functions within the company. From the point of view of the purchasing professional, overseas travel has historically been the exception and not the norm as most purchasing staff are typically stay at home people. Secondly, purchasing staff tend to be comfortable managing suppliers but not so comfortable or accomplished managing cross functional teams of their peers.

From a wider organisational point of view, purchasing has traditionally been viewed as a relatively minor service function. Typically reporting through the production or finance departments; it has generally been a low status subordinate function. Consequently, some companies have found it difficult to accommodate a higher status for purchasing staff within the organization or to recognise the additional responsibilities with greater resources and higher pay.

Nevertheless, some companies have recognised the widening role and importance of the purchasing function by adapting it to the changed circumstances. This has included elevating the status of the department and by creating specialists aligned to specific business needs. It is now increasingly common to find buyers specialising in a particular role such as strategy, new product introduction, overseas buying or commodity specialist.

Some companies have gone a step further and adopted the concept of supply chain management (SCM). In most companies this typically means that the functions of planning, purchasing, material's control and outbound logistics are grouped together under one manager. In the changeover, purchasing departments have become supply chain management departments and purchasing managers have become supply chain managers.

For the company, the concept of a single supply chain manager, controlling all aspects of material control and supply chain relationships is logically appealing. From the board of directors' standpoint, it means they can look to a single person who is ultimately responsible for coordinating company planning and supply. Production departments find it particularly appealing because it allows them to lose responsibility for logistics and to concentrate purely on production matters.

However, the successful adoption of supply chain management within companies has sometimes been hampered by:

- Insufficient business planning, in particular identification and provision of the resources necessary to effectively manage the wider range of activities and responsibilities.
- Insufficient numbers of qualified and experienced staff with a broad range of practical experience and management skills to successfully fulfil this highly demanding role.

In practice, unless the role of supply chain manager is adequately supported by specialist managers in the fields of purchasing, customer services, warehousing, planning and logistics, its scope is probably too wide to be effectively controlled by one manager.

In summary, the rapid changes in the world economy we are living through present great opportunities for ambitious purchasing professionals. To succeed often requires more than the traditional purchasing of yesteryear and in some instances greater personal commitment. However, purchasing will become more varied and rewarding if we as a profession can rise to the challenge.

Why purchasing

"The harder I work the luckier I get". Samuel Goldwyn

Not so long ago, purchasing was regarded as a staid administrative type of activity, populated by solid dependable types (if not a little dour). They were the steady full backs of the business, clearing the ball up the field to the midfield players in the production departments who then worked the ball onto the centre forward sales force who went on to score the goal and claim the glory.

The traditional role of purchasing, could be summed up as; the right product, in the right quantity, at the right place, at the right time, at the right price. If you got these elements right you were 99% home.

However, times have moved on and new business theories have been developed that emphasize a more prominent role for purchasing. At the same time, improved IT systems have freed up buyers from a number of their traditional time intensive administrative duties. The result is that whilst still retaining the core responsibilities of traditional purchasing, the nature and scope of purchasing have become much more strategic and wider than previous. Purchasing is being re-appraised in the light of these 'strategic' opportunities and is now being judged on its ability to shape business fortunes and create value for the company. If proof were needed of this change just look at the number of job advertisements for purchasing managers were companies are looking for people with experience of 'strategic' buying.

There are some good business reasons why purchasing and effective buying have been re-assessed and is now taken seriously by senior managers and boards of directors alike.

It is now recognized that purchased goods and services are often the single largest item of a company's costs. Indeed, it is not uncommon for manufacturing companies to spend 50 – 60% of their total revenues on bought-out goods and services. In some industries, such as the airline industry individual commodities can represent a sizeable proportion of the company's costs. In 2009 British Airway's fuel bill rose to £3 billion on total revenues of nearly £9 billion. It is not surprising that the dramatic increase in fuel prices during that year contributed significantly to the losses posted by British Airways.

Not only do purchasing operations account for the largest share of company expenditure but the growing popularity of sub-contracting and outsourcing of business operations has resulted in companies becoming ever more reliant upon suppliers for day to day operations. The move toward greater sub-contracting and outsourcing is a response to growing specialization in markets and the perceived need of business to concentrate on core activities. The direct result of this trend has been to increase the ratio of purchasing spend to total company revenues and to transfer the responsibility for activities previously performed by the likes of internal production departments to the purchasing departments.

Unlike most functions of the business, purchasing can directly affect the bottom line profit through its buying operations. If a company spends 50% of its total sales revenue on bought out materials and the purchasing department reduces the cost of bought out materials by 10% the company will gross 5% greater profit. To put this in perspective, if the company makes a 10% profit margin, sales would have to increase by 50% to achieve the same impact on the bottom line profit.

There has also been a growing recognition that in the context of globalisation and increasing business specialisation, success more than ever before is dependent on having the right suppliers and effectively managing their contribution to your company's market competitiveness. This belief has been behind the growing interest in partnership sourcing one of the methods that have proved so successful for the large Japanese car companies.

In summary, purchasing staff have never had a better opportunity to contribute to the success of their organisations and in doing so enhancing their reputation, status and pay. When boards of directors look around their organisations for the best person to lead lean manufacturing programs and integrate their supply chains, the people who often have the most relevant skills and knowledge of the issues are the purchasers.

Purchasing responsibilities

"As I grow older, I pay less attention to what men say, I just watch what they do". Andrew Carnegie

Traditionally purchasing was treated as an administrative function whose principle purpose was to organise the flow of materials into the company, and providing other business functions with a service. However, as the function has developed and the demands of business have increased, the profession has responded by widening the range and complexity of tasks undertaken.

It is possible to identify these stages in the development of purchasing as; traditional or transactional, tactical and strategic purchasing.

Transactional purchasing

Task orientated purchasing, largely reactive with little or no long term planning. Tasks could include:

- Defining and setting up a purchasing procedure.
- Identifying immediate company materials requirements.
- Identifying potential suppliers.
- Supplier selection.
- Sending purchase enquiries to suppliers.
- Performing bid analysis on quotations.
- Negotiation with suppliers to achieve 5 rights (right price, right quantity, right quality, right place and right time).
- Issuing purchase orders and spot buying.
- Progressing purchase orders.
- Contract administration.
- Resolving supplier disputes.
- Managing supplier warranty claims.
- Manage purchasing staff to ensure they meet basic purchasing standards.
- Maintaining up to date computer records for suppliers and prices.
- Maintain stock records and stock accuracy.
- Vendor rate suppliers and maintain any records for ISO accreditation.

Tactical purchasing

This is a proactive form of purchasing. Tactical purchasing activities could include:

- Actively managing staff on proactive projects in addition to routine day to day tasks.
- Developing commodity buying and encourage deepening of skills and specialists.

- Identifying and utilising individual team member skills and creating personal development plans. Tailoring training programs to individual staff requirements.
- Identifying and actively manage important product categories.
- Identifying and actively managing key suppliers.
- Carrying out risk assessment and developing fall back plans in case a key supplier fails.
- Actively seeking to identify and develop new sources of supply, new products and processes.
- Investigating and if possible developing group buying opportunities.
- Researching supply markets, identifying medium and long term risks to supply.
- Putting in place department objectives and targets. Regularly reviewing purchasing methods and operating costs and setting cost reduction targets.
- Setting key performance indicators, monitoring and using market research to inform purchasing decisions.
- Being involved at the outset of new products to guide sales and technical departments on the best materials and bought-out products.
- Driving standardization and simplification of products with other departments. Using value analysis and value engineering (VA / VE) methods.
- Holding regular forums with staff to discuss purchasing issues, performance and direction.

Strategic purchasing

This concentrates on broader issues and long term alignment of purchasing activities with the needs of the company. Strategies could include:

- Identifying suppliers that could provide competitive advantage, developing partnership relations with them and setting up long term collaborative ventures.

- Setting long term purchasing objectives to match long term company objectives.
- Rationalizing the supplier based and consolidating purchasing spending power.
- Providing the company the option of outsourcing non-core business functions.
- A decision to resource key materials, components or production overseas.
- Choice and developing integrated supply chain and IT systems.
- Reorganisation of the purchasing function.
- Succession planning.

Purchasing manager's checklist

"If you've got them by the balls their hearts and minds will follow". John Wayne

Just as you would expect a salesman to know certain basic information about his products, his customers and his prices, so it is normal for your boss to expect a purchasing manager to know certain information relating to the purchasing department. Below are some examples of what your boss may reasonably expect you to know:

- Do you know how much your organization is spending on goods and services per annum? Has it increased or decreased over the last 12 months? If there has been a large change in spend what are the reasons for the change?
- Who are the key suppliers? How much does the company spend with them? What is the proportion of your spend to their total sales? What management strategies are in place to maximize the benefits and minimize the risk associated with using each of the suppliers? Which suppliers do you expect to spend more with during the coming year and why? Which suppliers do you expect to spend less with and why?

- Which commodities or product groups does your company spend most on? What are the main factors influencing the price of each of commodity groups? Are you able to monitor the movement of these factors? Can you accurately forecast the movement of these inputs?
- Which individual parts are critical to your business? Why are they important? What are the risks associated with these parts? How do you manage the risks?
- Which parts or commodities are supplied by single source suppliers? What strategies do you employ to control the power of these suppliers? Have you researched alternative sources of supply, parts or commodities?
- What are the risks when buying each of the categories? Have you graded the risks? If problems arise with your suppliers that cannot be overcome, do you have fall back arrangements?
- How is supplier performance measured? How do you compare the performance between different suppliers?
- How are outsourced suppliers managed?
- How are new suppliers identified? How are they assessed and qualified?
- How do you decide what should be bought-out and what should be manufactured in-house?
- What percentage of spend is made by non-purchasing staff? What procedures are used to monitor and control delegated buying?
- Who is in the purchasing team? What are their skills and experience? Are they employed to their full effect?
- What targets do you set your team? How do you measure and record staff performance?
- Is the purchasing department organized in its most effective way? If not, what is stopping change? How can you make the necessary changes?
- Do you have a medium or long term purchasing strategy? Is it compatible with the organization's business strategy?

- What factors limit the effectiveness of the purchasing team? How do you plan to overcome any limits on the purchasing department's effectiveness?

Signs that the purchasing performance is underperforming:

- Basic purchasing information is patchy and or unreliable.
- Procedures are disregarded or non-existent.
- Different buyers doing similar jobs use different systems.
- There are no regular reviews of purchasing activity or performance.
- Too much time is spent on areas of little or no cost advantage.
- Regular invoice queries occur caused by price discrepancies.
- Buyers spend the majority of their time on routine paperwork.
- Buyers seldom visit existing or new potential suppliers.
- There never seems to be time for proactive projects.
- Buyers claim to be 'snowed under' with work.
- Suppliers never change and there is resistance to change them.
- There is no structure of purchasing leadership or reporting.
- Buyers do not have or know their individual objectives
- There is no understanding amongst staff of overall purchasing objectives.
- Deliveries are regularly late, quality problems are repeated and prices appear to rise every year.
- Other departments consider that the purchasing department is unresponsive and detached.
- Morale in purchasing is low, maybe reflected in high turnover of younger staff.

Key performance indicators (KPIs)

"An ounce of performance is worth pounds of promises".
Mae West

It is important to measure both supplier performances and the performance of your purchasing organization. Most measures should be recorded and reported on a monthly basis both to your boss, possibly the board of directors and as feedback to the purchasing team. Supplier performance measures can have a number of uses:

- To allow effective management of suppliers, by identifying areas where performance is below standard and need to be improved.
- Can be used as a point of negotiation by identifying strengths and weaknesses.
- They will help identify suppliers for removal from approved suppliers list.
- May have commercial or legal implications in a performance measured contract, for example service level agreements or liquidated damages.
- Previous measures of performance can indicate a trend and may be used in setting future targets or contract terms.

To be effective and workable, supplier performance measures should be:

- A true indicator of a valuable attribute. Identifying what matters to the business.
- Easily measurable and doesn't take too much time or money to collect data.
- Easily understood and accepted by the supplier.
- Realistic, targets should serve to motivate the supplier not demotivate.
- Wholly or mainly within the supplier's control.
- Assessed at pre-determined, regular intervals. Records must be kept for future reference.
- Periodically reviewed for relevance and cost effectiveness.

Measures of supplier performance

- Prices benchmarked against: the last price paid, competitive quotations or a recognized market index.
- Deliveries on time in full. Measure against contracted to delivery date.
- Lead time requirements including time to market for developing new products.
- The quality of goods. Measures may include the number of non-conformances registered against suppliers or could be measured as defect rate per thousand/million.
- Service levels. Supplier response times, availability of staff, quality of service.
- The number of customer complaints related to supplies or services rendered by suppliers.

Measures of purchasing department performance

- Price compared to the last price paid, against a budget estimate, against standard cost or other accounting measure.
- The level of ancillary spend (delivery, certification, packing costs)
- Aggregated savings, to give the cost saving benefit over a period of time.
- The cost of operating the purchasing department.
- The response time for sales or estimating enquiries.
- The number of active or inactive suppliers.
- Total purchase orders placed over a period.
- The average purchase order value.
- The percentage of customer commitments controlled through the purchasing department rather than informally within the rest of the organization.
- The number of purchase orders overdue for ordering.
- Purchasing cycle time e.g. time to process a requisition.
- The total number of orders or order lines placed.
- Orders delivered on time and in full.

- Parts not available at due date or kitting date.
- The number of quality non-conformances notes (NCN) registered against the purchasing department or suppliers.
- Clear up and cash recovery rates for supplier warranty claims.
- The number of invoices not supported by a valid purchase order (leakage rate).

Measures of stock management

- Average stock = starting stock level + finishing stock level /2
- Stock turn = cost of goods / average stock
- Stock days = (stock / cost of sales) x 365
- Percentage obsolete and slow moving stock to total stock.

What is strategic purchasing?

"In the long run we are all dead". John Maynard Keynes

The term 'strategic purchasing' is an over-used term, apart from anything else it sounds very impressive, but trying to pin down what strategic purchasing is, is not an easy task. Definitions are not much use as they tend to be unclear, use lots of jargon and are almost exclusively different. It seems that everybody has their own idea of what strategic purchasing is or what it is not and everyone is agreed on wanting to practice it.

Strategic purchasing to my mind means a planned course of action which has some long term aim, which will have an important impact to the way purchasing is conducted within the business and which could have a significant impact on the organisation. A clear distinction should be drawn between purely operational buying decisions and strategic buying. Strategic buying is not concerned with day to day issues but with the long term organisation of the purchasing function and the management of suppliers.

Strategic purchasing decisions may include:

- A decision to change from a decentralised purchasing organisation to a centralised or vice versa.
- A decision to develop partnerships with key suppliers.
- A decision to out-source key functions or elements of the manufacturing process.
- Agreeing to fix the price of a key component for a long period.
- A decision to rationalise the supplier base.
- A decision to change the materials planning system.
- A decision to resource company critical supplies.
- A decision to switch from domestic to overseas suppliers.
- Decisions that have serious ramifications on other functions, for example, introducing bar coding would affect stores and possibly production.
- Decisions that permanently change the need for resources in the purchasing department or another department.

Setting a purchasing strategy

Your purchasing strategy should be compatible and reflect the wider needs of the company. The starting point is therefore a broad analysis of the company's position in the market, its current organisation and its goals. Sometimes this is easy to establish because companies publish their long term aims, vision and goals; this is often the case with publicly listed companies. In other cases, especially in small to medium enterprises (SMEs), plans are not generally made public and sometimes even senior managers are not briefed as to the long term strategy of the company. In this case, consider the 'mission statement', which most companies now have as part of their quality procedures. However, mission statements are often not that helpful because they are too broad in their aims and objectives to be of any practical worth.

Of course the most direct way of aligning purchasing and company strategy is to discuss the matter with your boss, who may seek the direction at board level. If this is an area that they haven't actively considered you may want to guide them. Companywide policies that may have a direct impact upon purchasing could include:

- What will be the long term organizational structure of the company? Will it have single or multiple business divisions? Will the purchasing function be centralised or decentralized? What are the lines of reporting?
- Does the company plan a policy of upstream or downstream supply chain integration?
- Will the company have its own manufacturing facilities or will it sub-contract production to third parties?
- Does the company want to reduce costs by sourcing in low cost countries?
- What are the company's financial objectives? For example, will it aim for growth at the expense of profit margin?
- What type of products and markets does the company want to develop in the future? Will it produce and sell highly differentiated products in niche markets or high volume, standard products into highly price competitive markets?
- How will the company be owned? What resources will be available to business functions and how will the resources be financed?
- Will the company be a conglomerate, operating in different product markets or will it concentrate its efforts on a narrow range of core products?
- What is the company position on risk?
- What specific long term objectives are there for purchasing?

Purchasing organisation

Purchasing or procurement

"Common sense is not so common". Voltaire

The process by which a company organises its supplies of goods and services is known by different names, the most common being: procurement, purchasing, buying, contracting and more recently supply chain management. Similarly, the department is usually known as; the procurement department, the purchasing department, the buying department and contracts. The head of the department may be known as the procurement manager, the purchasing manager, the buying manager and contract manager. But which one is correct in any particular situation?

Dictionary definitions of 'procure' are numerous and quite diverse. Unfortunately, most standard definitions suggest underhand or illegal activities. They range from 'the act of getting possession of something' to 'arranging sexual partners for others'. This is clearly, not the image business professionals want to portray. A more acceptable business meaning could be, the process by which the resources (goods and services) are acquired, including the development of a procurement strategy, selection of suppliers, preparation of contracts, and management of the contracts.

By contrast, the term 'purchasing' has a narrower definition, often referring to the transactional task of placing orders, contract administration and the arrangement of payments. Or even more narrowly as the transfer of ownership in exchange for money or value.

Clearly the best term to use for professionals engaged in wider supply and materials management activities is 'procurement' despite its dubious historical origins. So, why do most people including myself, still use the terms; purchasing, purchasing manager and purchasing department? I would suggest that this comes down to ease of recognition and familiarity, both inside and outside of the profession.

Often what determines the title given to the department is determined not by what the function it performs but by the business sector, the size of the company or the latest thinking in business management.

Public sector organizations and large engineering concerns particularly defence industries, frequently use the term procurement. Retail organisations tend to have buying departments and buying or product managers. In general engineering and manufacturing industry the terms purchasing department and purchasing manager are most commonly used.

Some people have, in my view mistakenly, imbued the term procurement with the idea it is somehow strategic whereas purchasing is simply transactional. However, evidence indicates that calling your department 'procurement' and yourself the procurement manager may raise your profile. A survey of advertised roles suggests that procurement managers tend to be paid several thousand pounds a year more than purchasing managers. This might be because larger companies tend to advertise for procurement managers rather than purchasing managers or it could be that the term 'procurement' does actually create a greater cache than the term 'purchasing.

In my experience, regardless of whether a department is called the purchasing or procurement department, they all have similar responsibilities and perform the same duties.

Centralised or de-centralised purchasing

"Today we know that centralization and big bureaucracies have not, as promised, been the answer for promoting better opportunities for society". Carlos Salinas de Gortari

Centralised purchasing is when the purchasing function has the sole authority for committing the company to purchases and is managed as an independent function. Normally it will be situated in one location, with a chain of command running through a head of purchasing to the board of directors. Typically this will be the finance director, the operations director or the production director and occasionally the managing director. In the case of retail organizations there will probably be a buying director.

Decentralised purchasing is where buying is devolved to individual business units and the buyers or administrative staff who place the orders report to the local business manager. In this scenario there is usually no direct link to the board of directors.

Some companies oscillate between both structures never quite happy with one structure or the other. More often than not this continual changing of structure has little to do with the performance of the purchasing but more likely reflects the changes in power of the individual business units relative to the central management. In simple terms, internal business politics and empire building has more to do with the structure of purchasing than practical business issues. In my experience business managers prefer to have their own buyers rather than rely upon a central purchasing organisation even though centralised purchasing in most circumstances has advantages for the company as a whole.

The benefits of centralisation could include:

- The concentration of the company's buying power, which if managed properly should result in economies of scale and lower unit costs for bought-out items and services.
- Increased productivity resulting from specialisation of personnel. Basic economic theory regarding the division of labour suggests that by employing staff who demonstrate a technical superiority over other people in a particular field and by allowing them to concentrate on those areas will result in improved performance.
- Decisions will be made for benefit of the whole organisation rather than a particular business division.
- More effective co-ordination of purchasing initiatives and simpler lines of reporting.

- Concentrating purchasing staff will allow managers to be employed, whose principle task is to improve purchasing organisation, develop strategy and co-ordinate staff effectively.
- Concentrating purchasing staff together in one location and under one management structure should allow better holiday and sickness cover.
- Procedures are easier to draft and enforce. Records can be kept more effectively, allowing easier audit trails.
- Grouping purchasing staff under a single management improves the likelihood of detecting purchasing fraud.
- Specialist IT and communications equipment can be employed and duplication of systems avoided.
- Ensuring suppliers and resources are not duplicated.
- A simpler line of communication to the board of directors.

Benefits of decentralised buying:

- Local knowledge and skills are used by the business units.
- The accountability of the business unit is increased.
- The buyer becomes part an integral part of the business unit. Local teamwork and motivation may improve.
- Purchasing at business unit level is likely to improve response times.
- Less centralised bureaucracy.

Some companies find that a mix of centralised and decentralised purchasing is the most effective solution. Items requiring very quick response times like maintenance, repair and operations (MRO) items are best delegated to local buyers because they can react more quickly and the opportunities for economies of scale are limited.

Other systems may locate buyers remotely at business units but assigned group responsibilities to buyers in addition to their local responsibilities. The greatest drawback for the buyer is that they can end having a matrix of responsibilities and more than one boss, which may complicate management.

Portfolio analysis (category management)

"Meetings are indispensable when you don't want to do anything". John Kenneth Galbraith

When deciding how to organize your team and how to use your resources most effectively you will need to consider the nature of the mix of products that you are tasked with procuring.

The Portfolio Matrix (Kraljic 1983), is a useful way to classify the mix products and suppliers you are responsible for managing. The classification of products and suppliers can then be used to inform purchasing organization and strategy to maximize buying power and minimize risk.

The model utilizes a 2x2 matrix. One dimension measures the financial impact and the other the level of supply risk measured by complexity of supply. Financial impact is high when the proportion of material cost in the final product is high and low when there the amount of value in the final product is inconsequential.

Supply risk is high when the markets for materials are complex or difficult. Perhaps the most common reason for a market to be difficult is when a limited number of suppliers control the supply of product into the market. Although laws against price fixing exist, it is often hard for the authorities to prevent or prove market control through more subtle means such as creating scarcity of certain product line by altering or reducing production capacity.

Not all difficult market conditions are engineered. Sometimes dominant or monopoly suppliers in the market are protected by law through intellectual property they have developed often at some expense. Others products may be difficult to source simply because they are subject to natural uncertainty such as international relations, climate or accident.

Using these parameters, the model characterizes 4 product types: leverage, strategic, routine and bottleneck items. Each category responds best to a particular style of purchasing management and negotiation strategy.

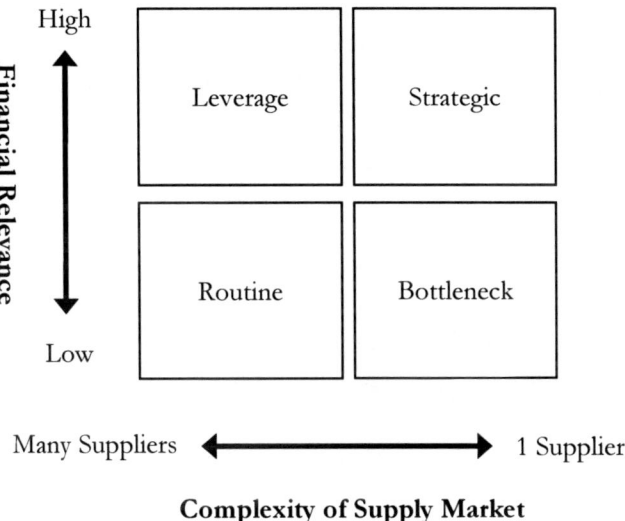

Complexity of Supply Market

Strategic spend items

These products are characterized by complex supply conditions but are also the parts critical to the end product or which absorb a high proportion of the raw material costs of the end product. These are the goods that the purchasing department should invest time and effort managing. Strategies should be geared toward building alliances with key suppliers with particular emphasis on joint product development and partnership.

Leverage products

These are golden nuggets for the buyer. These products allow buying power to be exploited whilst minimising supplier risk. Products falling under this category are likely to be standard, with multiple supply sources and easily substitutable. The most common examples of leverage products are commodities. The market for commodities is characterised by effective price competition and generally the buyer is in a dominant position.

Effective purchasing strategies would include using competitive enquiries and tendering. Volume is king, so consider grouping annual requirements or pooling group wide requirements to maximise the attractiveness of your enquiry package of requirements. Auctions work particularly well in the supply of standardised homogenous products, where there are many suppliers. This is why auctions work well for the setting up of gas and electricity contracts.

Bottleneck products

These are products were there are low profit opportunities but high supply risks. These products may often be single source items, or on long lead time with no alternative suppliers or substitute products. The supplier generally controls the price and there is little scope for cost reduction. Purchasing policies should in the short term aim to prevent shortages and ensure supply, through the use of forecasts, holding capacity, forward orders and insurance stocks. In the longer term, the aim should be to reduce dependence on the supplier or the product through development of alternatives. Bottleneck items are best dealt with at the design stage of product development through use of industry standard products, generic products and substitutable items. If possible avoid products with high technical novelty, made to specification designs or products that are being phased out.

Non-critical items

These products have a low impact on profits and low supplier risk. They are likely to be high volume items with low individual cost, which are available from multiple suppliers, for example, standard fasteners and hand tools.

The main strategy with these items is to reduce the unit transaction costs by processing them as cost effectively as possible. Processes should be automated, simplified, standardised and delegated. The aim is to reduce the amount of time spent managing them. Typically, these types of products are ideal for supplier managed inventory or blanket type orders, both of which take advantage of the supplier's specialist skills in handling these types of items and economies of scale.

The purchasing team mix

"No man will make a great leader who wants to do it all himself or get all the credit for doing it". Andrew Carnegie

Getting the right mix of team members is important to the effectiveness and cohesion of the department. Every team needs a balance of both ideas people and backroom staff keeping the engines going.

A simple and appealing way of doing this is by using a 2x2 matrix. With one axis measures ability and the other motivation, staff can be categorized in one of the 4 personality types according to these two personality traits a version is shown below.

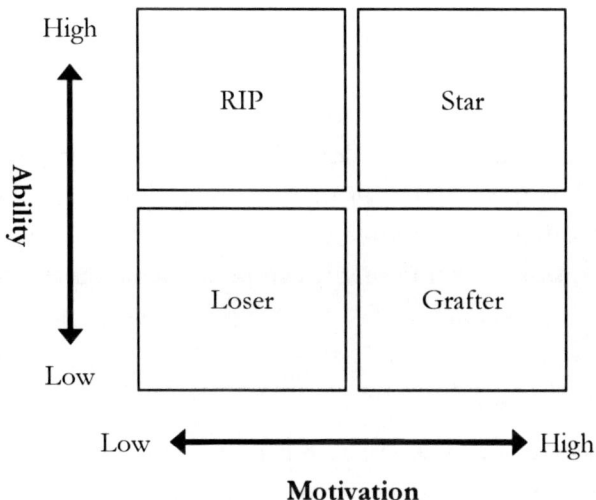

The star

This person is highly motivated with high ability. If managed properly this person will be an attribute to the team and the organisation. Stars respond well to praise and recognition of good work. This person needs on-going challenges so keep supplying new projects and greater responsibilities. This person is an ideal mentor to train other staff.

Avoid petty criticisms. Do not over control and avoid paternalism. Be prepared to recognise good work with promotion and remuneration. Be careful that colleagues do not detect favouritism. Perhaps because these people are potential future managers, some supervisors may find the ability and ambition threatening.

Retired in place (RIP)

This person has high ability but low motivation. They are maybe someone who has great experience but who has achieved as much as he or she wants to achieve. They are happy enough to take a back seat and coast along. Possibly an older member of the team, they may be reasonable well paid or at the top of their particular pay scale. Additional pay and responsibility are not normally motivators. This person is likely to be a bit cynical and maybe risk averse preferring not to draw attention.

They may have a tendency to sit back and wait to be told what to do, so it is important to set clear objectives and work rules. Avoid unsupervised work and monitor performance, although this is likely to be resented. Often these people channel much of their energy into an out of work passion. If this energy can be harnessed then the RIP can become highly productive.

The grafter

This person may have low ability but is strongly motivated to get on. Maybe a junior who wants to progress but lacks the experience to be really effective. This person needs direction and support so consider appointing a mentor for this person to develop their potential and provide encouragement. The best mentor would be a star with management aspirations, the worst mentor would be a RIP as prolonged exposure may induce premature cynicism within the grafter.

This person responds well to praise, so accept small mistakes as part of the learning process and provide reassurance. Incremental targets and rewards are useful to develop this person. Avoid overloading with objectives and avoid prolonged unsupervised activities.

The loser

Low performance and low motivation characterize this person. They often require constant help and support. Clear objectives and ways of improving performance need to be agreed and a development plan needs putting in place. Avoid overloading with work or placing any sensitive work with this person, until their performance improves. Sink or swim may work with the 'grafter' but not with the loser. If the person's performance doesn't improve then consideration should be given to whether or not the person is in the right job. Their poor performance can reflect badly on you.

The team mix in practice

Putting aside the fancy theory, few managers have the opportunity to build up a team as they would like it. In most circumstances, the team you inherit is a mixture of people you would not have necessarily picked yourself. Often the only chance to develop your own team is piecemeal when people retire or when younger staff find new jobs. Often periods of redundancy are good times to restructure a department.

When recruiting, managers will usually only seek to employ proven 'stars' or young 'grafters'. 'Stars' are accomplished and are hired at a premium; grafters are cheap to hire and often willing to learn the manager's ways.

Although it is against the discrimination laws, it is my experience that purchasing managers rarely employ people older than themselves except in clerical functions. Similarly, they rarely employ candidates that have previously held purchasing management positions or are more educationally qualified than them. Self-preservation runs as deeply through purchasing manager's veins as most other professions.

What makes a good buyer

"Integrity has no need of rules". Albert Camus

Good buyers tend to have the following characteristics:

- They have good analytical skills, particularly the ability to identify the bottom line issues.
- They are good at researching information, and can prepare a strategy based on that knowledge.
- They have the courage to question and challenge statements by others.
- They have an ability to make decisions in an objective and dispassionate way.
- They have confidence in themselves and do not feel the need to be liked.
- They can accurately summarise a position and communicate well gaining the confidence of their colleagues.
- They have the ability to deal with conflict and difficult people in a calm, reasoned way.
- They have an ability to listen to others and patiently draw out the bigger picture.
- They have knowledge of the subject matter.
- They tend to be task orientated.

If the buyer is going to be working in a team the following attributes would be useful:

- Has a positive attitude and reinforces other positive attitudes within the group.
- Works for the benefit of the team goal and not personal motives.
- Respect for the opinions of other team members and patience.
- People who don't form cliques.
- People who share knowledge and expertise and do not hoard information.
- Someone who shares the workload and responsibilities.

- Be enthusiastic and committed to the team's purpose.
- Someone who has integrity and can be trusted with confidential information.
- Someone who can be relied upon to carry out their actions following meetings.

One important aspect is whether the prospective team member will fit in with the mix of skills and personalities in your current team. There have been a number of studies into personality types and the team mix, below are some of the more interesting ones.

Staff motivation and objective setting

Spottswoode: Remember there is no "I" in "Team America". Intelligence: [pause] Yes, there is.
Team America: World Police 2004.

When considering motivation, one of the most influential ideas was proposed by Abraham Maslow. In his book 'Motivation and Personality' (1954), Maslow proposed that people are motivated by their needs and that people have a hierarchy of needs. Maslow identified 5 stages, from lowest to highest these are:

- Basic physiological needs. Food, water, shelter and sleep.
- Safety considerations including personal and financial security.
- Friendship and belonging to a group, maybe teamwork.
- Self-esteem, achievement, confidence and peer respect.
- Personal growth and self-fulfilment.

Another respected motivational theorist was Frederick Herzberg. Hertzberg's 'Motivator-Hygiene' theory (also known as the Two Factor theory) suggests that certain factors act to motivate staff but others are required just to stop the employees from becoming dissatisfied. Motivational factors would include:

- Recognition of achievement.
- The provision of interesting work.

- Advancement to higher level jobs and responsibility.

De-motivators or 'hygiene' factors would include:

- Salary levels and pay differentials.
- Working conditions.
- Security of employment and the absence of arbitrary rules.

When both theories are considered together, it seems that in order to retain staff, basic conditions need to be met including a good working environment, belonging to group, and pay. However, to get the most from staff, work needs to be interesting, challenging and good work recognised and appreciated by staff and colleagues.

Objective setting

Most people need to know and perform better when they understand what performance is expected of them. Therefore it is important to:

- Provide basic details of employment (employers are required by law to provide such details with 13 weeks of the employee commencing work).
- Make it clear what the scope of their day to day job is and the standard of work expected.
- Set challenging medium term objectives and regularly review progress.
- Agree a long term plan of development and progression.
- Be clear about rewarding good work.

Ideally, appraisal and mentoring should be an on-going process with manager and employee meeting informally at least once a week. The manager should keep a file on the employee and keep a record of projects, planned, underway or completed.

Appraisals

A formal way of reviewing staff performance and setting objectives is the company appraisal procedure. The normal format is for the manager to complete an appraisal form detailing aspects of the employees work during the previous period. The manager and the employee then meet face to face to discuss the appraisal, exchange expectations and agree a way forward. The meeting should be a two way dialogue and the employee should be encouraged to self-appraise. More specifically the appraisal will at least look at:

- Performance during the period and agreeing targets for the coming period.
- Tackling areas of weakness identified by either party.
- Identifying developmental and training needs.

Some basic rules for an appraisal:

- Criticise performance not personality.
- There should be no surprises for either party.
- Goals and targets should be achievable.

Types of manager

"He was a self-made man who owed his lack of success to nobody". Of Colonel Cargill, Catch 22, Joseph Heller

Detailed below are common stereotypes of managerial styles. Although they are clearly stereotypes, sometimes there are lessons to be learned about managers who share some of these characteristics and hopefully help reduce the number of bad practices and managers out there.

The micro manager

This manager scrutinizes every level of the job, often intervening unnecessarily. They want to be involved in all decisions and copied in on all correspondence. The micromanager is unknowingly driven by the need to control. They may appear to be a bit paranoid and obsessive. Taken to an extreme these managers can be compulsive obsessive but often fail to recognize the symptoms in themselves.

Micromanagement can result in subordinate staff feeling disempowered, because responsibility and control pass to the manager.

Often the result is that the member of staff is disengaged from active work. In the worst case scenario, subordinates are so intimidated by the micromanager that they enter a work paralysis, too afraid to do anything without the say so of the boss.

The key to managing the micromanager is not to fight them this will be counter-productive, but to co-operate with them. Give the micro-manager what they want but begin to manage the demands. Bombard them with correspondence, include them in all the detail you can, the aim being to make their monitoring of you practically impossible. Micromanagers love being asked for advice so take it a step further and ask them to deal with a project that is particularly difficult, this will keep them busy and maybe get them to appreciate what you do on a daily basis. The ultimate goal is that they will lose interest and perhaps realise that you can do the job without them sitting on your shoulder.

The fire-fighting manager

These managers don't have any short term plan or long term strategy. Direction and support are often lacking instead their style is to use frequent emergency type situations to cement their authority. Indeed this sort of manager appears to thrive on chaos and panics. Typically these managers are often quite forceful. They are often good negotia-tors and are politically adept. They tend not to be very supportive but ironically are often considered to as good leaders. Their motto could be laboris gloria ludi (work hard, play hard), outside of work they are often interesting fun people.

This type of management can lead to risk aversion in staff and the stifling of initiative however in some circumstances it can raise the game of staff by demanding high standards. Results are often achieved through fear of failure.

The non-manager

These managers are devoid of plan or strategy. They tend to shoot from the hip with frequent priorities which are often inconsistent with other recently issued priorities. After a while it becomes clear that they do not have their own ideas but are merely responding to criticism or initiatives launched by other managers. More often than not these managers are easy to work for if a little undemanding, often preferring to talk about anything but work. More often than not this type of manager is technically weak and is viewed as incompetent and out of touch by subordinate staff. However, do not underestimate, often a survivor because they are politically adept and know which horse to back in the boardroom. Don't expect backing up in tight situations if the non-manager sees it as expedient.

If you can withstand the lack of direction and inconsistency, this is probably the easiest manager to work for, but don't expect bonuses based on department performance. On the positive side plenty of scope to take the initiative and shine especially so since non-managers tend to have subordinate staff who coast along.

The political manager

In some respects the political manager is similar to the non-manager. They both have little real competence and rely upon working office politics to get by. However, the political manager takes office politics to a higher level of sophistication in building up political networks and useful information. They are adept at delegating and rely upon picking people who make them look good. If things go right don't expect recognition and if things go wrong don't expect any loyalty.

Since political managers don't necessarily have great technical skills you can become invaluable to them by being the person who makes them look good. Political managers have good networks of contacts, so use the political manager to widen your own network of contacts. If they get promoted your chances of promotion are good, just remember if things turn bad you are expendable. The political manager is a master backside coverer, so remember to document any projects or instructions from them.

The ego manager

Often confident and maybe arrogant, these managers can falsely inspire the confidence of their peers and their boss. The attention of these managers is on their own personal performance and recognition. They tend to focus on short term appearances rather than long term results. They are not team players, often they have been promoted to management because they are technically good at the job however they are not necessarily good people managers.

Consequently, these managers do not develop good teams since they do not build a mutual trust with their team. Having a highly competitive nature they sometimes lose sight of who their friends are, ambition is everything.

The weak manager

This person is not a natural leader or manager. Maybe they have been over promoted. They will tell people what they think they want to hear but are unlikely to keep to their word. Treat any feedback with caution even if it sounds positive. Don't expect support when the going gets tough.

Even though you are unlikely to learn anything directly from the weak manager the situation does present an opportunity since they are likely to welcome help managing the department. This allows you to gain management experience without actually being obviously accountable for any learning mistakes. Opportunities will arise to stand in on meetings and in this way raise your profile within the company. Try to avoid being too closely associated with this manager as you will pick up bad practice and maybe harm your own reputation.

The team building manager

Take all the positive points of the other manager types and you may have an ideal. They are competent in what they do. They listen to staff and encourage creative contributions. They take a real interest in their development and support them in their day to day work. Team-builders will coach you while letting you grow at your own pace. The best way to work with a team builder is to be open with them. Don't hold anything back. Tell them what you want and what you think. Don't be afraid to share your ideas and creativity. They may not always agree with you, but know that they will respect any idea you bring to the table. Ask them for help when you need it. Don't expect them to fix your problems for you, but know that they will be there to help you think through problems and provide you with additional resources so that you can solve them. Be aware that team builders delegate and empower their team members, and in exchange they expect commitment and involvement.

Purchasing leadership

"I believe in benevolent dictatorship provided I am the dictator". Richard Branson

Paul Thornton's book 'Be The Leader, Make The Difference', presents ideas which can be readily applied to the role of Purchasing Manager.

Thornton suggests that staff may be guided in what they can achieve and how they can achieve their goals using his 3-C Leadership Model. The essence of the model is that leaders provide Challenge, Confidence and Coaching for staff. When applied to a purchasing environment the following ideas could be appropriate:

Challenge

- Setting 'high' targets. Particularly during negotiation.
- Encourage people to question assumptions (a former Managing Director never tired of telling me that to assume makes an ASS of U and ME).
- Provide examples of good practices to guide staff.
- Change the rules of the game, for example, occasionally switch commodity groups and buyer's responsibilities.

- Set medium term and long term objectives as well as day to day tasks.

Confidence

- Praise employees for good work.
- Focus on achievements and be positive.
- Stress the personal achievements and their value.
- Provide worthwhile training.
- Keep records of past achievements.

Coaching

- Keep employees informed about company initiatives and the role of purchasing in achieving company objectives.
- Set a personal example. Avoid giving certain staff all the dross work. Don't ask people to do things you couldn't do yourself.
- Try to make work stimulating.
- Provide relevant training opportunities.
- Encourage self-improvement particularly for junior team members. Agree personal development plans with staff.

The GROW model

Some management consultants recommend using methods like the GROW model to guide the manager in coaching staff in problem solving. GROW stands for Goal, current Reality, Options and Will.

- Goal is where the team member wants to be.
- Reality is where the team member is currently.
- Options are the ways by which the team member can get from Reality to Goal.
- Will is the commitment and ability of the team member to travel to on their journey.

The GROW model has been attributed to several people including John Whitmore, Alan Fine, Graham Alexander and Max Lansberg.

Trustworthiness

You don't have to be the best friend of your staff, in fact, it is probably better if you are not. However, what you do need to have, is the confidence of your team. In particular, they need to know that you are fair and working in their best interests.

The subject of trustworthiness has been the subject of academic research (The Trusted Leader, Galford and Drapeau (2002). It is suggested by trustworthiness can be described by the equation.

$$\text{Trustworthiness} = C + R + I / S$$

C = Credibility earned by expertise, by the ability to obtain the required expertise, and by being up-front about one's limitations.

R = Reliability, consistency and dependability. Reliable leaders provide a sense of comfort to their subordinates.

I = Intimacy, which is not about revealing personal details, but rather, making the business of the organization personal and understanding the sensitivities of others.

S = Self-Orientation which is the degree to which one focuses on one's own concerns when interacting with others. Self-orientation decreases trustworthiness. Those who are motivated by duty or achievement tend to be more self-oriented than those motivated by meaning or who gain pleasure from the work itself.

Trust is often built through finding common ground and by sharing common objectives. Make time for staff, listen to them without distraction. Discuss issues that are important to them and identify problems that prevent them doing their job effectively. Discuss ways of resolving the problems, identify an achievable and positive outcome and convey this to your staff and in doing so sharing a common goal.

Trust is destroyed by being seen as a person pre-occupied with their own success. Gaining trust is always going to be difficult for someone who cannot empathise with staff or take a real interest in helping them achieve their objectives and helping them see through problems.

Self-management

"When you blame yourself you learn from it. If you blame someone else, you don't learn nothing, cause hey, it's not your fault, it's his fault, over there". Joe Strummer

Organising your day

- Try to make a list of tasks and objectives for the day. Prioritise if possible and put difficult items at the top. Don't overload your list because other matters will arise during the course of the day.
- Try to divide your day up into 90 minute slots. After 90 minutes or so most people's level of concentration tends to dip, so allow yourself a 5 to 10 minute break and then carry on your task or if you can move onto something new.
- Alternatively, set yourself tasks to complete and if a task is likely to take all day, try to break it down into 4 parts. Set yourself a reward for completing each part of the job, for example allowing your-self a drink or a snack.
- Most people are at their most focused and energetic in the morning but are more relaxed and open to ideas in the afternoon, so try to organise your day to get the most out of your own body clock. For example, I tend to feel a little lethargic around 2:00 pm, so I often pick this time to be on my feet, checking stores, production or something similar.
- Similarly, people tend to be more relaxed on Friday, so the best time to put in a holiday request to your boss is Friday afternoon.

Tackling difficult issues

- There are a number of ways we avoid doing things we don't like doing. We keep finding easier jobs to complete or we may put pre-conditions on ourselves before we start work. Don't allow yourself to put off tasks you don't like.

- The best policy is to do them straight away. You may still dislike doing the job but at least when it's complete it won't be a worry at the back of your mind.
- Often the hardest part is starting a new job. If this is the case, start with the straightforward elements, building up confidence and momentum before moving on to more difficult parts.
- If a problem is proving difficult to solve, try breaking it down into smaller parts. The parts are invariably easier to approach and solve than trying to tackle the problem as a whole.
- Another way of dealing with difficult problems and if you have a little time, is to sleep on it. It is remarkable how good sleep and the sub-conscious are at unscrambling complex issues.
- When dealing with difficult people, pick your time and venue carefully. Picks times and places when they will be relaxed or at ease.

Manage your paperwork

- Avoid clutter. Only keep your current papers in front of you. Keep other papers filed but accessible.
- Be ruthless with duplicates and unnecessary paperwork, bin or shred it.
- Set aside some routine time every day to sort paperwork, send it on, file or bin it.
- For regular meetings use a hardback note book rather than loose paper.

Manage your own expectations

- Balance perfectionism with getting the job done, don't become work paralysed through the fear of getting things wrong. Purchasing managers have to make lots of decisions and you won't get them all right.

Delegate

Used effectively, delegation can not only free up your time but it can motivate and develop junior members of staff by widening their range of skills and responsibility. However, used badly it can de-motivate staff and result in poor work. Some simple rules for delegating:

- Be clear about the task and if necessary provide training.
- Never delegate a job because you cannot do it yourself. Similarly, never delegate a job because it is risky and you want to pass the buck.
- Don't just delegate dross; it's not an excuse to dump boring jobs. By all means delegate mundane jobs but mix it with some tasks which are more interesting and will develop your staff.
- Don't delegate work and then take it back because doing so will leave people confused, undermined and de-motivated. If someone is struggling with the work delegated to them, provide support. People will not learn or gain confidence if they don't see through a task themselves.
- Provide feedback on results achieved.
- If you are increasing the workload, the skills required and responsibility, you must be prepared to reward good work at some later stage.

Managing monkeys

"The way to keep weeds from overwhelming you is to deal with them constantly and in their early stages".
George Schultz

One of the most influential works on the subject of managing workload is 'Management Time: Who's got the monkey' by William Onken and Donald Wass, first published in the Harvard Business Review in 1974.

Onken and Wass suggested that there were three types of activity that put time pressures on a manager; boss imposed activities (tasks your manager has set you), system imposed activities (routine tasks to perform your job) and self-imposed tasks (tasks you voluntarily accept from colleagues or subordinates).

The first two time pressures are in a sense obligatory, failure to comply will result in disciplinary action or will reflect badly on you or your department. However, the self-imposed time pressures are discretionary and the manager's penalty for accepting and carrying them is stress.

Onken and Wass, describe the process of upward delegation of problems by employees to managers by the analogy of monkeys jumping from the backs of employees to the back of the manager. If not controlled, the manager can quickly become overburdened with monkeys. This will reduce the performance of the manager and more importantly prevent the employee from learning how to deal with their own monkeys. The best way to deal with monkeys is:

- Be aware when someone is trying to pass a monkey to you.
- Resist accepting the monkey. Some managers just can't resist being helpful.
- Encourage employees to take responsibility for their own monkeys.
- Provide advice and support to the employee in dealing with the monkeys.
- Have regular update meetings, offer advice and support but don't let the monkey jump on your back.

Staff Development

Purchasing roles and pay

'We have to hate our immediate predecessors to get free of their authority'. DH Lawrence

Assistant buyer

Provide clerical support to buyers, typical tasks may include: data input, preparing paperwork, filing, sorting post, expediting orders, resolving simple invoice queries, arranging samples, looking after office stationery. No direct reports. No particular experience or qualifications are required.

Trainee buyer

A trainee buyer should be capable of progressing to be a buyer and should be studying for professional qualifications. Duties are similar to a buyer but product categories or commodities may be of lower importance. Trainee buyers will generally be overseen and guided by a more senior buyer or the purchasing manager. A good general education with a business orientation is a good start; some sectors may require further education in a particular field.

Stock controller

Stock controllers are responsible for the efficient management of stock within the company. Typically they will manage a particular range of commodities or goods. The main duties of a stock controller will be the analysis of stock control reports and preparation of requisitions and schedules for buyers. Key performance indicators will include the contradicting aims of maximising stock availability whilst minimising stocks and stock obsolescence. Some stock controllers will be responsible for placing repeat orders or maintaining order schedules.

Materials planner

Responsible for provisioning materials for production processes. Within a manufacturing environment they provide the link between the production planners and the buyers.

Materials controller

The principle responsibility of a materials controller is the efficient management of the company's inventory. Normal duties include: operating the company's stock control systems (MRP etc), control of goods receipt, storage, kitting, issue of materials and preparation of goods for despatch to customers. Normally, the materials controller is responsible for the company's stores and stock control staff. The title is not regularly used today having been superseded by the supply chain manager.

Junior buyer

Somebody joining the purchasing profession at this level, these days may be required to have a higher education background and a business or related qualification either at HND or degree level.

Buyer

Buyers perform the day to day purchasing activity of the company. The main responsibility of a buyer is to manage suppliers to ensure that purchase product arrives on time in the most cost effective way for the company. Usually buyers are responsible for a particular category / commodity group of products or supporting a business division. A buyer will usually have a degree of independence how they manage the purchasing of those parts and will be accountable for performance.

There is a view that the term buyer should only be used to describe someone who has a creative or active role in deciding what product is bought rather than merely seeking the best supplier for a specified product. This is certainly true of the retail sector and the salaries in this sector reflect that fact. Sometimes buyers may have responsibility for a small number of direct reports such as purchasing assistants or stock controllers.

It is quite common to pre-fix the term 'buyer' with another word to better describe the role, for example, commodity buyer, new product introduction (NPI) buyer, lead buyer and strategic buyer. There also appears to be a trend to substitute 'specialist' in place of 'buyer', so we get commodity specialists rather that commodity buyer.

Merchandiser

The role of merchandiser is usually found only in wholesale, mail order and retail companies. Typically, the role will include a mixture of the tasks performed by the buyer and the stock controller, in buy to make industries. Merchandisers will usually be responsible for managing the availability of stocks and also placing repeat orders with suppliers. Merchandisers will often work alongside and report to the buyer who sources the suppliers and places the initial orders.

Senior buyer

This role has similar duties and responsibilities as a buyer but may have greater experience and manage higher value and / or more complex commodities. Sometimes, senior buyers will have junior managerial responsibilities particularly with respect to mentoring and monitoring the day to day work of junior buyers, trainee buyers and purchasing assistants.

Chief buyer

A chief buyer will usually be responsible for buying a category of products but will also have managerial duties with respect to day to day management of the buying team. Additional managerial duties will probably include representing the department at meetings and may include development of purchasing strategy. When there is nobody higher in the purchasing organisation, this role is more akin to a purchasing manager, which begs the question why a company doesn't want to call somebody in charge of purchasing, 'manager'.

Purchasing manager

The title 'purchasing manager' is used to describe someone who has control and responsibility for the entire purchasing function of a company. Sometimes this responsibility extends and includes the company's stock control and stores functions. Generally, purchasing managers with supervisory responsibilities will not be responsible for a commodity group or day to day purchasing as such but will be involved with planning and negotiating higher value contracts, important suppliers or serious supply problems.

In a medium to large company, the purchasing manager's role will be predominantly advisory and supervisory, however, at the other extreme it is quite commonly used to describe the sole person carrying out the purchasing operations in a small company.

Supply chain manager

The role of supply chain manager is a relatively new one and reflects the growing influence of supply chain management in company strategies. Logically, a senior role which brings together all of the parts of a company's supply chain; planning, purchasing, inward logistics, storage, distribution, outbound logistics and sometimes customer services is a very attractive proposition. It is also attractive to boards of directors because this role seemingly removes the need to employ 3 or 4 other middle management positions. However, it must be recognised that this is an extremely wide range of responsibilities and in companies with any degree of scale or complexity, it is virtually impossible for one person to cover all of these responsibilities except in a purely supervisory role. To make this role successful, requires it to be a co-ordinating and supervisory role, with individual specialists responsible for logistics, purchasing, planning and customer service. The supply chain manager will normally report to the operations director.

Purchasing director

A purchasing director directs and oversees the purchasing function with an emphasis on strategy and organisational planning. The person fulfilling this role should be experienced in a wide range of management philosophies and practices. This role is usually only found in larger companies or where buying and selling is the principle activity of the business as in wholesale or retail. Generally and unfortunately, purchasing directors rarely make it to full board members.

Supply chain director

A supply chain director will be responsible for the implementation of supply chain policy across a number of business divisions. Consequently, planning and integration of supply chain systems are likely to be the principle occupations of this role. Divisional supply chain managers will report

Purchasing pay

"If you pay peanuts, you get monkeys". James Goldsmith

The following are approximate average salaries for purchasing staff in the UK, 2010, taken from job advertisements.

Assistant buyer	£15-18,000
Trainee buyer	£18-20,000
Stock controller	£20,000
Junior buyer	£20-27,000
Materials planner	£23-28,000
Buyer	£25-35,000
Merchandiser	£25-32,000
Materials manager	£28-35,000

Senior buyer	£32-37,000
Chief buyer	£38,000
Purchasing manager	£35-45,000
Supply chain manager	£35-45,000
Purchasing director	£50-70,000
Supply chain director	£50-100,000

Due to the economic recession in the UK, salary levels across the board are under pressure, this is particularly noticeable in the private sector and in particular sectors like manufacturing and retail sectors. At the time of writing, the public sector appears to have escaped from this effect but this may change as the year progresses.

Purchasing salaries are typically 15% to 20% higher than the average in London and the South East. The poorest paid region is the North East where salaries are about 12% below the average. Buyers working in retail, financial services, IT and food generally get paid more those in general services, manufacturing or engineering. Professional qualifications will increase your average pay by about £2000 to £3000 for middle ranking purchasing staff. Purchasing managers work about 40 to 45 hours per week. Private sector buyers generally work more hours on average than those in the public sector.

Training for purchasing and supply chain staff

"Without education, you are not going anywhere in this world". Malcolm X

The Chartered Institute of Purchasing and Supply (CIPS)

The Chartered Institute of Purchasing and Supply is the principal professional body in the UK for those engaged in purchasing and supply. The CIPS Graduate Diploma is the standard by which other qualifications should be measured.

The CIPS has 6 levels of qualifications:

- Level 2, Introductory Certificate in Purchasing and Supply
- Level 3, Certificate in Purchasing and Supply
- Level 4, Foundation Diploma (Foundation Stage)
- Level 5, Advanced Diploma (Professional Stage). Degree level
- Level 6, Graduate Diploma (Professional Stage). Degree level
- Level 7, Member of Chartered Institute in Purchasing and Supply (MCIPS) requires 3 years buying experience.

Student membership is a pre-requisite when entering examinations.

Chartered Institute of Logistics and Transport (UK) (CILT)

CILT (UK) has 5 levels of qualification:

- Level 2, Introductory Certificate, aimed at students in secondary or further education. Equivalent to NVQ level 2.
- Level 3, Certificate, aimed at the supervisory level. Equivalent to NVQ level 3, OND, A Level
- Level 5, Professional Diploma, aimed at graduate entrants or middle managers. Equivalent to NVQ level 4, HND or Ordinary Degree.
- Level 6, Advance Diploma. Aimed at senior managers. Assessed by project or assignment. Equivalent to Honours Degree, post graduate
- MSc in International Logistics and Supply Chain Management. Post graduate.

National School of Government / Office of Government Commerce (OGC)

- Government Certificate of Competence in Purchasing and Supply. Gives exemption from level 4 CIPS foundation stage.

Edexcel

NVQ Supply Chain Management, levels 2, 3, 4, and 5. Level 3 and above allows access to membership of the CIPS.

Interviewing for purchasing jobs

*"If you work for NASA or the Cosa Nostra, I bet it's all
the same. Why's his chair bigger than my chair".*
Ricky Gervais

Preparation

The first hurdle at an interview is to demonstrate that you have
carefully planned for the meeting and researched the company. You
wouldn't expect to place an order for millions of pounds with a
supplier you hadn't researched, so why wouldn't you research a
potential employer? In particular, understand their product(s), know
their market(s) and know what products they spend most of their
money on. Additionally, be aware of any significant changes in the
business during the previous year. Make yourself aware of any current
initiatives or challenges the company faces. Be prepared to link your
skills or experience with the issues affecting the company.

At the interview

- Be prepared to demonstrate your previous achievements. Have
  at least 3 examples where you have made a difference and
  saved money or created additional value.
- Be prepared to explain a difficult situation you have faced and
  how you managed the situation. In particular, how you managed people more senior in the organisation and also more junior than you.
- Be prepared to show how you successfully managed staff or
  suppliers, what objectives you set, how you motivate them and
  how you measure their performance.
- Explain how to set and measure purchasing key performance
  indicators. Be prepared to give examples.

It is becoming increasingly common for purchasing candidates to be
subject to Competency Based Interviews (CBI).

With Competency Based Interviewing, the recruiter will establish a set of core competencies and characteristics for a particular job. Each competency will usually be categorised as either essential or desirable and ranked. Points are awarded to each candidate on the basis of their ability relative to each category.

The best way to answer competency based interview questions is to use the STAR method when relating your practical experience:

S Situation (describe)
T Task required (as a result)
A Action taken (to resolve)
R Results (the outcome of your actions)

What employers are looking for

When recruiting buyers, employers will be looking for someone whose personality is a good fit for the challenges of the purchasing role. In particular, they will be looking for people who are:

- Practical and realistic rather than creative and innovative. Candidates will usually have a good memory for details such as prices, names and people. Not only should buyers be good at remembering facts but they should also be good at sifting the relevant facts and getting to the root of an issue.
- Analytically minded when involved in decision making. Decision making is guided by logic based on principle and practical experience rather than sentimental feelings. This allows buyers to make quick, dispassionate decisions without dwelling on the personal consequences.

On the downside, these personality traits sometimes give the impression that buyers are cold and unsympathetic. Since most organisations value teamwork and maintaining good relations with suppliers, good buying candidate must also show that they can communicate well and build the trust of fellow employees and suppliers.

Some don'ts

- Unless you are interviewing for a buying job where individuality or creativity are required, dress soberly. Dark suit, plain shirt or blouse, un-patterned tie and few embellishments, avoid jewellery.
- Do not talk badly about your last or current employer, colleagues or suppliers.
- Avoid being over familiar with the interviewer. Don't be over confident, when applying for purchasing jobs modesty is not a bad trait.
- Do not lead the interview, the interviewer should always feel in control of the process.
- Don't bring up pay and conditions unless you are asked directly. If you are asked about your current pay try to turn the question around. For example, "how much are you currently paid?" is answered by, "how much does the position pay?" or "what are you offering?" Try to avoid discussing what you are prepared to accept until the company makes an offer.

Negotiating a job offer

"Do your duty and a little more and the future will take care of itself". Andrew Carnegie

Timing is perhaps the most important factor in securing a larger salary and by far the best time to get an employer to improve your remuneration is before you have actually joined the company. Some basic rules of negotiating with potential employees:

- If possible, don't bring up pay and benefits until you get an offer.
- A short delay before responding to an offer may be a good move, especially if the employer burns their bridges with other candidates.

- Remember, there is more to negotiate than just salary, consider other valuable benefits such as: car allowance, fuel allowance, mileage allowance for private car use, pension arrangements, share options, saving schemes, notice period, private health insurance, performance bonuses and death in service benefit.
- Consider negotiating an individual bonus based on your performance reducing costs or levels of stock.
- Remember to discount any remuneration by the costs of working at a particular company. Commuting 30 miles a day in a private car will cost you about £6,500 a year, or about £9000 in gross salary. Also, consider the cost of your time sat in traffic.
- If you are being placed by a recruitment agency, consider using them to negotiate for you. If they work regularly for the employer, they often have a stronger position than you and what's more they can reduce any potential conflict.

Negotiating a pay rise

"What you want and what you get are two different things".
Pat Garrett and Billy the Kid, (1973)

Assuming that you are not moving job, the best time to get a pay rise is when the company you work for is making money, has had a good year and at a time when budgets are being reviewed. It goes without saying that getting a salary increase when people are being made redundant is a) very difficult b) unpopular with your work colleagues.

Most companies have annual staff performance reviews; this is an ideal time for employees to agree targets and rewards with their employers. Indeed, some companies recognise that these reviews can create expectations of higher pay. For this reason, companies who want to keep staff costs down sometimes avoid annual reviews. The simple message is, if you have a performance review, plan for it properly and use it to frame recognition of your performance with higher pay.

Another good time to look for a pay increase is when other people are leaving the company, particularly those in your department. This of course assume you are not the reason those people are leaving!

Building the case

You need to provide your boss with good reasons for giving you a pay increase. Remember your boss may need to justify any pay increase or promotion to other members of staff and their bosses.

- Demonstrate your value to the business. Doing excellent work, taking on extra responsibility and putting in extra effort. Explain to your boss, what extra effort you will provide. Keep records that demonstrate your performance, the cost savings that you have made, additional responsibilities you have taken on and improved working practices you have introduced.
- If you need to exert a little more pressure, benchmark your value in the market place. Find out how much people get paid in similar companies, at your level, in the area. Taking it a bit farther, find out how much your peers earn (be careful it may be considered confidential by your bosses). Use the information gained with discretion and tact. Avoid personal comparisons, "John earns ten grand more than me and he's rubbish".
- As a last resort, either, let it be known you are looking for another job or find another job and try to negotiate using this. However, be careful, many bosses or companies will react badly against threats, even veiled threats.
- Prepare your boss in advance. Often bosses have to clear increases in pay with their boss. By giving advance notice of your aspirations, your approach will not come as a complete surprise to your boss and more likely to be well received.
- Be positive and assertive but not aggressive. A confrontational approach and threats will be counter-productive.
- If you don't achieve your salary aspirations, don't take your bat and ball home.

Basic Purchasing Tasks

Sourcing

"Suppliers and especially manufacturers have market power because they have information about a product or a service that the customer does not and cannot have, and does not need if he can trust the brand. This explains the profitability of brands". Peter Drucker

Sourcing is the process of identifying suitable suppliers for the organisation's needs. If you already have a pool of good suppliers it is usually best to concentrate on developing them but if either the pool is too small or you suspect they are not the best then checking the market for other potential suppliers is necessary. Given that time is short and raising and checking enquiring is time consuming, the process below is an effective way of identifying likely suppliers with the minimal amount of time.

Identifying possible suppliers
- Use your own historic records to identify sources but also draw the knowledge of your colleagues past and present.
- Suppliers often have a wealth of information in their particular markets. If there are no conflicts of interest, it doesn't cause any harm to ask them who they use for particular products.
- When interviewing potential new suppliers, ask them to confirm who their main competitors are, it is surprising how many will tell you.
- When touring supplier's premises, try to note who they buy their materials and equipment from. This can be used later for sourcing leads or costing purposes.
- Who do your competitors use?
- Use a search engine.

- Every day you will receive cold calls from potential suppliers. Most can be assessed for their usefulness in a few minutes. If a contact sounds good but you don't have an immediate need, ask them to send a fax, email or brochure. This can then be placed in your current supplier's file for future reference.
- Trade journals and trade shows. Search trade associations on the internet, use www.taforum.org.
- Government organisation like Business Link and Chambers of Commerce.
- Sourcing agents and trading companies may be useful or necessary in some overseas markets for example China.

Send an enquiry

After identifying your shortlist of potential suppliers, send an enquiry for the supply of a part or range of parts. Choose parts for the enquiry that may have a reasonable volume and are typical of the type of work you would expect the supplier to do. Accompanying the enquiry should be your standard supplier qualification forms such as your quality questionnaire.

Assess the quotation

On receipt of the enquiry, screen out the suppliers who are uncompetitive or non-compliant and if any remain you may choose to visit the supplier's premises or invite them to your works, the former is much more preferable if practical as you will discover much more about the company. Some suppliers will give you the contact details of other companies they supply, so you can take up references.

Request a sample

Assuming that you are still satisfied, request a free of charge sample or place a trial order. The physical sample and any certificates or test reports should be fully checked for suitability. Records of measurement and performance should be taken and an inspection report logged with a copy to the supplier. Low value samples could be retained along with the inspection report for future reference. Some companies may require formal production part approval process

(PPAP) which must be successfully completed prior to proceeding with full production.

Proceed to full enquiry

If the supplier is competitive and satisfies your other approval criterion either progress to a part or full enquiry for other similar parts.

Negotiate to clarify any queries and to improve the offer

Negotiation can and should be taking place throughout the process of qualifying a supplier not just at the end. Judge the best time to further negotiate prices and other terms. Remember, whilst the potential supplier is still 'potential', your purchasing leverage is at its greatest. Unless it is unavoidable, do not let the supplier contact or receive feedback from another function within your company.

Purchasing enquiries

"Learn from yesterday, live for today, hope for tomorrow. The important thing is not to stop questioning". Albert Einstein

Request for quotation (RFQ) is normally the first step in forming a binding contract with a supplier. The RFQ is a document that details the materials or services the buyer is interested in purchasing from the seller, and the terms and conditions he would like to use in any subsequent contract.

Quotations provided by suppliers in response to RFQs are not normally construed as outright offers which if accepted will bind the offeror. The normal rule is that any subsequent purchase order would be the offer to buy and the supplier's acknowledgement, acceptance of the order. This can be contrasted with an invitation to tender (ITT), which invites the submission of tenders which if accepted will generally bind the offeror.

When forming a contract, it is important that both parties have a meeting of minds as to the subject of the contract and the terms under which they agree to trade. It is therefore important that when drafting a request for quotation, all the aspects that will eventually make up the contract are detailed. Normally an enquiry will include the following information or requests for information:

- The enquiring company's details including: addresses, contact person and contact telephone numbers.
- The date of the enquiry and an enquiry reference number.
- Details of the head contract (if there is one) or purpose of the contract.
- Details of the goods, services or works to be provided , including quantity, description, part number.
- Commercial requirements, including method of quoting, the nature of pricing, cost breakdowns, delivery due dates, terms and conditions of contract including notes on the order of preference if there is a conflict.
- Technical clauses and standards to be observed.
- A list of documents that should be supplied with the goods for example; test certificates, certificates of conformity, drawings, technical manuals etc.
- An enclosures list detailing documents accompanying the enquiry for example, drawings, terms and conditions, schedules of work.
- The latest date a quotation should be returned by the seller. The method of reply (if important) and the format of the quotations.
- The required validity of the quotation (period it is open to acceptance).
- The buyer's signature or approval.

If the enquiry and subsequent quotation result in an order, both should be referenced in the purchase order document. This helps to bind the parties to the agreement and can be used in interpreting the intention of the parties if a disagreement occurs.

Invitation to tender (ITT)

"Some people find oil, some don't". John Paul Getty

This is a formal written statement of requirements sent to short listed suppliers, inviting the submission of a formal proposal for completing a particular piece of work. An invitation to tender will normally be broken down into different sections, similar to those below:

Introductions

- The title of the tender.
- A definition of the contract.
- Pre-amble. This summarises the purpose and objectives of the document. The preamble may include background information about the contracting party and the project.
- Guidance to bidders on how to complete their proposal. This is necessary to ensure all bidders approach the bid in consistent way.
- Bid compliance and qualifying conditions.
- Details of the time, place and method for submission of tenders.
- Details of how the bids will be assessed and timescales.

Details of the work

- A summary statement of work / scope of the work (SOW) to be completed by the supplier.
- A detailed statement of the work or deliverables to be provided by the supplier.
- Technical requirements such as performance and functionality characteristics.

A commercial pack

- Pricing schedules.
- Legal documents including a draft contract and the contractual terms and conditions the supplier is expected to sign.

- Statutory conditions and regulations such as health and safety and environmental policies.
- Compliance statements.
- An enclosures pack including any drawings and pre-addressed reply stationery.

Timings

The sequence of events for a typical invitation to tender (ITT) may be:

- Defining the work packages to be subject to the invitation to tender.
- Drafting the commercial and technical specifications.
- Selection of the tender panel (short listed suppliers).
- The issue of the invitation to tender to the tender panel.
- A clarification stage with discussion about the details of the invitation to tender with the tender panel.
- Submission of tenders by the tender panel.
- Evaluation of the bids.
- Post tender negotiations to clarify any uncertainties and non-compliances.
- Final negotiations.
- Final presentation by the preferred supplier.
- Award of the contract.

Forms of tendering

Open tendering

The contracting party advertises for suppliers interested in tendering to apply for a tender pack. Any supplier may submit a tender.

Restricted tendering

Any supplier can request to be included on the tender panel but the contracting party has discretion which suppliers are included in the tender panel. When deciding who is included in the tender panel the contracting party may make use of qualifying conditions such as previous experience, technical expertise or commercial considerations.

Sealed bid invitation to tender

A sealed bid is where the supplier's submission is presented in a sealed envelope. Generally, all sealed bids received in time and in compliance with the invitation to tender will be opened at the same time. It is not uncommon for the opening of sealed bids to be witnessed. Usually interested parties are invited to the bid opening.

Sealed bids are most often used where public money or government agencies are involved and were fairness must be seen to be done. Sealed bids may be a requirement of some tendering processes.

Acceptance of tenders

Invitations to tender are normally worded in such a way to elicit unconditional offers from tenderers and hence open to immediate acceptance by the buyer.

Bid analysis

"Knowledge is a process of piling up facts; wisdom lies in their simplification". Martin Fischer

After receiving supplier quotations you will want to compare them. The best way of doing this is to draw up a spread sheet which lists the different bidders and the key factors you want to consider. If a particular factor is important to your assessment of the bid, you need to make sure that you specifically request it in your enquiry document.

Simple bid analyses will look at only a few factors, price, delivery costs, lead time. What is important is to try to ensure that all bids are assessed on the same basis and that you are comparing apples with apples. This is not always an easy process and suppliers will often do their utmost to differentiate their product in some way to avoid direct comparisons. Suppliers know that the more a product is standardised the greater the competitive pressure which will often lead to lower prices and gross margins.

Table 1. *Simple bid analysis*

	Qty	Supp 1	Total	Supp 2	Total
Product Y	5	**44.55**	222.75	48.05	240.25
Product Z	9	**30.99**	278.91	41.05	369.45
Product X	15	20.15	302.25	**15.12**	226.8
Carriage			15		0
Packing			20		0
Total			**838.91**		**836.5**

The above analysis lays out the negotiation options open to the buyer, which could include:

- Choose supplier 2 and save £2.41 over using supplier 1.
- Cherry pick the lowest priced items from each supplier saving £73.04, over supplier 2 alone (carriage and packing included).
- Ask supplier 1 to match supplier 2's free delivery and packing saving £32.59 over option 1.
- Ask the lowest overall bid to match the other supplier on expensive items possibly, saving £108.04.
- Ask the lowest bid to improve their offer.
- Ask supplier 2 if product Z is subject to a price break if 10 are ordered.

Total cost of purchasing or total cost of ownership (TCO)

Sometimes, just looking at the initial buying prices is not the best guide to the true cost of a product. With products that have significant in-life running costs it is often better to consider the total cost of ownership, which may include the initial acquisition costs, operating and disposal costs. This may be particularly important when dealing with capital equipment purchases, buildings or service contract. Even for low cost items like printers it is sometimes better to look at the total cost of ownership rather than the simple purchase cost, for example:

Table 2. *Printer example, total cost of ownership (TCO)*

	Printer 1	Total	Printer 2	Total
Price	250	250	100	100
Toner price	20	400	30	600
Printer life	40000		40000	
Toner life	2000		2000	
TCO		**650**		**700**

Based on 20,000 pages per annum

The point is that the initial purchase price does not necessarily give the best indication of cost effectiveness over a products entire life. When considering more complex machinery, with long lifetimes, the buyer should consider taking account of:

- Supplier's warranty, what is covered and for how long?
- The availability and cost of spare parts. Many OEMs sell their products at cost in order to make profits on overpriced spares.
- Regular maintenance requirements and cost.
- The efficiency of the machine and the consumption of raw materials.
- The average amount of downtime.
- Depreciation in the value of the machine.

More complex bid analyses

With big ticket or complex products or services, the range of issues for the buyer to assess will be greater.

- Projects with staged payments or large down payments will create risk and the need for finance.
- Suppliers quoting projects of long duration may seek to protect themselves from rising material and labour costs by quoting prices subject to variation or by time limiting the validity of the quotes.
- Some purchases may require subsidiary or enabling purchases, like tooling or patterns.

- Shipping costs may be significant.
- Quotations from overseas suppliers may be in foreign currency and may require assessment of incoterms, duties and additional shipping and port costs.
- Delivery lead time and damages for late delivery may be important.
- The length of warranty and the scope of cover offered may be a consideration.
- Technical or commercial compliance may be important.
  Table 3. Refers.

Cost breakdowns

A useful request at the enquiry stage is to ask the supplier to support their quoted prices by providing a cost breakdown. To encourage the supplier to comply, it is good practice to provide them with a pre-printed form for them to complete (Table 4.) Such a form would normally request details such as product weight, the base price of raw materials, manufacturing or assembly costs, overhead costs, distribution costs and profit. Comparing different cost breakdowns can be quite enlightening and help preparation for negotiations.

Another reason to request a price breakdown is to challenge supplier price increases. Don't expect all suppliers to roll over and provide this information some may even get hostile and claim confidentiality of information. Far East suppliers in particular are uncomfortable with such request and may even appear affronted that you have asked them form such information.

In most cases, sales directors simply don't know how their prices relate to costs let alone explain how a price increase reflects changing costs. Often all they know is that their managing director has told them to get a certain price increase from customers. In any case make it bloody awkward for them, the more awkward the less likely they will be to repeat the request without serious thought.

Table 3. *XY Machine*

	Supplier A	Supplier B
Quote reference	pst dated 17.9.10	jj/11 dated 19.9.10
Currency	GBP	EUR
Price	15000	20000
Price basis	Firm	Firm
Tooling	3000	3500
Ownership	100%	100%
Shipping	0	500
Handling and clearance	0	200
Duties	0	180
UK shipping	400	500
Total GBP @ 1.1 EUR	**18400**	**22616**
Lead time wks	12	16
Warranty period mths	12 from commissioning 18 from despatch	12 from commission-ing
Staged payments	10% with order 40% materials ordered 40% on shipping 10% 60 days receipt	100% sight bill of lading
QA compliant	Y	Y
Technical compliant	Y	N see notes
Commercial compliant	Y	N see notes
Quote valid until	31.10.10	31.10.10

Table 4

Enquiry number XY12359   Currency GBP

	Part number	Description	A weight kg	B Mat'l rate per kg	C Total mat'l price (AxB)	D machg time mins	E machg rate mins	F Total mchg price (DxE)	G OH	H Other	I Carriage and Packing	Total piece price (C+F+J+H+I)
1	ABCDEF-1001	Casting aluminium	0.56	1.8	1.01	1.5	0.8	1.2	1.32	0	1	4.53
2	ABCDEF-1002	Casting aluminium	0.49	1.8	0.88	1	0.8	0.8	1.01	0	1	3.69
3	ABCDEF-1002	Casting aluminium	0.533	1.8	0.96	1.2	0.8	0.96	1.15	0	1	4.07
4	ABCDEF-1002	Casting aluminium	0.61	1.8	1.10	1.7	0.8	1.36	1.47	0	1	4.93
5	ABCDEF-1002	Casting aluminium	0.353	1.8	0.64	0.8	0.8	0.64	0.77	0	1	3.04
6	ABCDEF-1002	Casting aluminium	0.79	1.8	1.42	2.1	0.8	1.68	1.86	0	1	5.96
7												

Material index used   LME primary aluminium cash unoffical confirmed   Currency conversion rate used   USD 1.45

Approved by   AN Other   Date   25.12.09

Types of purchase orders (POs)

"Labour was the first price, the original purchase - money that was paid for all things. It was not by gold or by silver, but by labour, that all wealth of the world was originally purchased". Adam Smith

A purchase order is normally a printed document produced by the buyer and sent to the supplier that sets out the details of the goods, services or works that the buyer seeks to purchase. In most circumstances it becomes the principal legal document forming the contract between the parties. It should be noted that in most circumstances a purchase order is only legally effective when it has been accepted by the seller. Acceptance may be made formally, for example by an acknowledgement or informally by the conduct of the seller.

Purchase orders will normally include the following information as a basic minimum: a unique or serial purchase order number, a description of the goods, a price, a quantity and a delivery date. Other details normally include: quality specification and contractual terms and conditions. Drawings and other related documents must be incorporated into the contract by clear reference in the purchase order.

It is normal to detail correspondence such as the supplier's quotation in the header and any additional documents sent with the order in a list of enclosures. Purchase orders are normally signed by the buyer to authenticate them although this is not necessary.

Purchase orders can be given verbally but wise suppliers should insist that on a purchase order number. Sometimes when buyers cannot access a purchase order number they will ask the supplier to reference their name on the order although this is not good practice. Printed orders that follow a verbal order should be clearly marked 'confirmation order' to avoid the requirement being duplicated.

Variations on standard purchase orders

Variations on the standard purchase order have been developed by buyers and salesmen usually to make the administration of regular requirements more efficient and provide supply stability over a period of time.

Blanket purchase orders

A blanket purchase order details the individual parts but is unspecific about quantities. The order will normally cover a period of time typically a year. It will set out the main terms of the agreement such as price(s) and expected service levels but the timing of individual deliveries are left open. Goods and services are then ordered by the buyer as and when necessary, using the blanket order number.

This type of order is best suited to low value parts. The principle benefit of this type of order is that it avoids the need to repeatedly raise repeat purchase orders and all the associated costs. Blanket orders lend themselves to periodic and structured annual negotiations which allow buyers to plan their workload and negotiate quantity discounts through consolidated quantity discounts. Blanket orders can incorporate monthly consolidation of invoicing, reducing the cost of administration further.

Open order

An open order is similar to a blanket order but the duration of the contract is not specified, instead the contract will usually allow termination by either party giving notice.

Call off order

Quantities are fixed (usually set at several months requirements) but with the exact timing of deliveries to be advised, usually with the caveat that the buyer will commit to eventually pay for all of the parts.

This type of order is suitable when it is cost effective to produce a larger batch of the goods than are immediately necessary. It allows suppliers to put down customer specific stock with the confidence that they will eventually be paid for the goods. It also allows the buyer to move stocks of supply sensitive items to supplier in the knowledge that goods are immediately available.

Scheduled order

An order which details a number of specific delivery dates, sometimes in a separate schedule which is updated periodically. Requirements are either firm (not subject to variation) or forecast (subject to variation). Typically, requirements are firmed up 2 or 3 weeks prior to the planned shipping date.

Useful when the buyer has fairly regular requirements. Benefits include: less purchasing administration (because fewer orders), flexibility and security. Suppliers have visibility of the customer's demand which allows them to plan their raw materials and reserve production capacity. In short, fewer surprises and consequent risks.

Limit of liability (LoL) purchase orders

This is a purchase order that restricts the commitment of the buyer in a specified way. The usual method to limit an order is to put a financial limit on the value of work authorised by the order.

This type of order is useful when it is either not practical to put an exact value on the work or there is not enough time to obtain a full quotation. For example, a machine breaks down and a part needs repair. Speed is important but it is not possible for the supplier to give a price without inspecting it. Issuing a limit of liability order controls the administration of the return and immediately authorises work to a specific value (beyond which value the repair may be uneconomic). The disadvantage of a limit of liability purchase order is that the supplier may push the price up to the limit.

Local purchase orders

This is a form of delegated ordering in which non-purchasing staff are allowed to order goods using something like a manual ordering pad.

This type of order is useful when speed and flexibility is required for example a maintenance engineer. The use of these orders will be allowed only in certain circumstances and usually limited to particular type of goods, up to a financial limit, with local suppliers and when it is impractical to organise a standard purchase order.

Expediting

*"If you set out to be liked, you would be prepared to
compromise on anything at any time, and you would achieve
nothing".* Margaret Thatcher

Expediting means to hasten or speed up something, in the case of
purchasing it means hastening or speeding up the supply of parts or
the provision of services. The goal of the expeditor is to make sure
that materials are delivered or services performed in accordance with
build or project schedule. Sometime the term 'progress chasing' is
used but it means the same thing.

Expediting can be one of the hardest jobs in purchasing and it is
certainly one of the most time consuming activities but all too often it
is given to a junior buyer or assistant to perform. This is common
practice perhaps because more senior people don't like to do it.
However, part of the expeditor's role is to identify when the seriousness of a situation requires the intervention of a buyer or manager.

Expediting can be broken down into two areas, routine progressing of orders and specific progressing of orders.

Routine Progressing

Routine progressing should be a daily or weekly activity and is as
essential to the smooth operation of the purchasing department as
placing orders. Essential to the task is the availability of an outstanding order report. This report can discriminate between particular
jobs and due dates, which will make the task of expediting much
easier. A good report should be able to group purchase orders by
supplier so only one telephone call is required. Typically, routine
progressing should include:

- Confirmation or receipt of the order. Shortly after the purchase
  order has been sent to the supplier the expeditor should confirm that they have received it. In most instances the supplier's
  acknowledgement of order does this. So it is important to ensure all acknowledgements are routed by the expeditor. The

expeditor should check the details on the acknowledgement, updating purchasing records such as lead times and resolving any simple inconsistencies by contacting the supplier. It is good practice to write the details of any conversation on the acknowledgement including the person spoken to and the date. For more fundamental disagreements the expeditor should refer the matter to the buyer. Some suppliers will not send a purchase order acknowledgement, if this is the case experience should indicate which suppliers are important and should be contacted to confirm receipt. It would be impractical and not cost effective for the expeditor to spend too much time chasing down all acknowledgements. Acknowledgements should be filed with the copy purchase order in case it needs to be referred to at a later point.

- Follow up progress enquiries can be made at any time but it is advisable to follow up deliveries a short time prior to the planned delivery date, maybe 1 week before. Try to speak to the same contact as used previously.
- Progress outstanding items shortly after the planned delivery date.

Urgent Progress

Emergency expediting is sometimes needed when it is clear that key materials are not going to arrive in time to meet a critical path. In these circumstances it is usually necessary for the buyer to get involved and maybe more senior managers.

After obtaining as much detail as possible from normal contacts, the issue should be referred up the supplier's chain of management. Make use of the supplier's external sales contacts, these people often have more of a personal interest in resolving the problem because they are likely to be the ones who will have to explain themselves face to face with you. It is best not to go to the top of the organisation straight away as this may prove counter-productive.

Explain that you wouldn't normally trouble the person but you felt it necessary to contact a more senior person because of possible consequences. Also explain the consequences of failure to the end customer and damage to future business but avoid direct threats. Investigate ways of bringing forward the delivery with the supplier, these may include:

- The supplier finding the item in their distribution chain or even from a competitor.
- Has the supplier supplied the item to another customer who may have free stock?
- Does the supplier have a similar specification item available?
- Can the item be shipped direct or by special courier?
- Can the supplier working overtime, weekends to complete the job?
- Can the supplier break down the run of an existing job to produce your urgent job?
- Request that you speak directly to their purchasing department or buyer responsible.
- Request to speak to their supplier direct (they will resist this and it may make them pursue the matter more actively with the supplier).
- The supplier offering a superior product at the same price.
- Threaten to go to the top person in the suppliers company.
- If all else fails go to the top person in the suppliers company.

Purchasing Issues

Small businesses and purchasing

"It is not from the benevolence of the butcher, the brewer, or the baker that we expect our dinner, but from their regard to their own interest". Adam Smith

When businesses are small it is common for the owner to perform the purchasing activities themselves, indeed it is not uncommon for the managing director of small medium enterprises to continue to maintain contacts with a few key suppliers. However, as a business grows it normally becomes necessary for the owner to delegate the purchasing activities to a company buyer or purchasing manager.

At this stage in a company's life, the small number of people employed means that it is normal for the buyer to have wider administrative duties within the company. Typically these other duties may include receiving goods, matching invoices with deliveries and logistics functions. It is therefore important to employ someone who is not too specialist and someone who will not mind putting their hand to a wide range of tasks.

Due to the vulnerabilities of small companies, the owner may wish to put in place simple procedures for the buyer to follow. Sometimes larger companies may want to incorporate similar practices.

- Implement rules on seeking competition. Whenever competition is possible three quotes should be sought. It is not necessary to repeat this exercise for every purchase of the same item(s) so long as the original price comparison or justification is kept.
- Bid analysis records should be kept with the copy order or details kept in the suppliers file.
- Make it clear who has authority for committing the company to contracts. Set out what can be ordered by the person and what cannot. If necessary create financial limits on the value of orders that

can be raised. If it is practical, make suppliers aware of these rules otherwise if the buyer goes beyond their remit, suppliers will be able to argue that the person had apparent authority to act as they did.

- Try to avoid the buyer being responsible for the complete purchasing cycle. One person should not be allowed to source suppliers, identify requirements, place orders, received goods and clear invoices. Even if it is not practical to split up the chain, introduce an outside check, for example, orders could require a second signature, raising cheques and signing off should be performed by another person.
- Make clear rules about confidentiality of information and where a conflict of interest might exist or develop.
- Make clear rules on accepting corporate hospitality and gifts

Low value orders

"Look after the pennies and the pounds will look after themselves" or "Pennywise pound foolish".

Sometimes when buyers should be focusing on reducing the cost of high cost items their time and energy is sapped by having to deal with high volumes of low value orders.

The first step in tackling this problem is to map out time spent against spend. If you want to display this graphically create a matrix with order value on one axis and number of orders raised on the other and plot the results by supplier or by product group. This should not really be necessary because we all know what the low cost high administration cost items are: office consumables, factory consumables, fasteners and minor electrical components.

Not only do purchasing managers dislike dealing with these items but also suppliers find them costly to process. Some OEM suppliers deal with this by transferring lower value accounts to distributors. Another way supplier managed them is by setting minimum order values, small order charges, quantity discounts and carriage charges for orders below a set value.

From the purchasing manager's point of view, the main problem arises because we try to handle them using the same system as we use for critical and high cost parts. We often spend more time and effort raising an order for 30 items costing £30 as we do for 1 item costing £1000. To solve this problem we must adapt our ordering systems to reduce the administrative burden. Ways of doing this may include:

- Purchasing cards (corporate credit cards) are issued to end users, like service and maintenance engineers. The supplier will accept the payment without the need for official documentation and at the end of the month a statement will arrive detailing the transactions which can be audited. The system is quick and there is no need to raise requisitions, await orders to be issued and in some cases book in goods. Accounts don't receive large number of invoices which in some cases have to be individually signed off. However, companies generally do not like the use of purchasing cards, I suspect because of the lack of control, the potential for abuse and the difficulty reconciling using cards with company costing systems. These risks could be reduced by setting strict limits on the maximum transaction value, a monthly limit and restrictions on the type of company the card can be used with.

- Using blanket type orders. In this case a single order number is raised which can be used many times reducing the need to raise order numbers by purchasing. However, purchasing staff remain in control of who the order is placed on, the timing and the terms of the agreement.

- Using supplier replenished kanbans. Bins are set up for particular materials, levels and replenishment cycles are agreed by the buyer. The supplier checks what has been used and raises a periodic consolidated invoice. A single purchase order is raised to cover the administration. A degree of trust and audits are a necessity for this type of arrangement to work but apart from reducing purchasing administration it also cuts out some stock keeping tasks and movement of materials within the factory.

Electronic Data Interchange (EDI)

"Computers are useless. They can only give you answers." Pablo Picasso

Electronic Data Interchange (EDI) is 'the automated computer-to-computer exchange of structured business transactions between a company and its customers and suppliers, in a standard format, with the minimum of human intervention'.

Normally businesses exchange data through a third party B2B e-commerce company. These companies provide a safe network for exchanging data such as purchase orders, demand forecasts, demand schedules and delivery documentation such as bar coded kanban cards. The system works by uploading selected data from you ERP system onto the e-commerce company's platform. Suppliers are able to securely log onto the platform and are allowed to upload the relevant data. When combined with the use of blanket or scheduled orders, automatic transfers of demand schedules to suppliers are particularly effective.

Perhaps the most commonly used application of EDI is reverse e-auctions. In reverse e-auctions, pre-selected suppliers log onto the e-auction providers site at a pre-determined time and are able to bid on pre-advised packages of work. The key factor of the process is that all suppliers can see bids being placed in real time and can re-bid. A good site for more detail of reverse e-auctions is www.ogc.gov.uk.

Facilities management (FM)

"Not only is there no God, but try finding a plumber on Sunday". Woody Allen

Facilities management is the operation, maintenance and security of a facility, usually performed by a specialist external contractor or contractors. FM services are sometimes characterised as 'soft contracts', those involving people like catering, cleaning, security pest control and 'hard services' which relate to estates management and maintenance of capital assets.

Responding to market demand, FM providers have in recent years widened the scope of their services to include many roles regarded by their customers as non-core activities. These 'outsourced' activities include: distribution and warehousing of goods, office supplies, catering, utilities, payroll, IT and in some instances elements of purchasing. The trend toward outsourcing has been driven by two beliefs, firstly, that overhead costs will be reduced and secondly that FM companies can bring improvement through the employment of specialist skills and economies of scale. I tend to believe that the former reason has been the main driver in most circumstances.

Consequently, facilities management companies have seen sustained growth in recent years and are a growing area of employment for purchasing professionals.

Outsourcing

"Strategy is buying a bottle of fine wine when you take a lady
out for dinner. Tactics is getting her to drink it".
Frank Muir

Outsourcing is where one or more business functions are transferred to another company to manage and perform day to day activities. The usual suspects for outsourcing include: company canteens, cleaning, security, logistics, some sales functions, IT. Often the responsibility for these functions is taken over by organizations specializing in managing other company's non-core activities. This activity is called facilities management or FM.

Companies choose to outsource because they expect to save money in the following ways:

- Allowing the customer to focus resources on core activities.
- Reducing overhead costs, by reducing the non-direct headcount.

- The FM provider is expected as a specialist employer to work its staff more efficiently. Efficiency is achieved by employing specialist skills, having greater staff utilisation and lower rates of pay and benefits.
- The FM provider is expected to benefit from economies of scale in the purchase and employment of specialised equipment.

At the same time the company should be aware of the principle disadvantages of outsourcing namely:

- The possible loss of control and risk to supply.
- The loss of key skills which are difficult to recover.
- The risks to confidential information.

Selecting a supplier for outsourced functions is in some ways the most challenging task a buyer can face because you are not buying a physical product with dimensions, performance characteristics and specification but a highly individualised service from a company whose main input to your company is people and skills. So buyers need to consider whether the supplier can actually deliver benefits whilst minimising the risks. In particular, the buyer must satisfy themselves that the FM supplier can:

- Complete all the tasks required and avoid the need for your company to retain some of the function internally?
- Provide a better service than your own staff?
- Reduce the overall cost of providing the service?

But additionally they should also consider:

- How the supplier and its staff would integrate with your company, your company practices and your existing staff?
- Would the supplier's staff be trustworthy or be a security risk?
- Would the supplier's staff present a good impression to customers?

So additionally, the buyer needs to check how the supplier recruits, manages and trains its staff. Since it is in part a subjective test, it is important to take up references from other customers.

Service level agreements

"Service to others is the rent you pay for your room here on earth". Muhammad Ali

The normal management tool for FM and outsource services is the Service Level Agreement (SLA)

A SLA includes the usual terms and conditions found in a sale of goods contract but in addition it will set out the elements of service to be provided and the way these service elements will be managed. In particular SLAs need to be clear on the following points:

- The scope of the service to be provided needs clearly specifying. If necessary, the outsource supplier should audit the existing service to establish the full extent of the job.
- The duration of the contract and the provision of break clauses allowing the buyer to end the contract if the supplier isn't performing.
- Performance measures should be clearly written into the contract, for example: the minimum level of quality, response times, clear up rates, staffing levels and skill levels.
- How contract and performance reviews will be carried out and when they will be carried out.
- Procedures to update and modify the scope of the supply.
- The procedure for modifying prices.
- What compensation is to be paid in the event of poor performance
- Responsibility for work carried out, and the liability for contractor's employees.
- The arrangements for protecting company confidential information.
- The application of statutory obligations for example health and safety regulations.

TUPE

"You cannot escape the responsibility of tomorrow by evading it today". Abraham Lincoln

TUPE stands for Transfer of Undertakings (Protection of Employment) Regulations 2006 enacted to put into effect the Acquired Rights Directive (ARD), (2001/23/EC). The aim of the regulations is to protect the rights of employees when ownership of a business changes hands. The main provisions of the Act are as follows:

- When work is transferred whilst retaining its identity, employees who had contracts of employment immediately prior to the transfer are automatically transferred to the new employer, on the same terms and conditions of employment.
- All rights and liabilities of the transferring employers are taken on by the new employer.
- Any dismissals related to the transfer are automatically deemed unfair dismissals unless it can be shown that the dismissal was necessary for economic, technical or organisational reasons requiring a change in the workforce.

Change of ownership could include the transfer of work from one employer to a new employer. The most likely scenario buyers will face is when work is outsourced to an external supplier. In such circumstances the buyer may need to consider the following:

Does TUPE apply?

TUPE applies whenever there is a transfer of all or part of a business to a new employer.

Staff consultation

IF TUPE applies, it is good practice to inform staff representatives and their trades unions. Regulations require that affected staff are consulted and informed of any change of employer.

Documentation

If TUPE applies, tender and enquiry documents should make it clear that tenders should be compliant with TUPE regulations and the Code of Practice.

Workforce information

Tenders should provide full details of the current workforce including: number, skills, age, and lengths of service. Details should include existing terms and conditions of employment and details of any pension schemes applying.

Bid Evaluation

Bids should be evaluated for compliance with TUPE regulations and Code of Practice. Tenderers may be required to submit TUPE method statements. As part of the evaluation process, tenderers should submit details of their proposed pension arrangements.

Following the Suzen case ECJ March 1997, ARD does not apply to outsourcing cases unless; there is a transfer of significant tangible or intangible assets, or, the new employer takes over a major part of the workforce, both in terms of number and skills.

Offshoring

'Say no to Bangalore and yes to Buffalo,' Barack Obama

A variation on outsourcing is offshoring which is where the business function is transferred to an overseas subsidiary. The principle economic reason for offshoring are the lower labour costs in developing countries. In 2010, a general worker in China is paid the equivalent of £1 an hour. In addition, the social and welfare costs associated with employing people in developing countries are much lower. It could also be argued that workers in some third world countries are now better educated, work harder and have a better attitude to work compared to those in the west. It is therefore unsurprising that the most commonly offshored functions are those that have a high labour content particularly services that can be provided by phone such as technical support and direct sales.

There is some evidence to suggest that the competitive pendulum is now beginning to swing back in favour of the west, reasons for this include:

- Control of quality. Quality is not always the highest priority in low cost countries. Often this is a deeply ingrained cultural issue and the only way of ensuring good quality is to employ western style practices and staff.
- Developing countries are becoming more expensive. During recent years Chinese wages have been increasing by 25% per annum.
- Exchange rate movements are making investment in developing countries more expensive.
- A growing adverse reaction by consumers in the west to offshored services.

How far and how fast the pendulum will swing is debateable, largely because the labour market in the UK remains relatively inflexible due in large part to the high levels of welfare provision.

Buying capital equipment

"Successful investing is anticipating the anticipations of others". John Maynard Keynes

Capital equipment expenditure sometimes abbreviated to CAPEX, is expenditure on items that are used by the company in creating its output but are not physically embodied in the product or output. Typical CAPEX items are: buildings, production equipment and vehicles. Companies often treat CAPEX spending differently to other forms of company spending because the items are classed as fixed assets of the business and subject to different financial rules.

From a buying point of view, there are a number of additional considerations that must be addressed when putting together a purchase enquiry document for CAPEX items, which may include:

- Commissioning, in particular, who is responsible for and the costs of unloading, siting of equipment, connection to services and commissioning. In some circumstances, it may be useful to arrange a site visit by the supplier(s) to check access, clearances and weight restrictions, in advance.
- The provision of instruction manuals and drawings in the correct language.
- What arrangements are there for training your staff?
- The availability of spares and consumables and an agreement on their prices.
- Ensuring that the product will comply with regulations and legislation. The principle requirements are embodied in Supply of Machinery (Safety) Regulations 1992. as amended by the Supply of Machinery (Safety) (Amendment) Regulations 1994. (SMSR). The product should be compliant and be CE marked. CE marking is the manufacturer's declaration that the product complies with relevant European health, safety and environmental protection legislation.
- Warranty considerations. When it starts (after successful commissioning and sign off?) What is the duration of the warranty period? What it covers and more importantly what is excluded? What is the expected response time for call-outs during the warranty period? Are both parts and labour included? What parts are considered to be consumables?
- What are the service arrangements outside of the warranty period?
- The inclusion of any licenses or rights to operate the equipment. Consider the case of the Chinook mk3 ordered by the UK mod for special operations. When they were ordered someone forgot to enquire about the software source codes to operate the navigation systems. It is rumoured that Boeing couldn't supply these because another company owned the rights and in any case their release was restricted by US laws on

the export of military knowledge. As a result the aircraft could not be used and sat in a warehouse for many years, eventually emerging at great cost but at an inferior specification.

- Any special terms and conditions you want to include. Terms and conditions tailored to specific purpose can be obtained through professional / trade organisations and solicitors.

- Are you buying off the shelf, or is the equipment tailored to your specification or needs? If the equipment is special to you, make sure that it is clear that the supplier is offering a product to meet your needs or purpose. This could be important legally if the product doesn't do the job it was expected to do.

- Timings may be critical, for example equipment must be installed when production has stopped and the area of installation is clear. This may only occur during planned factory maintenance shutdowns, so it is critical to meet delivery schedules. To achieve this supply milestones linked to staged payments should be considered. Alternatively, liquidated damages (damages paid by the supplier in the event of late delivery) could be considered to achieve the same end.

- Performance guarantees to cover the risk that the equipment doesn't perform as well as promised. Often performance guarantees will set out the minimum required level of service and damages associated with failure to meet that criterion. Normally performance guarantees relate to either consumption of inputs or quality / volume of outputs. In the former case a company may specify a particular level of energy consumption. Therefore a typical condition of contract may be that if the energy consumption exceeds a certain predicted level, for example 5%, for every 1% additional energy usage the supplier would pay damages of X%. Similarly with output, if the equipment didn't reach the right temperature, speed, or volume of output then a similar damages clause could apply.

- Buildings and equipment by their nature are used by the company for a very long period of time. It is therefore necessary when considering different bids to assess the overall lifetime cost of the offers. For example a new building may cost more than an old one but the maintenance costs and heating may be substantially less. Fuel for a company car over two or three years may outweigh the cost of the original purchase. Spares for plant and equipment may be extortionately expensive, some capital goods suppliers make a point of selling the original equipment at an artificially low cost on the basis they will recoup money on tied in spares and operating expenses.

Buying tooling or patterns

"Capitalist production, therefore, develops technology, and the combining together of various processes into a social whole, only by sapping the original sources of all wealth - the soil and the labourer". Karl Marx

The supplier will often ask for tooling costs or a contribution to tooling costs. This is not unusual when the product you are buying cannot be produced from the suppliers existing tools or patterns. Before committing to such a purchase you should consider the following:

Questions to do with ownership

- Will the property in the tooling become 100% yours on payment, or has the supplier stipulated 'part tooling costs'. Without agreeing that the tool will be completely owned by your company you will have difficulty enforcing any rights in the property. Avoid 'part tooling' payments.
- How will the supplier identify the tooling as your property?
- Does the supplier confirm that you have the right to transfer the tooling to another supplier and that they would make the tooling available for collection on request?
- How will the tooling be stored? Who will pay for insurance? Will the tooling be held by the supplier on your behalf free of charge?

- What is the likely lifetime of the tooling and who will maintain the tooling? How will repair maintenance or repair costs be controlled?
- Who owns the design rights in the tool and the product it produces?

Financial assessment

Before committing to any new tooling you should consider whether it is a financially sound decision. One of the most practical methods to use is the 'payback period' or a variation thereof. This method is a very simple way for calculating the period of time it will take to recoup the investment on a project which has a defined annual benefit.

Payback period (years) = Investment required / net annual benefit

Suppose the investment is £10k and the net annual benefit is £3000 then the payback period is 3 years 4 months. This method is only really suitable for short term decision making since projects with much longer periods for return on investment should take account of other factors like the cost of money and inflation. Some companies have rules whereby they will not invest in a product if the time to payback the investment is longer than a set period e.g. 3 years.

In respect to buying, this method is particularly useful when making decisions on tool purchases. Two scenarios are typical:

1   A purchased item currently costs £20 / unit, your annual demand is approximately 1000. By investing £5000 in tooling the supplier will be able to automate the production and reduce the cost to £19 / unit. Applying the payback formula gives: Payback period = 5000 / (£1x1000units) = 5 years.

2   Your supplier provides you with a choice of tooling; a low cost tool but higher unit price and higher cost tool but lower unit cost, which do you choose? For example, a supplier may offer a unit price of £10 with a tooling cost of £1000 or alternatively offers a unit price of £5 if you purchase more expensive tooling at £3000.

Assuming you have no other options:

Additional investment required / net unit benefit = minimum quantity of units

$$2000 / 5 = 400 \text{ units.}$$

So, if your likely demand is above 400, it is worth investing in the more expensive tooling, but ask yourself how long will it take to use 400 units? It seems quite straight forward but you may be wise to consider some other questions which may have a material impact.

- Is demand likely to fall or increase over the 5 year period?
- Will you still even require the product in 5 years?
- Will the tool last 5 years?
- What are the maintenance costs over the period?
- What are the storage costs over the period?
- Will it affect your choice of supplier?
- Have you put in place a system of controlling the unit price charged?

Paying for tooling

The supplier will want to find a way of covering their costs whilst your aim may possibly be to avoid a lump sum payment or to delay payment. The starting point for any negotiation on new tooling is why does the supplier need payment at all? By setting up tooling with the supplier you are usually committing yourself to buying product from the supplier. Failing this line of approach try one of the following:

- Amortize the tooling cost over an agreed number of parts. For example, if tooling costs £5000 and the normal price of the output is £4, agree to pay £5 for the first 5000 units after which the price will revert to £4.
- Guaranteed business. Agree to take a particular output, over a particular period of time, at a particular price
- Apply staged payments, for example, 40% with order, 40% on sample approval, 20% with the completion of the first order.

Buying maintenance, repair and operations (MRO) parts

"Guys usually know immediately that I'm high-maintenance". Yasmine Bleeth

MRO items are all the goods and services (excluding capital items) required to transform raw materials and other bought-out parts into the finished product. MRO items are sometimes called indirect items because they are not physically embodied directly into the finished product. The purchasing of these items is an often overlooked area because individually MRO purchases tend to be low value. Consequently, the buying of these parts regularly gets passed to junior buyers which is not only unfair but bad management because if all the minor orders are taken together, they can often amount to a sizeable spend. Some integrated manufacturing plants may have MRO budgets of 10 to 20% of the total purchasing spend. Secondly, purchasing MRO items is one of the most difficult fields to effectively manage because of their particular characteristics.

MRO items cover a very wide range of parts from spare engines to paper clips but in general can be classified as either spares or consumables.

Spare parts

This buying is characterised by unpredictable demand, poor technical information, large numbers of potentially active suppliers, large numbers of potentially active parts, low volumes and often the need for immediate availability.

Consumable parts

This buying is typified by regular purchasing of high volume, low value items such as grease, fasteners, stationery, drill bits, hand tools and safety equipment. Demand for consumables is relatively predictable and ordering is repetitive. The main problem with consumable buying is that it can be disproportionately time consuming.

Both spares and consumable buying suffer from often being outside of the normal requirement identification systems used for direct materials and so manual requisitions and orders are commonplace. Methods of effectively managing each of the above issues are set out below.

Unpredictable demand

Holding spares stock in case of breakdown is the insurance policy companies take out to cover the risk of breakdown, but there are ways of reducing your premium.

- Organise parts into manageable groups. Methods such as ABC analysis should be used to identify critical, long lead or high value parts that require the majority of purchasing time.
- Develop effective lifetimes and replacement plans for high value and critical parts. Suppliers should be asked to provide details of expected lifetime of major parts.
- Co-ordinate spares purchases and stocks with scheduled maintenance plans.
- Stock safety calculation should be systemized and periodically reviewed for group 'A' type parts.
- Equipment should be standardised as much as possible. By reducing the range of parts required to maintain equipment, the overall demand is likely to be higher and more consistent. Being involved at the time of equipment specification is important to achieve this.
- Availability information with respect to spare parts should be kept current, including supplier lead times, warranty periods of equipment, supplier product support periods.

Poor Technical Information

Often company part numbering systems do not extend to MRO items with the result that parts do not have fully maintained descriptions and records. In addition, equipment manufacturers will want to sell you spares with very high mark ups and will often use their own part numbering system to conceal the original source.

- Where possible, use a part numbering system, if one doesn't exist create one or at least find a way by which records of spares can be organised. When you have a system you can start building up useful records of usage, prices, original source and other details.

- Often spares are engineered specifically with a machine in mind. It is therefore important to have the supplier provide drawings, part references and the original source if possible. If the OEM stops supplying for whatever reason you will not necessarily be high and dry if you have this information.
- Send sample parts out to likely sources for identification and quoting.

Large numbers of suppliers and parts

In my experience a medium size manufacturing company may have 250 direct material suppliers and 5000 active direct raw material parts but maybe 2000 indirect material suppliers with 20,000 parts but amounting to 10% of the total spend. To manage this imbalance:

- Rationalise suppliers by using specialist distributors.
- If you use specialist distributors effectively, you can reduce the number of parts you carry but still retain rapid access to parts. The additional costs of the distribution network are partly or wholly offset by their greater efficiency and competitiveness in their particular field of excellence. Distributors create efficiency by pooling together demand from a wide range of customers, making economies of scale notably in purchasing. Having a wide range of customers allows them to reduce the risk of obsolescence.
- Delegate the management of your low value parts to your suppliers. In particular, consider vendor managed bin fill systems. This may be appropriate particularly for low value bulk items.
- Consider consignment stocks from suppliers. These stocks remain in the ownership of the supplier until the point when you use the item. From the point of view of the supplier they save storage space but retain the flexibility of owning the stock. From the buyer's point of view, parts are only invoiced when used but are not tying up capital.

Low order values

- Arrange blanket type order to reduce the amount of order processing.
- To obtain the best prices and reduce long term administration, group parts into logical packages. Negotiate sole supply agreements with suppliers based on the annual estimated quantity.
- Order spares when ordering original equipment to leverage lower prices.
- Agree spares prices or discount structures when you are negotiating the purchase of the original equipment

Notification of requirement

Since MRO type items are not included in most integrated manufacturing systems, notification and authorising of requirements are notoriously difficult to manage and can be ad-hoc. Requirements are often signalled through manual requisitions from user department. User departments sometimes use requisition numbers in lieu of order numbers, consequently the official order acts purely as a confirmation of the commitment. If not controlled properly, this practice can lead to confusion and duplication. Often the buying department only discovers this when an unmatched invoice arrives on their desk.

Since breakdown spares are usually required at very short notice, and sometimes outside office hours it is best practice to delegate some purchasing responsibilities. Effective ways of doing this are:

- Agreeing preferred suppliers with end users.
- Set up annual supply agreements or blanket orders with preferred suppliers.
- Agreeing limits of liability (maximum spend limits and authority) with end users and suppliers.

Buying software systems

"The first 90% of the code accounts for the first 90% of the development time. The remaining 10% of the code accounts for the other 90% of the development time." Tom Cargill

The main consideration when buying an ERP system is to capture the total cost of acquisition. The cost of the actual software is often less than half of the total cost of acquisition. Other significant cost elements are:

- Hardware costs including upgrades, networks and peripherals. For example, if you are thinking of barcoding your inventory, consider £1500 per station.
- Implementation costs, these include surveying, installation, migration of data, training and project management. Allow approximately 40% of your budget for implementation costs.
- Special report writing to integrate with existing business systems. This is the honey pot for any ERP system developers and a real danger for buyers. Don't expect much change from £1000 a day for the services of a system specific software engineer.
- Annual licenses, service support and upgrades. Typically count on about 15 to 20% of the initial software costs.
- The cost of employing your own IT specialists to run the system.
- By far the greatest cost of introducing a new ERP system is the opportunity cost of your staff's time and the disruption that is likely to be caused to your business.

It is important to ensure that you have fully specified the functionality that you require. This is perhaps the most difficult task when purchasing new software because every company's requirements are different and suppliers are not generally forthcoming about their system' deficiencies. There are two practical measures you can take:

- Involve all departments in determining the functionality required. This can most effectively be achieved through forming a multifunction team to capture as broad a range of functionality as possible. Invite each of the software suppliers to a 'discovery' meeting where users from different functions can quiz and probe each of them technical questions with respect to function in their particular field of expertise.

- Draw up an exhaustive list of functions required. Creating this list can be laborious but it is invaluable in determining what the supplier's software will and will not do. This document is an important record of what has been offered and should be included in any subsequent purchase order. If you don't go through this process you can be assured that the software company will offer missing features but at an additional cost.

When comparing a number of different systems, thought should be given to:

- The degree of complexity of the system. You do not necessarily need the most expensive and complex system if your needs are simple.
- Consider the level of ability in your staff to operate the system. Some systems are so complex they can only be effectively operated by employing on or more full time system specialists.
- The lifetime of the technology and the risk of the technology being superseded.
- The timescale for introducing the system, basic systems will take about 3 months complex ones years.

Environmental purchasing

Green purchasing

"Approximately 80% of our air pollution stems from hydrocarbons released by vegetation, so let's not go overboard in setting and enforcing tough emission standards from man-made sources". Ronald Reagan

There is a concept called 'cultural relativism' which maintains that there is no universal moral code and that we should not impose our moral codes on people from countries. However, the reality is when your ultimate market is sensitive to such issues, buyers must reflect this in the choices they make. Indeed, many companies incorporate ethical purchasing considerations when sourcing suppliers. The main areas to be aware of are:

- Human rights including the use of child labour and force labour.
- Animal welfare such as dolphin friendly fishing and destruction of animal habitats.
- Environmental considerations for example buying recycled products and use of low carbon modes of transport.

The following sections are taken straight from the Mayor of London's Green Procurement Code, which is an accessible statement of what environmental purchasing is and guidelines on implementation.

Green procurement is the selection of products and services that minimise environmental impacts; it's about using your purchasing power to promote productive use of resources and materials. This involves integrating environmental considerations into all stages of the purchasing process: from avoiding unnecessary purchases and identifying greener products, to the specifications you use for contracts and whole life costing.

What makes a product green?

Green products are made or operate in a way that:

- Uses fewer natural resources.
- Contains fewer hazardous or toxic materials.
- Has a longer life span.
- Consumes less energy or water in production or use.
- Can be reused or recycled on disposal.
- Generates less waste, for example be made from recycled materials, use less packaging or be recycled by the supplier.

How to implement green purchasing

Green procurement needn't be complex. Use this action plan to implement green purchasing in your workplace through a simple step by step process.

- Question the need for the purchase in the first place. Can existing products or equipment be used instead of buying new goods? Can the requirement be met by hiring or sharing instead of purchasing?
- Appoint an environmental champion to spearhead your green procurement strategy.
- Agree green purchasing objectives and integrate them into a simple green procurement policy that clearly states your intentions. Ensure this fits in with your environmental policy.
- Get top level support for your objectives from the chief executive or finance director.
- Communicate your strategy and processes to staff and suppliers so they are clear on what is expected of them.
- Regularly audit your purchases.
- Develop green specifications and contract weighting tools.
- Assess the environmental impact of your purchases against emissions to air and water, waste to landfill, resource use and environmental quality.
- Engage existing suppliers who may be able to provide products or services to fit in with your new procurement policy. Seek their feedback before targeting new suppliers or contractors.

- Ask your supplier for sample products.
- Incorporate green procurement criteria into all key contracts focusing on those which are high spend, have a high environmental impact and are easily influenced.
- Incorporate environmental specifications into contracts including: energy and water efficiency recycled content, reusable packaging and products, REACH and carbon neutrality. Sometimes there are industry organized schemes such as the Forest Stewardship Council (FSC) or Program for the Endorsement of Forest Certification (PEFC) certified.
- Award new contracts on the basis of value for money and whole life costing, not the lowest price. This takes into account whole life costs; green purchases may lower operating or disposal costs. Choose products that use less energy (minimum A-rated energy efficient), have a long life span and can be easily repaired or reused.
- Implement contract and monitor performance, including the environmental benefits of your new product or service.
- Improve performance such as minimising delivery frequency and miles, and reducing packaging.
- Further advice is available from schemes such as the Local Environmental Management Systems and Procurement (LEAP) toolkit or European Union Green Public Procurement.

Environmental management standard ISO14000

"I know they are all environmentalists. I heard a lot of my speeches recycled". Jesse Jackson

The ISO14000 series of standards provide companies with a framework for developing and managing their environmental impact with the aim of minimizing their impact on the environment and complying with current and future legislation.

The standards have been widely adopted internationally and in the UK. The main standard is ISO14001 which details the requirements of an environmental management system (EMS), its implementation and its continual improvement.

The basic methodology behind ISO14001 is based on the so called 'Deming cycle' of Plan-Do-Check-Act. In brief this would include:

- Plan - Setting environmental objectives and establish measurable targets. Objectives and targets may be guided by national or international requirements.
- Do – Basic organisation, who is responsible for managing the system, documenting the procedures and training staff.
- Check – Regularly monitor progress in respect to targets, reestablishing new targets if necessary and updating staff. Establishing a system of internal audits to prove the validity of the system and procedures.
- Act – Regular management reviews to assess the effectiveness of the system using the data from the checking stage. The system is updated as necessary and targets refocused to reflect performance and changing circumstances.

Environmental taxes

" but in the world nothing can be said to be certain except death and taxes" Benjamin Franklin.

Buyers may find themselves subject either directly or indirectly to a range of environmental taxes, the main ones are detailed below:

Energy taxes

- Duty on hydrocarbon oils.
- VAT on duty.
- Fossil fuel levy.
- Gas levy.
- Climate change levy (CCL).

Transport

- Air passenger duty.
- Vehicle excise duty.

Pollution

- Landfill tax. For 2010-11 the rate was £48 / tonne and due to increase by £8 / tonne until 2013.

Resources

- Aggregates levy. Applies to sand, gravel and crushed rock. The rate from April 2011 is £2.10 / tonne.

REACH and CoSHH

Every change results (at least initially) in productivity Improvements. The Hawthorne Effect.

REACH stands for Registration, Evaluation, Authorisation and restriction of Chemicals. Reach was introduced in 2007 to consolidate a number of EU Regulations regarding the control of chemicals. It is being phased in between 2007 and 2018. REACH applies to substances that are manufactured or imported into the EU (minimum quantity limits apply). It covers:

- Individual chemicals.
- Preparations of chemicals.
- Chemicals embodied in articles which in the normal course of events are emitted from the article.

It does not cover the following which may have their own specialist regulations:

- Radioactive substances.
- The transportation of substances.
- Substances under customs supervision.

- Waste.
- Naturally occurring low hazard chemicals.
- Non-isolated intermediates (substances manufactured solely for the purpose of being transformed into another substance and is used up in the process).
- Human and veterinary medicines, food additives, plant protection chemicals.

REACH requires that the manufacturer or importer registers the product with European Chemicals Agency (ECHA). The registration process requires that a standard set of information is disclosed about the substance. Goods cannot be sold legally if they have not been registered (no data, no market). The main stages for approval are:

- Registration. Companies submit data on the substances to REACH. Companies supplying generic substances can collaborate and produce a joint set of data.
- Evaluation. This is dealt with at 3 levels: compliance checking (quality of information provided), dossier evaluation (the testing methods are reviewed), substance evaluation carried out by national competent authorities.
- Authorisation. Substances considered to be very high concern, must apply for an authorization. Decisions on authorization are made by the EU Commission based on advice from REACH and member states. Restrictions on production or use can be placed on substances deemed to be high risk.

Safety Data Sheets (SDS)

Importers and manufacturers must provide information on substances using SDS if the substance is:

- Classified as dangerous under the Dangerous Substances Directive or Dangerous Preparations Directive.
- Persistent, bio-accumulative or toxic (PBT) or Very Persistent or Very Bio-accumulative (vPvB) as defined by REACH.
- Included in the European Chemicals Agency's Candidates List of substances of very high concern.

- Not classified as dangerous under the Directive but has certain concentrations of substances with known risk factors.

Control of substances hazardous to health (COSHH)

Like REACH, COSHH seeks to control hazardous substances by imposing responsibilities for assessing risk and creating suitable risk management measures to control the risk.

The main differences are:

- COSHH places the responsibility for risk assessment on the employer, whilst REACH places it on the manufacturer or importer.
- COSHH looks are the level of risk in a particular workplace whereas REACH measures risk based on hypothetical exposure conditions.

Supplier Management

Supplier visits

"It is better that one's customers come to one's shop than to have to look for them abroad". Manfred von Richthofen

There are times when a meeting at a supplier's premises is the best course of action. Circumstances when supplier visits are advisable include: the appraisal of new suppliers, quality assurance audits, milestone progress checking and expediting goods. In addition, occasionally a supplier's performance deteriorates for no apparent reason often the only way of finding out the root cause of the problem is to visit the supplier. It is not generally advisable to carry out commercial negotiations at a supplier's premises.

In most cases, it is good manners and good business to send the supplier details of matters you would like to discuss, areas you would like to inspect or people you would like to meet.

Often it is good practice to invite a colleague from another department to accompany you on the visit. Not only may they be able to provide specialist knowledge but it allows your colleagues to build up useful contacts and familiarize themselves with the supplier's systems and products. In my experience, the ideal partner for a supplier visit is the quality manager. At the very least, inviting a colleague will help to break up a journey and build up relationships with colleagues.

It is important to make a record of the visit. You may want to make notes on the following:

Basic details

- Date of the visit, name of company, address or premises visited and the contact for the visit.

- Sales turnover, useful to establish your relative importance to the supplier. The number of employees and the split between shop floor and office staff.

General management

- Make a simple organisational chart.
- Identify the main contacts including: the internal sales contact, the external sales contact, the sales manager, the quality manager, the production / operations manager and maybe the managing director.
- Identify key decision makers who affect supply decisions.
- Does the company appear busy? A company with a weak order book will often be keen to retain your business.
- Do employees appear well organised and motivated?
- Is there sufficient equipment and does it appear well maintained?
- Is there a clear system of work and flow of materials?

Technical requirements

- Does the supplier correctly understand your technical specification, including testing and paperwork?
- Does the supplier correctly understand the commercial terms and conditions?
- Review of performance over the period and make enquiries into the reasons for any failures.
- Who are your supplier's main suppliers? Check labels on goods, maybe you could go direct or consider using the same supplier.

Quality systems

Does the supplier hold any recognised third party quality accreditations? If the supplier doesn't have third party accreditation, do they have any unaccredited systems and if so do they cover the following:

- A system of approving their suppliers?
- A system for checking the quality of goods inwards?

- A system for checking the quality of finished goods?
- Do they work to an industry standard and do they mark up their approved product in a particular way?
- A system for tracing output back to a production batch, operator, batch of raw materials or raw material order?
- A system for training and qualifying staff? Consider whether staff need nationally accredited training for example welders.
- An effective system of record keeping?

Other points to note

- Does the supplier have any prestigious customers? Inspection of goods despatch areas may reveal who your competitors are, the quality of their supplies and the types of products they take.
- Is demand for the supplier's products seasonal? Do lead times fluctuate during the course of the year?
- Check your company's property, such as tooling and patterns. Are patterns or tools owned by your company marked up with your companies details? If the company goes into administration this could be instrumental in whether you take claim ownership.
- Are materials, work in progress and finished goods marked up with customer names and job numbers?

Most buyers do not visit their suppliers enough but the benefits can be great, both in terms of relationship building and market research. Another, less obvious benefit, is that it gets people who are often office bound out of their protective cocoon. Out of the office environment, buyers may have time to reflect more objectively about their role, objectives and opportunities.

Single or multiple sources

"Competition is the keen cutting edge of business always
shaving away at costs". Henry Ford

Traditionally, buyers have followed a price driven, competitive approach to supplier selection. However, more recent thinking has emphasised the benefits to be gained from single source or partnership sourcing. Advocates of supplier partnerships and co-operative supply strategies suggest the following gains will be made:

- Buying power will be concentrated making your company's spend more attractive to suppliers wanting to become your single source of supply for a product group. This should create greater leverage over the suppliers and result in lower prices.
- Benefits will accrue from supplier rationalisation including more time to concentrate management efforts on a smaller number of key suppliers.
- Supplementary costs like carriage will be reduced by consolidating deliveries.
- Fewer suppliers generally results in less paperwork for purchasing and other functions like accounts particularly when paperwork like invoices are consolidated.
- The specification of materials or parts will be more consistent if you stick with one supplier.

In addition, benefits will arise from growing co-operation and trust:

- Departments within your company will become familiar with the capabilities of the single supplier leading to better co-ordination and transfer of information. Incidental benefits may include the speed by which new products can be brought to market.
- A long term commitment to your supplier should create conditions in which they would have the confidence to invest in new equipment and products. The end result should be better products at a lower cost.

- You may be able to persuade the supplier to strike an exclusivity agreement and therefore limit the supply options of your competitors.

On the negative side, unless properly managed the following problems may arise:

- The supplier becomes complacent and takes the account for granted.
- The supplier cheats, increasing prices, reducing quality or service and consequently takes a greater share of any mutual benefit.
- There is an increased risk of supply interruption if you only have a single source of supply. It is advisable that if you plan to make a supplier a single source, choose a supplier that has a relatively large supply capacity relative to your demand, as this will tend to reduce the risk but this doesn't take account of freak events. Toyota, widely acknowledged leaders JIT techniques and single sourcing, had a supply crisis in 1997 when its sole supplier of brake valves was destroyed by fire. Following this event, many key components were dual sourced. Similarly in 2002, Land Rover's chassis supplier UPF (UK) Ltd got into financial trouble. Land Rover couldn't afford to lose the supplier and ended up agreeing a much higher price with UPF's receivers.
- There is some scepticism that trust is ever achieved, and that collaborators will always be looking to gain advantage under the smokescreen of the partnership agreement. It is remarkable that more sales people are advocates of partnership sourcing than buyers.

Key factors when deciding whether a commodity or part is suitable for 'partnership' sourcing may include:

- The size of spend. If you only have a limited budget for a particular product, the scale of your demand may make dual sourcing uneconomic. Suppliers may simply find the level of your demand too unattractive to make a competitive offer.

- Consider what the economic order quantity (EOQ) is. Splitting orders between multiple suppliers may not make economic sense.
- Availability of competition. If there are few suppliers in a market, the ability to generate effective competition may be limited but the risks of upsetting scarce suppliers high.
- Does the partnership create synergies which will increase the overall benefit to both parties?
- Will the partnership create competitive advantage in the finished goods? Or put it another way, will a partnership arrangement, give you a comparative market advantage over your competitors?

Partnership sourcing

"The poor man who enters into a partnership with one who is rich makes a risky venture". Titus Maccius Plautus

Partnership sourcing is a policy of close collaboration with key suppliers. It is based on the presumption that working together will generate greater benefits than the traditional adversarial approach. It is sometimes used as part of a lean manufacturing program but more commonly as a stand-alone purchasing strategy.

The aim of partnership sourcing is to gain commercial advantage by reducing long term cost and increasing the long term effectiveness of the supplier base.

Partnership sourcing is not suitable for all supplier relationships partly because it can be very time consuming. It is a strategy best suited to suppliers where a close collaboration can result in significant mutual benefits. These circumstances are most likely when:

- The product supplied is one which if developed in collaboration can give the buyer a competitive advantage in the market
- The product can be differentiated and can specifically be tailored to suit the buyer's specific requirements.

- There are large investments required to develop a world class product. Investment may not be forthcoming without an assured, long term market for the supplier and their product.
- There are high risks which may prevent the supplier developing the product without sharing risks in a long term relationship. Even nation states have partnership arrangements when the costs and risks are high. In the Euro fighter programme, the UK, Germany, Italy and Spain all share the costs and risk.
- The sharing of information and collaboration can significantly reduce the supply chain costs of all the parties. JIT methods can be employed by sharing market and production planning information.
- By collaborating, and using each partner's strengths, product can be brought to the market quicker.
- Both parties can expand their markets, margins or some other benefit by collaboration.

For a partnership agreement to work it is necessary that both parties believe that they will gain from the arrangement. Consequently there needs to be jointly agreed goals, jointly agreed plans, jointly shared risks and benefits. Of course this requires that both companies work and share information across a number of business functions not only purchasing. In particular it requires a degree of openness with respect to costs and maybe other financial information. It is this aspect that causes most companies difficulty in accepting. In Japan, where some of the larger automotive companies employ lean methodology, this particular problem is not such an issue because many of the 1st tier suppliers are at least part owned by the buyer.

Partnership relationships generally require more input than traditional competitive type scenarios. Unlike competitive suppliers who only need to know a limited amount of information, the partnership supplier needs to be treated like a quasi-internal company department. This may include regular meetings and updates across a wide range of business functions and across different levels within both companies. To cement partnership agreements they are often recorded in a partnership agreement.

Typically the buyer will gain the following from a partnership agreement:
- Confidence that they are not being overcharged through transparency of costing.
- Improved security of supply through mutual dependency.
- The supplier's technical and product expertise.
- The sharing of development costs and risk.
- A reduction in administration due to fewer suppliers and fewer purchase orders.

Typically what the supplier will gain:
- Security of demand for its products.
- Longer term planning horizons particularly for new product development.
- Shared development costs and risk.
- The customer's market expertise and access to markets.
- A test bed to develop new products.

Ultimately, partnership relationships may develop into strategic alliances which are characterized by:
- Extensive cross company co-operation at all levels.
- Mutual dependency of the parties for example buyers will have a single source of supply for supply critical items.
- The supplier may have dedicated production facilities for the customer's product.
- Companies share a common corporate vision.
- Very long term agreements.
- Shared ownership.

Partnership sourcing is not without critics in particular it is criticized for:
- Dulling the competitive edge of the supplier.
- One side can cheat and play a competitive game.
- Suppliers may become dependent on the buyer.
- If one party fails financially it can create big headaches for the other partner.

Supplier Management Spectrum

	Competition	Good relationship	Partnership	Strategic alliance
Relationship	Arms length	Regular meetings	Regular scheduled	Shared project management
Suppliers	Many	1 to 3	1 + competitive fringe	1
Exclusive supply	No	No	Possibly within market	Yes
Shared information	RFQ only	Some shared	Shared + trust	Shared
Design	Fully specified	Mainly specified	Joint,	Shared design Development
Product development	Buyers	Buyers	Some shared	Shared
X company contact	No, commercial only	Some	Regular	Frequent
Transactions	e-procurement	Discreet orders/VMS	Reserved capacity	Dedicated production
Contract length	As required	Annual	1 - 3 years	5 years +
Parts	Bulk items commodities	MRO items	Some competition critical items	Competition critical items

Pricing and Costs

Pricing strategies

"The real price of everything, what everything really costs to the man who wants to acquire it, is the toil and trouble of acquiring it" The Wealth of Nations". Adam Smith

Salesmen talk about the 4 Ps of marketing; product, place, promotion and price. Although salesmen are trained to avoid selling on price alone, for buyers it is perhaps the most important factor. There are a variety of ways sellers will arrive at a price.

Average cost pricing

Prices are set such that average costs are covered which should result in the supplier breaking even. Average cost pricing can be worked out by dividing total costs by total production. This type of pricing is sometimes imposed by government and regulatory authorities on natural monopolies to avoid abuse of monopoly power.

Break-even pricing

This method sets the price at a level where total revenue is equal to total costs at a given level of output (assuming you can sell everything you produce!).

Cost plus pricing

Prices are based on marking up costs, usually be a set percentage. Regularly used by defence contractors, suppliers prefer cost plus when quoting for new products with an element of uncertainty or on-going development. From a buyers point of view it is not an attractive pricing strategy. Cost plus pricing shifts all the risk to the buyer and it provides the seller with no incentive to be efficient.

Cross-subsidisation

This occurs when the price of two products is linked. Typically one item is sold with a low margin and the related product on a high margin. The aim is to entice the buyer into purchasing the low margin product and then more than recoup any loss on sales of the high priced subsidiary product. Examples of this would include the sale of equipment and linked consumables or spares. Office printers are often sold well below the cost price on the basis that the supplier will recoup on the sale of high priced ink cartridges. To combat this deception, the buyer needs to focus on the total cost of supply rather than the headline price of the equipment.

Geographic pricing

The basis of geographic pricing is that the supplier is able to separate geographic markets and therefore able to charge different prices in each. The supplier may justify this by claiming that each market is subject to different costs. These claims are usually complete bunkum. Products particularly susceptible to this type of abuse are those with some degree of local differentiation. For example, cars in the UK always used to be more costly than in Europe. Informal cross border trade which would normally correct this imbalance could not occur because UK cars are handed differently to European cars.

Goldilocks pricing

Standard products with embellishments are offered for sale at premium prices to make highly priced standard products appear relatively good value even when they not. Examples could include business class air travel which appears good value when compared with first class air travel.

Another psychology factor at work here is the aversion people have to extreme options. When faced with a premium product, a standard product and a budget product, most people subject to accountability will choose the middle option even if the middle option is overpriced.

Historic pricing

Prices are based on what has been charged previously. This happens more than salesmen would care to admit. This may be because there is comfort in charging a historic price. They don't have to face awkward questions from buyers and they can justify their decision to their bosses. The more resistance buyers put up, the more likely sales people will stick with the historic price.

Learning curve pricing

Often suppliers price new products at a premium price, often to reflect the additional costs and risks when setting up new parts. It is not unreasonable for a buyer to insist that in subsequent years prices should be reduced to reflect the lower costs of production resulting from learning how to operate or produce a product more efficiently.

Loss leaders

Loss leaders are products offered at prices below cost with the aim of selling other higher priced products to the customer at the same time. This is a tactic used regularly by supermarkets. They sell staple items like bread and milk at cost in order to get people into the stores to buyer higher margin product. In the stationery market the staple would be A4 copier paper.

Lump sum pricing

A bundle of products or services are offered as a complete package at a lump sum price. In doing so, the seller can hide high margins on some products within the bundle. To counter this, buyers should ask for breakdown of prices and break up bundles by cherry picking.

Marginal cost pricing

Prices are based on the incremental cost of producing items. This is good for the buyer since he is not usually paying for any of the supplier's overhead costs.

Monopoly pricing

A monopolist is able to set prices by restricting supply, the buyer has no option but to pay the price the monopolist offers.

The monopolist derives his power from the lack of alternatives available to the buyer. The best way the supplier can control the monopolist's power is to develop alternatives.

Nuisance pricing

The supplier doesn't really want the work, it is a nuisance either because the company already have enough work or they prefer not to work for the buyer. The resulting price is unrealistically high.

Peak pricing

When capacity is fixed but demand is flexible, prices may be increased above the average rate to encourage purchases at off peak times. Typically used in the supply of utilities and services.

Penetration pricing

The aim of this policy is to gain market share by offering low prices. This strategy is used when the price elasticity of demand is highly elastic (small change in price leads to large change in demand). Sometimes it may be used in a relatively new market where there is a threat of new entrants into the market. In effect it acts as a barrier to entry.

Predatory pricing

It may employ predatory pricing, to undercut other suppliers to gain market share and make it unprofitable for competitors to remain in the market. Companies can only do this for a short time unless they have other profitable lines which can cross-subsidize the low price. This strategy in export markets is called dumping.

Prestige pricing

Product is offered at the higher end of the price spectrum to attract status conscious customers, who see a snob value in paying high prices. Prestige pricing often relies upon product branding to create an image of exclusiveness and product reputation. The astute buyer should factor out any price premium based on hyped reputation.

Price discrimination

Different customers are charged different rates for the same product. Price discrimination occurs when the supplier can segregate its various markets and customers. The most obvious example is the separation of OEM and distributor markets. Another example is in the provision of personal services. In both these cases, price discrimination relies to a large extent upon the supplier maintaining confidentiality of pricing agreements.

Price points

This strategy works on the basis that the customer's price elasticity of demand will shift significantly at different points along the price spectrum. Selling something at £20 may be a psychological block for some buyers but £19.95 may be perfectly acceptable.

Price lists

A tool often used by the market leading supplier. One purpose of the price list is to set the direction of pricing, usually upwards. The result is that price lists often bear no relation to actual market prices. When this happens buyers need to keep on top of the level of discount received. Discounts of 80 to 90% are common in some industries. Often the net price following discount bears no relation to the published price list. Advice to buyers, ignore published price lists, it is the net price that really matters.

Price to meet competition

This pricing strategy may be used in a market where there is strong price competition between suppliers. This situation approximates to the perfect competition models found in classical economics. Many suppliers, none of whom can individually affect the market pricing of a homogenous type of product. In this situation suppliers have to follow market trends and accept the going rate for their product.

Promotional pricing

This is a low price usually limited by time, quantity or availability of stock. The strategy is based on creating a fear of scarcity due to limits on supply for example 'when it's gone, it gone' offers (WIGIG).

Retrospective (contingent) discount pricing

This is where the buyer and seller agree that at the end of the contract period a discount will be applied, usually on the basis of volume purchased and a sum rebated to the buyer. This is often popular with buyers and sellers alike, the buyer can show a saving to his bosses and the seller can point to a higher volume of sales. Salesmen like to tie retrospective discounts to year on year increases in spend. If the buyer goes along with this any savings will be a one off saving rather than an on-going cost reduction.

Skimming

This is a profit maximising strategy in which prices are set high to cream off buyers who are not price sensitive. This strategy would suit a seller with limited supplies or a product that does not lend itself to high volume low cost manufacturing. Alternatively the strategy may be appropriate for a product which is early in its life cycle.

Sticky pricing

Prices do not change to reflect changing market circumstances. Prices are usually sticky downwards, that is suppliers are keen to raise prices when costs rise but slow to reduce prices when costs fall.

What the market or buyer will bear

The highest price the market can bear is called the ceiling price. The ceiling price will be higher the greater the price inelasticity of demand (inelastic demand is relatively unresponsive to price changes). The profit maximising strategy for the seller is to establish the price each individual buyer will bear. To be successful the seller must have very good market intelligence both of the customer's attitude and competitor pricing. This is a real battle of knowledge, bluff and nerve between the buyer and the seller.

Price points

"Price is what you pay, value is what you get".
Warren Buffet

The relationship between the price and quantity demanded can be plotted to create a demand curve. It is normally depicted as a smooth line, sloping down to the right with a slight convex to the origin.

The gradient of the demand curve measures the sensitivity of demand to changes in the price this is what is described as the price elasticity of demand. The price elasticity of demand (PED) can be worked out using the formula:

% change in quantity / % change in price = PED

If the PED is less than 1, then a change in the price results in less than proportionate change in demand and if greater than 1 a price change result in greater than proportionate change in the demand. If price elasticity of demand is 1 then price changes result in an exactly proportionate change in the quantity demanded.

In reality, the demand curve is unlikely to be smooth but a series of mini curves, as shown below.

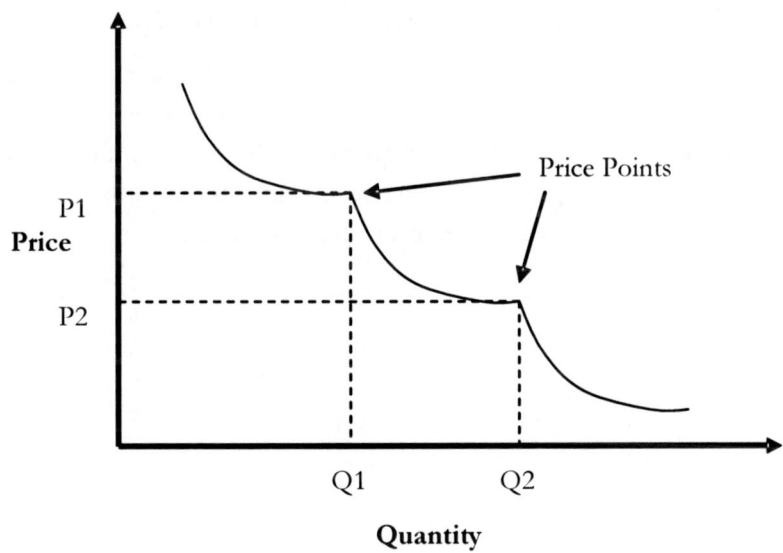

This pattern occurs because demand doesn't behave in a regular way when price changes. There are some points on the demand curve were demand is particularly sensitive to price changes, these are called price points.

At prices just above the price point, demand tends to more elastic (greater demand changes) and just below the price point demand is relatively inelastic (lesser demand changes).

- Psychological prices. These are prices some people may be unwilling to exceed for a particular product. They tend to be at round numbers, which is why supermarkets price goods at £0.99 rather than £1. A variation on this theme is the concept of a 'ceiling' price, "I'll never pay more than £10 for a cd". Ceiling prices are often specific to particular demographic groups and can sometimes become institutionalised. The marketing rationale of 'pound shops' is entirely based on the concept of ceiling prices.

- Price points can sometimes be interrelated to the price of close substitute product. For example, when the price of Pepsi rises higher than the price of Coca Cola the demand will fall off markedly. This effect can be measured by using cross price elasticity of demand (CPed) and can be calculated as follows:

  CPed = (% change in demand X) / (% change in price of Y)

- The market may get use to a particular price for an item. When the price increases above a customary level the demand for the product will decline more proportionately than the increase in price. For example, if a burger restaurant increases its price of its basic hamburger, this effect is likely to happen.

Simple break-even analysis

"Benefits should be conferred gradually; and in that way the taste better". Niccolo Machiavelli

Table 5.   *Calculating the break-even point.*

Output	Total costs	Sales Revenue
0	£40,000	£0
1000	£42,000	£10,000
2000	£44,000	£20,000
3000	£46,000	£30,000
4000	£48,000	£40,000
5000	£50,000	£50,000
6000	£52,000	£60,000
7000	£54,000	£70,000
8000	£56,000	£80,000
9000	£58,000	£90,000
10,000	£60,000	£100,000

Method 1 Plot graphically

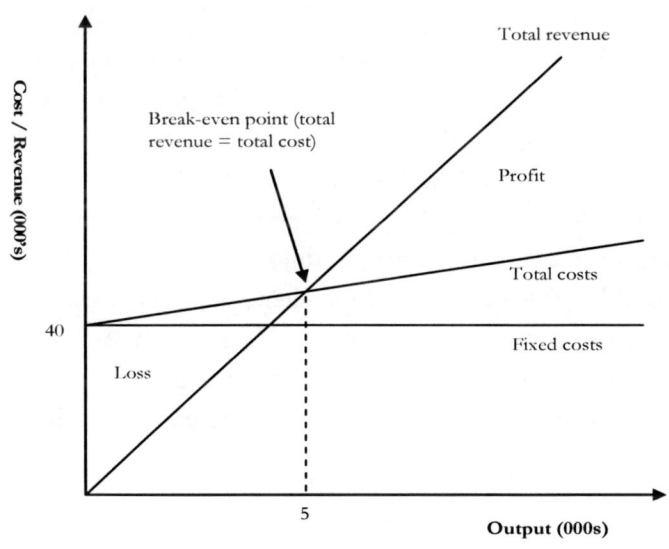

Method 2 (unit basis)

B/E point   = Fixed costs / 1 - (variable unit costs/sales price per unit)
B/E point   = £40,000 / 1 – (2/10)
B/E point   = 50,000 units

Method 3 (total basis) assume output 8,000

B/E point   = Fixed costs / 1 – (total variable costs / total sales rev)
B/E point   = £40,000 / 1 – (£16,000 / £80,000)
B/E point   = 50,000 units

Contribution   = Sales (1-variable cost per unit / selling price per unit)
                = 80,000 (1 – 2/10)
                = £64,000
Profit   = Contribution – fixed costs
                = £64,000 - £40,000
                  = £24,000

Variation of price (VOP)

"Beware of geeks bearing formulas" Warren Buffet

Variation of price formulas, sometimes called contract price adjust-ment (CPA), are used to take account of changes in prices from the time the prices are originally agreed to some date in the future when payment is due. Normally VOP clauses are used on contracts for the supply of goods with very long lead times or contracts for services provided over an extended period of time.

A typical VOP formula has three elements, a fixed element some-times called a non-variable element (NVE), a materials element and a labour element. However, there is nothing to stop any relevant factor being used (currency, interest rate) and there can be more elements than three.

A simple VOP formula may be:

$$P = 0.45 \times \frac{L1 - L0}{L0} + 0.45 \times \frac{M1 - M0}{M0}$$

Where:

P is the percentage adjustment for labour and materials
L0 is the base labour index
L1 is the labour index at the end of the period
M0 is the base material index
M1 is the material index at the end of the period

In this case labour and materials are equally weighted and the fixed element is 10%. The split should reflect the particular circumstances of the contract.

Using the example above, if the relevant indices for labour and material are:

L0 = 110 and L1 = 120 = (120-110)/110 = 0.0909
M0 = 115 and M1 = 125 = (125-115)/115 = 0.0869
Then P = 0.45 x 0.0909 + 0.45 x 0.0869 = 0.0409 + 0.0391
      = 8% variation in price

The formula above is similar to the most commonly recognised VOP formula produced by BEAMA (British Electrical and Allied Manufacturers). BEAMA release indices on a monthly based on UK Government Central Statistics Office (C.S.O.).

VOP formulas are normally preferred by the sellers because it allows them to offer prices based on current information rather than speculate on future price movements. The best advice to buyers is to get a firm price for products or work, however, if there is a risk of inflation, buyer's shouldn't unreasonably refuse a VOP clause because the supplier may otherwise load the price from the start, allow for large contingency costs or even refuse to quote.

When considering what form of VOP clause to accept, a buyer should consider:

- Choosing price indices that accurately reflect the industry or sector which best represent the conditions facing the seller.
- Making the fixed element as large as possible by identifying elements of the price which are unlikely to vary. The higher the fixed element the better it normally is for the buyer.
- Choosing the base dates for the variable elements. Check the indices first to see whether seasonal or other factors make them particularly low. If you agree base dates with exceptionally low indices then you are likely to face larger adjustments in price.
- Get the right balance between the labour element and the material element. In most cases for the supply of physical goods, the material element will be greater than the labour element.
- Dates for reviewing movements in indices should reflect real milestones in the work. Raw material purchases tend to be front end loaded whereas labour costs tend to be incurred later in a project.

Costing systems

"When a variable factor is applied to a fixed factor in increasing quantities, for a time the marginal product may increase but eventually will diminish". The law of diminishing returns

When trying to understand how a supplier has arrived at a particular quote, it is good practice to take the price and attempt to deconstruct it into its cost components. The aim of price deconstruction is to establish whether the offer is reasonable or whether there are flaws in it which the buyer can challenge. In performing this task, it is useful to understand some of the methods suppliers use to determine their prices.

Direct costs

These are costs incurred directly in making the product, including: direct labour (assembly workers), direct materials (raw materials), direct expenses (often a minor category which includes things like special equipment or royalties paid to use a particular process). All the direct costs make up the 'prime cost' of the product. Direct costs are sometimes thought of as variable costs because they vary with the level of production.

Indirect costs

This generally refers to factory overheads, including indirect labour, materials and expenses. Indirect labour will include the wages of all the support staff like buyers and accountants. Indirect materials will include materials like safety clothing, cleaning equipment, etc. Indirect expenses include costs such as rates, heating, lighting, equipment depreciation costs etc. Indirect costs are sometimes called fixed costs.

Absorption costing

Also known as 'full costing', this is where all costs, both direct and indirect associated with the production of the product are applied to normal output levels to give a unit cost. Since all costs are used it is a better method of costing for a company's long term planning. However, from a buyer's point of view, absorption costing can lead to selling prices that seem unreasonably high.

Budgeting

This is a financial plan detailing every major expense associated with a project or cost area. Budgets as a management tool are particularly useful for comparing projected and actual expenses. As a buyer, budgets are more likely to be a constraint upon your purchasing choices than a consideration of supplier costing. From a negotiation standpoint, budgets can always be used as a legitimate reason to request a price reduction from your supplier.

Marginal costing / variable costing / direct costing

This is where only the direct costs of the product are included, for example, direct material, direct labour and variable manufacturing overhead. Buying at the marginal cost price is advantageous since the buyer is not paying for all the costs incurred in making a product. However, in the long term, a supplier must recover all costs and make a profit or it will go out of business. Consequently, marginal costing cannot be anything other than a short term policy.

So why would suppliers consider marginal cost pricing? Sometimes companies adopt marginal cost pricing as part of a planned marketing strategy based on price discrimination. If a company can cover its total fixed costs from other lucrative contracts, it may employ marginal costing and sell extremely competitively into target customers or markets. As a buyer you need to be aware that if you are a target customer, you may be able to exploit this strategy and get lower prices than some other customers, maybe even other competitors.

The buyer should also be aware that marginal cost pricing is appealing to sales people, particularly those rewarded on sales volume rather than company profits.

Job costing

This method is often used to measure the costs on small production runs of customized products. With this method all costs associated with the production of a particular job are recorded. Set-up times, patterns and tooling requirements may have a disproportionate affect on the total cost. Consequently, price breaks may be an important factor in the quantity a buyer chooses to purchase.

Process costing

This costing method is most commonly used in continuous processing environments. Costs are monitored for each individual process in the production cycle over a specified period of time. Unit costs are the net costs in the activity divided by the number of units produced. Add together the individual process step unit costs to arrive at the total cost for the entire process.

Standard costing

This is a system for predetermining product cost by using cost standards for labour, materials and overheads. Cost standards are usually based on historical records. The advantage of standard costing is that it is usually stable for a period of time and allows comparison of actual expenditure against expected expenditure. This can be expressed as a cost variance.

From a buyer's point of view, a supplier basing his selling price on standard costs may underestimate the real cost of a product, especially during times of high inflation or when standards are allowed to lapse. On the downside, companies sometimes uplift all standard costs by a fixed amount across the board. This can result in costs and hence prices that don't reflect market realities.

Activity based costing (ABC)

"All money is a matter of belief". Adam Smith

ABC seeks to trace all expenses incurred by individual activities and match them to a process, product or customer. The typical method is:

- Define activities and establish cost centres. Activities can be defined as narrowly as individual processes or as widely as whole functions.
- Activities can be further sub-divided and so on, depending on the degree of definition that is required.
- Allocate all expenses (direct and indirect) to a cost centre during a defined period. Total expenses for each activity.
- Calculate the unit cost by dividing total expenses for the period between total the number of units produced by the activity during the period.

Advantages of ABC

- Analysis of activity data will allow more detailed and practical recommendations than global costing systems.

- Line managers and staff are more likely to be involved in the data collection process and results will have greater relevance for staff.
- It helps to improve efficiency by hi-light both wasteful and value adding activities.
- By concentrating on activities it makes benchmarking easier and allows performance metrics and scorecards to be developed.
- It is more accurate than using global total costs.
- It encourages accountability.

Disadvantages of ABC

- It is an internal management tool rather than a costing measure which can be used externally
- Since the conventional forms of costing often have to be maintained there is a duplication of effort.
- Operational managers may view it with suspicion
- It can be costly and complex to collect data and administer

Attempts to rectify some of the problems operating ABC have been addressed in Time Driven Activity-Based Costing

Target costing or engineering costing

The starting point for this method is identifying a viable selling price and working backwards through the costs rather than the conventional approach of analysing an existing product and identifying the costs associated. This approach engages a wider cross section of skills from within the company and involves them in designing, manufacturing and marketing a product for a particular market.

Cost estimation

"Work expands to fill the time available for its completion".
Parkinson's Law

Estimation is the act of predicting the physical quantities of resources required to complete a project or product. Cost estimation goes further by assigning costs to the resources identified. Estimation is normally used because establishing the actual cost of something would either take too long or would be too costly.

Cost estimates are important because they often form the basis by which suppliers decide their sales prices. Understanding the methods of estimating may provide the buyer useful information when negotiating with the supplier. The most common methods of estimating costs are detailed below:

Estimation by analogy

This method is often described as a 'top down' approach to estimating. It uses previous projects or products as comparators by which to estimate the current job. This method depends upon having both reasonably similar projects to compare against and good cost records on previous projects. Estimating by analogy is usually quick but accuracy depends on how similar the project is and how good your records are. For example, building a power station in the UK in 2010 may be a completely different cost to building a replica power station in Africa in 2008. Currency and interest rates may have changed, price inflation may have made equipment more expensive and local land, labour and materials will all be different.

When the nature of the project or product is qualitatively similar but quantitatively different, estimators will either scale up or down the comparator project. However, care must be taken because in many cases an increase in scale will not necessarily lead to a proportionate increase in costs. Different industries have from experience developed formulas which take account of such matters as physical principles of scale and economic economies of scale.

Estimation by analysis of inputs

This is a 'bottom up' approach that works by breaking down a project into its components, estimating the cost of each of these and then aggregating the results. The lower the level of detail estimated the more accurate the estimate but the longer and costlier it is to arrive at an answer.

As a minimum, records should break down cost into the main constituent elements, direct materials and labour and indirect costs like overheads. Better still, these broad categories will be broken down into their sub-assemblies and individual parts. The full implementation of this approach would result in a fully itemized, structured and costed bill of materials.

Sometimes, when economy of effort is required, it may be expedient to estimate only the top 20% of items by cost, knowing that you will probably be covering 80% of the total costs. Similarly, in most medium size projects you will tend to find that there are probably less than 10 items that actually make up the bulk of the cost. Experience of your own industry will usually tell you what items you need to price up.

Adjusting estimates for price changes

Most forms of estimating which use historic data will lose accuracy over time due to price inflation. It is therefore an important part of estimating to allow for escalation in raw material, labour and overhead costs.

If the date the original costing is known, it is usually a straight forward task to look at the inflation rate during the period and adjust prices to take account of this. Raw material prices are readily available on the internet and changes in labour rates for different industrial sectors are published regularly by the Central Statistics Office (C.S.O.).

One of the most common tasks of a buyer, is to assess a supplier's quotation against an earlier price. If you know the major components of your supplier's price then you can follow the method above. However, in most circumstances you will not know the proportion of the price made up by each of the main cost elements. To help you avoid this situation, it is always wise to ask suppliers to provide a break-down of their selling price at the time of quotation. Often the split is similar across all suppliers of a similar product, so once you have this information you can assess a wide range of suppliers.

If you cannot find out this information from a supplier, I suggest a good rule of thumb for general industrial items is that materials will account for about 50% of the costs, direct labour about 25% and the balance overhead and profit. Of course this is only a very rough guide, some products will have a higher material content than this, some less and some industries, notably defence, will have overhead rates several times the level of all direct costs.

Parametrics

Costs are sometimes estimated used parametric models and standards. For example, the cost of a buying land or storage space may be estimated by £'s per square foot.

High-low method

If you know the total costs for a range of quantities it is possible to estimate the variable cost of a product using the high-low method. Take the following cost pattern.

Quantity	Total Cost
2,000	£15
3,000	£13
2,000	£14
4,000	£12

Subtract the highest cost from the lowest cost (£15-£12) = £3 and divide by the highest demand less the lowest demand (4,000 – 2,000) = 3/2,000 = £0.0015 estimated variable cost per unit.

Expert opinion

Perhaps the simplest way is to ask a number of experts in the field to make their best guess of the cost. This can then be refined by either, feeding back the results to the experts and asking them to revise their own guesses or by removing any extreme guesses and averaging the remainder.

Estimating the mass of materials

"If a commodity were in no way useful, - in other words, if it could in no way contribute to our gratification, - it would be destitute of exchangeable value, however scarce it might be,or whatever quantity of labour might be necessary to procure it".
David Ricardo

The specific gravities (SG) of all materials are benchmarked against pure water which has a specific gravity of 1 and a mass of 1000 kg per cubic meter at 4 degrees C (some standards use 60 degrees F). Density changes with temperature and 4 degrees C was chosen as this is the temperature at which water is most dense. Similarly, glass has a SG of 2.5, which means it has will have a mass of 2500 kg per cubic meter. Likewise steel has a SG of 7.85 and a mass of 7850kg / m3.

To calculate the mass of a solid piece of material we can use the formula: volume x specific gravity. For example, A mild steel plate 3000 x 1500 x 15mm, the calculation would be:

Length (m) x width (m) x thickness (m) x mass per m3
3 x 1.5 x 0.015 x 7850 = 530kg approximately

Alternatively,

Length (m) x width (m) x thickness (mm) x SG
3 x 1.5 x 15 x 7.85 = 530kg approximately

Table 6. *The approximate specific gravity for some common engineering materials*

Aluminium bronze	7.7
Aluminium extrusion	2.71
Brass rolled	8.7
Cement	1.5
Concrete, Portland and limestone	2.371
Chromium	7.19
Copper rolled	8.95
Glass	2.5
Gold	19.32
Gypsum	2.3
Iron	7.85
Iron cast	7.2
Lead	11.34
Magnesium	1.738
Manganese	7.35
Molybdenum	10.188
Monel	8.36-8.84
Nickel	8.9
Nylon 6	1.12-1.14
Phosphor bronze	8.9
Platinum	21.4
PVC rigid	1.45-1.5
Sand silica	2.6
Silver	10.49
Steel carbon rolled	7.85
Stainless steel 304	7.9
Tin	7.28
Titanium	4.506
Tungsten	19.6
Tungsten carbide	14.29
Vanadium	5.594
Water at 4 degrees C (benchmark)	1
Zinc	7.135
Zinc cast	6.9

Material costs

"Markets are constantly in a state of uncertainty and flux and money is made by discounting the obvious and betting on the unexpected". George Soros

Raw material markets are notoriously volatile, prices rise when demand exceeds supply and fall when there is an excess of supply over demand. There are many factors affecting supply and demand of raw materials, the main ones are detailed below:

- Loss of capacity, due to strikes, plant closures, accidents, natural disasters and wars will often have significant effects on the world price of materials. For example, the price of nickel rose dramatically in 1978 and 1979 due to a strike at Inco. Part of the problem lies in the fact that capacity is often concentrated in only a few countries. For example, Chile is the source of about a third of the world's total copper output and Peru 15%. Conditions affecting the mining of copper in this part of the world have a significant effect on the world price.

- Speculation. Investors buy and sell metals in anticipation of future price changes. Prices driven by speculation often lack any firm underlying causes but once started speculation can create its own momentum driven by the herd instinct and human emotions, not least fear and greed. Invariably, speculation causes the market to exaggerate price movements and in the worst case create price bubbles that invariably end up bursting.

- Fundamental, long term, changes in supply or demand. Additional processing capacity, more efficient extraction technologies or discoveries of new deposits will all tend to drive prices down. The main cause of increasing demand is often the natural growth of economies. The massive increase metal prices during the last decade, was largely due to increasing demand from Asia and in particular China.

- Security. Sometimes physical goods are demanded because they are a relatively safe store of wealth during uncertain economic times. In stable political and economic circumstances gold is not normally the investment of choice because it doesn't earn interest. However, the recent global financial and economic crisis has made gold (and scarce commodities in general) an attractive store of value for those seeking security.

Case study - nickel

Nickel prices are a classic case of market volatility, driven in some way by all the factors noted above. Used extensively in the production of steels, nickel typically accounts for 60-70% of the end cost of stainless steel. Historically the market has been dominated by a limited number of producers in a small number of countries (Australia, Canada and Russia).

Prices fell to a low in 1986 causing producers to cut capacity and reduce supply. In 1987, the demand for stainless steel increased dramatically. At the same time, the Dominican Republic imposed large duties on the export of nickel. The resulting shortage caused nickel prices to increase five-fold reaching a peak in 1988. Production was ratcheted up by suppliers leading to nickel prices falling just as dramatically as they as risen. The fall of the Soviet Union in 1991, released large amounts of nickel onto the world market which further depressed prices. In 1995, the destruction of a power plant in Finland seriously reduced the processing capacity and hence the supply of nickel from Russia. In the same year, high demand from Japan, following an earthquake, caused prices to again surge. Prices fell back again until 1999 when strikes, technical problems and cold weather in Finland reduced supply below demand which firmed up prices. After stabilizing in 2005, nickel prices increased massively in 2006 reaching a peak in 2007, driven up by strong demand from Asia, particularly China. Speculative purchasing at this time financial instability no doubt multiplied this effect. Prices fell sharply in 2008 before recovering some ground in 2009. At the time of writing, prices are about 50% off the peak prices.

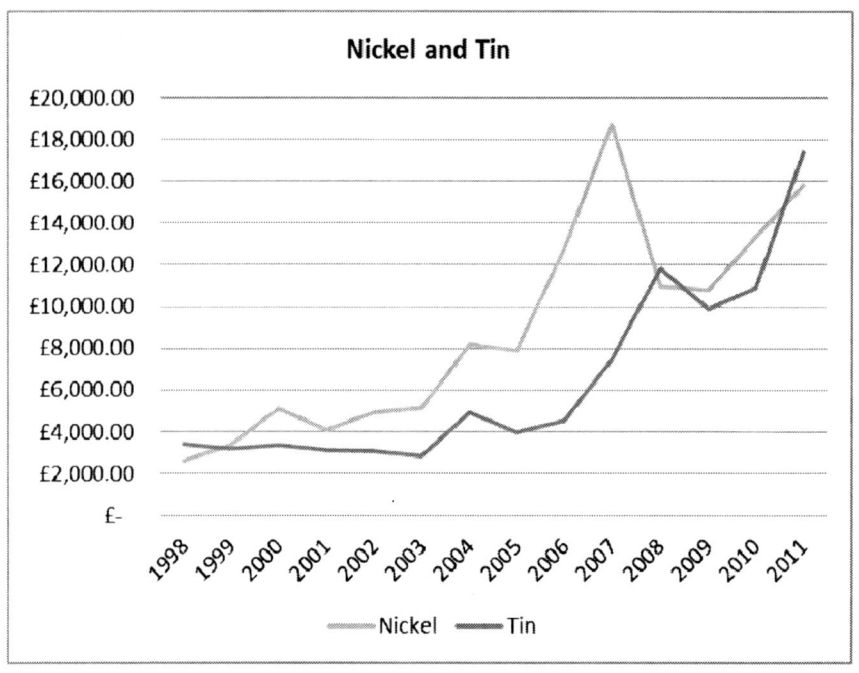

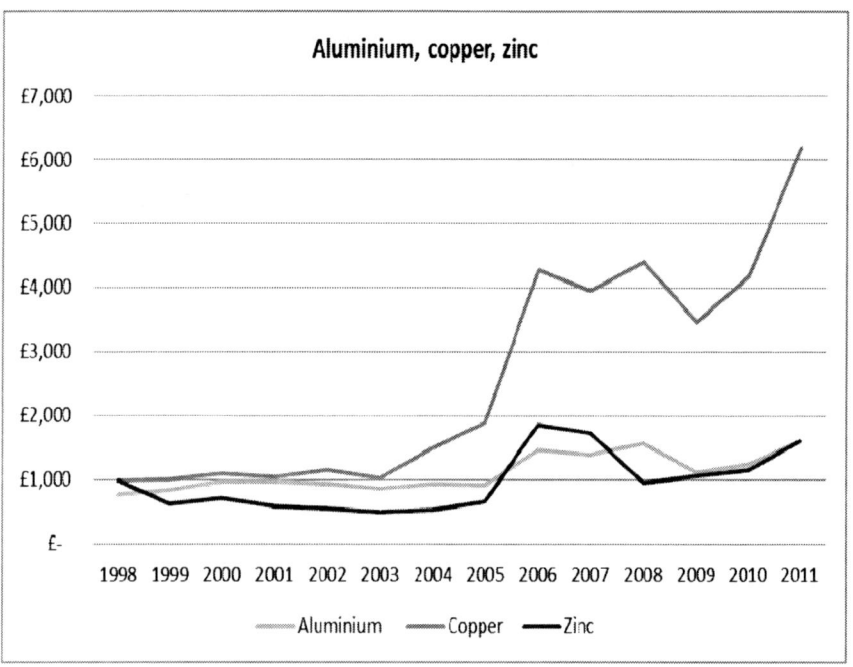

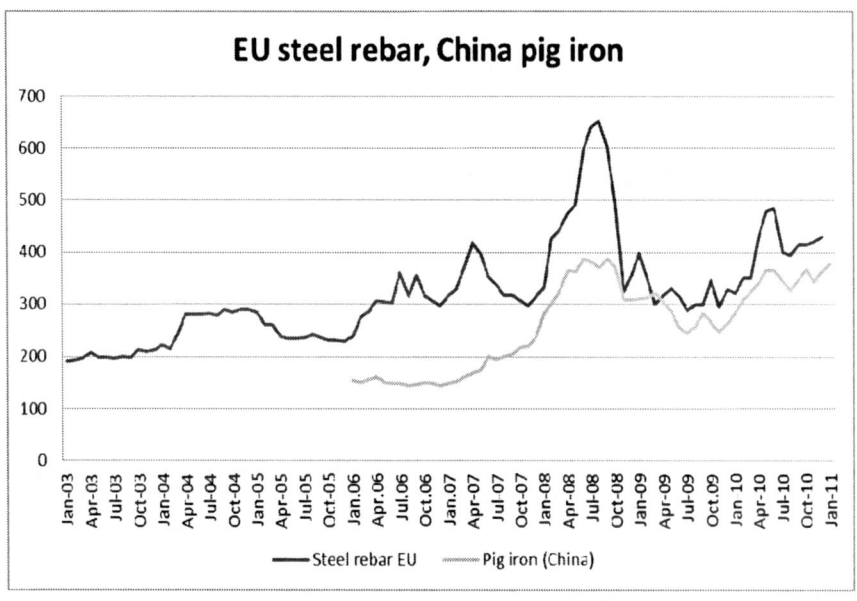

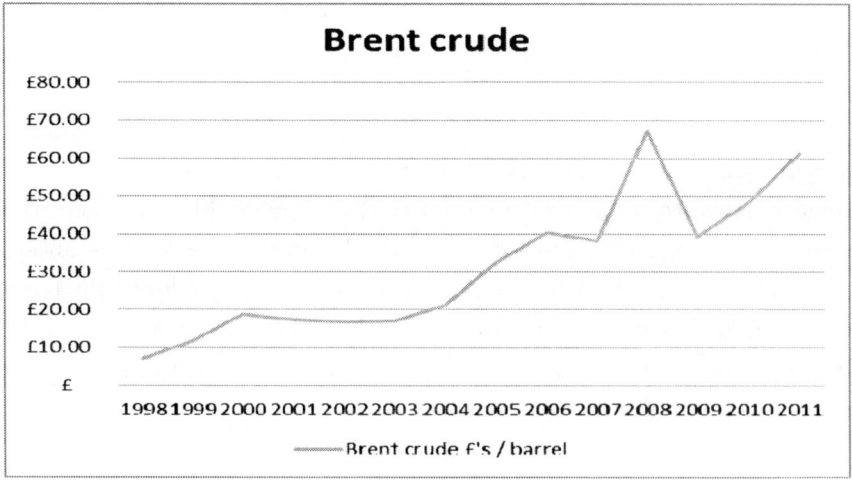

The prices are approximate and for general guidance only, to indicate general market trends over the period. The source of data is either stockholder prices or the BBC reporting on the London Metal Exchange (LME). The figures for 2011 are based on or about the 1st of January, at which time the price of commodities were rising rapidly.

Quality

Quality standards and purchasing

"Quality is not an act, it is a habit". Aristotle

ISO9000

The recognised quality procedure in the UK is ISO 9001. There used to be three versions ISO 9001, ISO 9002 and ISO 9003, often referred to generically as ISO 9000. The three standards were consolidated into ISO 9001 in December 2000. The latest update is ISO 9001: 2008.

With respect to purchasing, the relevant part of the standard is section 7.4. Comprising of 3 sections, 7.4.1 which deals with purchasing process, section 7.4.2 which covers purchasing information and 7.4.3 which describes the verification of purchase product. The 2008 update has not changed from ISO 9001:2000.

The first point to make is that the sections that refer to purchasing are drafted very broadly. They are brief and not particularly detailed instead they are written in such a way that they could be applied to a very wide range of circumstance. On the positive side, this allows great scope when drafting the purchasing quality procedure to make it suit your operating circumstances. On the downside, it provides little guidance on what an auditor will be looking for. When drafting your procedure consider the following:

Purchasing process

- Define what is important to you in achieving your final product.
- Suppliers should be assessed on their ability to meet your defined requirements.
- There is no requirement that you only use ISO 9001 approved suppliers.

- Suppliers are evaluated against supplier performance standards set by you.
- There is no specific requirement for a supplier questionnaire but it is a good basis for starting a quality records file.
- It is acceptable to approve a supplier on previous good performance.
- When organising suppliers, differentiate between those whose performance directly affect the end product and those that don't. For this reason, many companies leave their indirect purchase outside the scope of their ISO 9001 procedures.
- Define who is authorised to commit the company to contracts and set levels of authority if necessary.
- Maintain approved suppliers lists and keep supplier performance records (maintain quality records).
- Regularly re-evaluate supplier performance.
- Create a mechanism for performance feedback to the supplier.
- Consider courses of action following re-evaluation. If the supplier fails the evaluation process, it may be necessary for the supplier to re-train, re-tool, re-organise or take other steps to improve.
- Have a policy for deciding why, how and when, suppliers are de-listed as an approved supplier.
- Demonstrate continual improvement by periodically checking that the purchasing policy is aligned to company needs and objectives.

Purchasing information

- Purchase documentation must clearly specify relevant details including purchase order, part specification, quantity, delivery, certification, etc.
- Part specifications must reflect the customer requirements and be consistent with design / engineering control. Ideally parts should be linked to a bill of materials.

- Consider the approval of supplier's quality systems and the training / qualifications of their personnel.
- Allow for purchase order review and checking of accuracy prior to release.
- Consider goods inwards inspection procedures and certification requirements.

Verification of purchased product

- Set up control systems to ensure that delivered product or services meet the standards specified.
- Procedures must be made clear to all parties.
- Goods should not be released until the goods have been verified in accordance with the purchase order and the procedure.

TS16949

ISO/TS16949:2009 is the international quality standard for automotive industries and service part companies. The latest version 2009 replaces the 2002 version and ensures compatibility with ISO9001:2008 and ISO14001:2004.

Automotive companies across the globe have adopted this standard to avoid the need for multiple national certification standards such as the American QS-9000, the French EAQF, the German VDA6.1 and the Italian AVSQ standard.

The ISO/TS16949:2009 procedure aims to emphasize:

- Continual improvement.
- Defect prevention.
- Reduction of waste.
- Minimization of variation.

Automotive manufacturers are required to pass on the requirements of the procedure to their tier 1 suppliers. Manufacturers and tier 1 suppliers are assessed by an International Automotive Task Force (IATF) accredited registrar and must demonstrate compliance of their quality management systems (QMS).

Root cause analysis (RCA)

"The love of money is the root cause of all evil".
Bible, Timothy 6:10

The aim of root cause analysis is to identify and systematically eliminate the root cause(s) of a problem rather than repeatedly dealing with the symptoms. The end goal is to improve long term quality of output.

RCA is used in many fields of work; with respect to manufacturing we are interested in production based root cause analysis, which is essential to effective manufacturing quality systems and is often an integral part of continuous improvement programs. Most continuous quality improvement programs follow the same steps:

- Identify the problem.
- Gather information on the problems.
- Establish the cause effect relationship.
- Identify causes which if removed would remove the problem.
- Identify solutions that don't have negative side effects.
- Implement solutions.
- Monitor revised performance and re-assess.

Often the most difficult part of this process is establishing the causal links between the problem and the manufacturing system, below are a few simple techniques for doing this:

5 whys

Define the problem, for example, the car has ceased up. Ask why about a problem 5 times, for example:

Why, no engine oil (led indicator)
Why, leak in the engine case (oil under the car)
Why, cracked sump cover (visual inspection)
Why, start of crack not spotted at service
Why, not serviced regularly

Of course you don't have to stop at 5 whys, go on for as long as the chain of causes keeps coming. For most simple problems, people ask themselves all the whys in a split second to come up with the answer but in more complex business situations it is often necessary to go through the process methodically to find the root cause.

Ishikawa diagram (fishbone/cause and effect diagram)

This method is used to identify all the possible causes and effects of a problem. Each of the major causes is represented by a major bone. Each of these main causes may have a number of contributory causes, which are shown as smaller bones. Each of the smaller bones may have contributory causes and these are shown as even smaller bones and so on. Against each new line the question why should be posed to expose all the possible causes.

Normally the starting point for a fishbone analysis is a brainstorming session by a cross functional team. To start the ball rolling the main causes need to be identified these may include for example:

- Plant and equipment
- Materials and physical products used in the process.
- Manpower. Anybody involved in producing the final product.
- Method (management). Includes processes procedures.
- Business functions or department

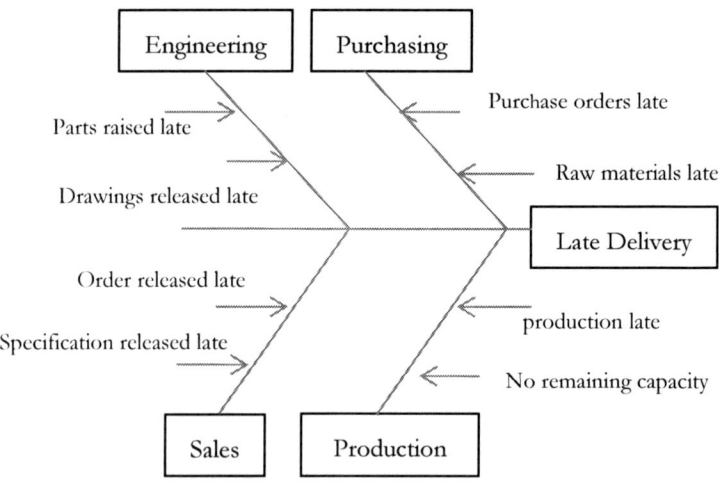

Total quality management (TQM)

*"Profit in business comes from repeat customers, customers
that boast about your project or service, and that bring friends
with them".* W Edwards Deming

The International Standards Organisation (ISO) define TQM as "…a
management approach for an organization, centred on quality, based
on the participation of all its members and aiming at long-term
success through customer satisfaction, and benefits to all members of
the organization and to society."

TQM has its origins in the theories and systems developed by W.
Edwards Deming in post-war Japan. Originally part of the occupying
forces, Deming stayed on to advise Japanese companies in the area of
quality management. The theories and practices he developed became
widely known as total quality management (TQM). In his book "Out
of the Crisis", Deming set out 14 points of quality management:

1   Create constancy of purpose. Make quality improvement
    to the product or service an on-going policy.

2   Make this policy a philosophy running through the com-
    pany from top to bottom. Previous standards of poor de-
    livery and quality are no longer acceptable.

3   Discard the need to inspect all products, quality should
    be built into the product and controlled production
    should ensure consistency.

4   Move toward single sourcing of parts and build close re-
    lations with suppliers with the aim of improving quality.
    Work should not be awarded only on the basis of the
    lowest price; other measures relating to performance
    should be included.

5   Commit to a regime of continuous improvement. Iden-
    tify the problems, improve the process or training, meas-
    ure the results and implement improvements. This is
    embodied in Deming's view of the quality cycle to Plan,
    Do, Check and Act (PDCA).

6   Train staff uniformly to a standard. Use statistical methods to measure performance.

7   Institute leadership, with supervision focusing on helping people to perform their job better by providing the right tools and working environment.

8   Remove management by fear, it damages quality. Encourage all levels of the company to contribute to change

9   Break down barriers between departments. Use cross functional teams to solve problems and improve quality.

10   Slogans are not effective by themselves; they should be supported by effective systems.

11   Eliminate volume driven production quotas and quantitative targets because they emphasise sheer output rather than quality output.

12   Remove barriers to pride in workmanship such as piece work based on volume rather than quality.

13   Institute education and self-improvement in the workforce.

14   Set in place a management structure and systems that entrench a permanent commitment to implement the previous 13 points.

Without doubt Deming's work was influential in shaping Japanese post war industrial development. It could also be argued that his work was the precursor of later management processes like lean manufacturing.

The success of Japanese companies practicing TQM and Lean Manufacturing, like Toyota, has of course led to a great deal of interest from companies outside of Japan. Some companies in Europe and America have adopted these practices but their success has been mixed. Why has it not always been possible to emulate the Japanese experience in other countries? It could be argued that TQM was successful in Japan because of specific conditions that existed there:

•   The unique nature of corporate ownership in Japan which links the largest companies and their suppliers.

- A homogenous workforce that placed great emphasis on teamwork and which was highly motivated to rebuild their country and prepared to accept personal sacrifices to succeed.
- Japanese industry was starting from a clean slate because most of her industry had been flattened during the war.

In contrast, Western countries that tried to emulate Deming's results have tended to have highly individualistic workforces, who don't tend to work well together particularly across functions. Furthermore, workers are generally not prepared to accept personal sacrifices for the long term good of the company. British and American industry came out of the war largely unscathed and brought with it a legacy of industrial practices that were more suited to mass production based on volume rather than supplying quality products that consumers wanted to buy. In such circumstances it is questionable whether Deming's work would have had the same impact as in Japan.

Where TQM and lean manufacturing philosophies have been successfully exported there are often common characteristics.

- The company has started from a green field site; the entire workforce has been completely new.
- The Japanese are the sole or principle investor and Japanese managers and management have been closely involved.

Taking these factors together suggest that TQM will be most successful where a complete change of culture can be fostered. However, since it is largely impractical for most western companies and employees to undergo such a dramatic cultural change, companies have instead chosen to pick out and use specific TQM tools and techniques that can be incorporated into the traditional western practices. The most common tools and techniques used are quality circles, multifunctional problem solving teams, brainstorming, performance benchmarking, cause and effect diagrams (Ishikawa diagram), statistical process control using methods such as six sigma, histograms, Pareto charts, flow charts and scatter diagrams.

Six Sigma

"Does experience help? NO! Not if we are doing the wrong things." W Edwards Deming

This is a statistical based management tool for reducing the number quality defects in output. It has its roots in the concept of a normal distribution curve first proposed by Carl Frederick Gauss in the nineteenth century. In the 1930s, Walter Shewhart, suggested that a three sigma variation from the mean should be used as a guide to indicate the need to improve a process. It was not until the 1980s, that the term six sigma was coined by Bill Smith at Motorola. It drew upon earlier philosophies and methodologies like TQM, zero defects and the work of people like Juran, Deming, Ishikawa and others. It is sometimes used as part of a lean manufacturing program and is best suited to high volume process manufacture.

The theoretical basis of Six Sigma is that process defects will be normally distributed about a mean point. The Greek letter sigma is used to denote the standard variation from this mean point. So a process that operates within one sigma of the norm would indicate a high level of defects with decreasing levels of defects the higher the sigma level. At six sigma level, the number of defects expected will only be about 3 DPMO (defects per million opportunities).

Sigma	Defect Rate	DPMO
1	69.1%	691,462
2	30.9	308,538
3	6.7%	66,807
4	0.62%	6,210
5	0.023%	233
6	0.00034%	3.4

It is important when developing a six sigma system, to define what is a defect? What is a unit? and what is an opportunity?

- A defect is normally defined by failure to meet a critical to quality (CTQ), customer driven specification or performance characteristic. Note, the customer may be the ultimate user of the product or the internal customers in the process chain.
- A unit has to be something that is capable of being measured, but it doesn't have to be a physical unit of output, it can also be a measurable process.
- An opportunity is every independent possibility of a CTQ failure per unit. Complex products or processes may have a high number of opportunities per unit.

Implementation

Six Sigma is often combined with a quality improvement programme. There are normally five steps in a six sigma style quality improvement programme. Sometimes these five steps are described by the acronym DMAIC: Define, Measure, Analyse, Improve, Control; another is DMADV: Define, Measure, Analyse, Design, Verify.

Define

- Who are the customers and what are the customer's critical to quality (CTQ) issues.
- The business processes involved and map them.

Measure

- Determining the metrics (measurements that quantify results), what you will measure and how you will measure it. Metrics should relate to CTQs and should particularly concentrate on weaknesses. Maybe use customer complaints, warranty claims or representative feedback to inform you choices.
- Establish the baseline reference points for your metrics.
- Establish a plan for data collection.
- Survey competitor's performance to benchmark you metrics.

Analyse

- Perform root cause analysis on data. Use methods like 5 Whys, Root Cause Analysis and the Ishikawa (Fishbone) diagram.
- Recommend courses of action. Decide priorities and implement improvements.
- Create controls which enable sustain the changes made.

Improve

- Solutions to problems identified in the analyse stage are developed.
- Solutions are screened for practicality and cost effectiveness, maybe used cost benefit analysis.
- Trials are used to measure the effectiveness of solutions.
- Develop an implementation plan and use project management tools to introduce.

Control

- Record lessons learned and document standards.
- Set up systems to monitor metrics and alert staff when standards fall below those acceptable.
- Train employees who own the processes.

Practitioners of Six Sigma methodology are sometimes described by reference to martial art belts. A black belt will usually be a six sigma project leader, whereas a green belt will be less experienced and responsible for only part of the project. Master black belts train and mentor other six sigma practitioners.

Six Sigma is another term which has been adopted by the supply chain management revolution, and it is now generically used to describe a business performance methodology. When it is considered in this way, it is not dissimilar to lean manufacturing or the supply chain operations reference (SCOR) model. However, it should be noted that Six Sigma is a registered trademark owned by Motorola.

Negotiation

The nature of negotiation

"Nine-tenths of tactics are certain, and taught in books: but the irrational tenth is like the kingfisher flashing across the pool, and that is the test of generals. It can only be ensured by instinct, sharpened by thought practising the stroke so often that at the crisis it is as natural as a reflex." TE Lawrence

Negotiation is the process whereby two or more parties choose to enter into discussions with the other(s) in the belief that in doing so, they will be able to gain advantage that would not be possible if they acted alone.

In a typical trading scenario, the buyer wants to give as little for the goods as possible and the seller wants to charge the highest price possible. However, there is often a range of outcomes that are acceptable to both parties. Negotiation is the process of finding these mutually acceptable outcomes and reaching agreement on them.

Buyer's acceptable range

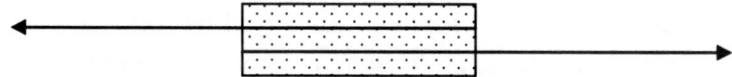

Seller's acceptable range

The shaded area is the mutually acceptable range of outcomes. Of course in some circumstances the buyer and the seller's objectives do not overlap and there is no mutually acceptable range of outcomes. In this circumstance, the lack of common ground should spur both parties to re-assess how realistic their expectations are.

Negotiations are essentially a dynamic process, as they unfold the parties gain new information, and modify their positions accordingly. The ease with which the parties are able to move to modified positions depends to a large extent on the experience of the negotiators, the trust and confidence they have in each other and the ease of communication. This is why face to face meetings are often the best format for difficult negotiations.

However, this doesn't mean that you should start off with low expectations and a low target, you should aim high. In my experience, the higher your target the better results you achieve when compared with lower initial targets. As a rule, start off with low offers and only move slowly to higher bids. However, be careful not to offend or show your ignorance by suggesting a non-sense offer.

The skill in negotiation is to achieve the maximum benefit for your company but still reach an agreement the other side is willing to accept. Some people are good natural negotiators; in part it comes from their personality and in part from experience. This does not mean to say that someone who is a poor natural negotiator cannot become a good negotiator or for that matter that a natural negotiator cannot lose their negotiating edge. Like rock bands, negotiators often do their best work when they are still striving to be recognised and do not have the comfort of success.

The two main personal characteristics of a natural negotiator are competitiveness and a degree of intelligence. Good negotiators tend to be ambitious and want to win; this is displayed not only at work but often in their private lives, particularly in sport or games. As well as competitiveness, buyers need to have a degree of intelligence. By intelligence, I don't mean they are good at algebra or some other academic subject, but that they are gifted at weighing up people and situations, and are can skilfully manipulate them toward a particular goal through persuasion, guile or strength of personality.

There are other core personal qualities that make a good negotiator that should not be overlooked:

- Analytical skills, in particular the ability to quickly recognise the main issue from subsidiary ones and to be able to identify the barriers to achieving the objective.
- Flexibility and creativeness. Good negotiators are adept at thinking of and trying different strategies to reach their goal.
- Good communication skills particularly presentational skills and persuasiveness. Negotiators have to convince the other side that they are both trustworthy and that their suggestions will be successful.

Styles of negotiation

"One of the things I learnt when I was negotiating was that until I changed myself I could not change others".
Nelson Mandela

There are many different styles of negotiation; some people approach negotiation as a joint problem solving exercise based on co-operation, others will see it as a competitive process in which they must prevail over the opposition and then there are some people who try to avoid conflict altogether and seek to avoid negotiation or to accommodate the other party by compromise. Each of these approaches even the last one can be the most effective style, it really depends upon the circumstances and in particular the strength of the different parties. Good negotiators have a range of styles they can draw upon, employing them individually or combining them at different stages of the negotiation.

It is widely accepted that the two main approaches to negotiation are adversarial and co-operative. The characteristics of each are detailed below:

The adversarial approach works on the assumption that there is a cake of finite size that must be carved up between the parties. It is the job of the negotiator to secure as much of the cake as possible for his side. This is sometimes called a zero sum game because one party's gain or loss is exactly balanced by the gains or losses of the other party. This view of negotiation is attractive to buyers because in most simple purchasing tasks this is self-evidently true. Ceteris paribus, if the seller increases the price of an item, your company loses that amount and the seller's company gains whole of the benefit.

A negotiator adopting an adversarial style will seek to exaggerate their strength and will talk down or undermine the strength of the opposition. Competitive negotiators share little information with the other side, start with high demands and only give small concessions, slowly when absolutely necessary. This type of negotiator may use silence, threats and coercion to achieve their aims. It is not unknown for a competitive negotiator to be overbearing and use force of personality to unnerve the other side.

An adversarial approach is best employed when the subject of the negotiation is a one off deal, in a highly competitive market with many suitably qualified suppliers. It is effective against inexperienced negotiators particularly those who don't like conflict. However, adopting an adversarial approach can be a high risk strategy when not used appropriately. Avoid using it when the other side has a lot of negotiating strength, particularly if their strength lies in the scarcity of the product or service. Avoid using it when you want to maintain a long and constructive relationship with a supplier. Specific risks of using an adversarial approach could include:

- The other party will remember and compensate in the future, for example, by quoting higher initial prices.
- People on the receiving end of an adversarial approach will be less willing to provide goodwill services like pulling orders forward.
- The other party may not be intimidated and may either close up, withdraw from negotiation, or fight back with threats.

Sometimes it is possible to play a competitive negotiation game but portray yourself as the good guy, for example, you can introduce the pressure of a cheaper alternative quotation by adding that you would prefer to deal with the supplier so long as the price is competitive. In this way, a robust message is put across but in a charming way.

The alternative view is that the size of the cake can be enlarged by co-operation and even if one party does get a larger slice both parties will still benefit. This is in essence the rationale behind the development of 'strategic' partnerships.

The nature of a co-operative negotiator will be to identify areas of common interest, in particular, problems that prevent the full benefit of the business relationship being exploited. For example, by identifying and exchanging concessions that have a relatively greater value to the other party. Co-operative negotiators will work to promote trust with the other party and develop a long term relationship, which is conducive to sharing information which may add value through improved products and better co-ordination of the supply chain.

The principal risk of adopting a co-operative type approach is that the other party does not follow suit and behaves competitively. This dilemma is best summed up by an analogy known as the 'prisoner's dilemma'. Two prisoners are held in isolation at the police station under suspicion of committing a crime. They each face a choice, confess or remain silent. If one prisoner confesses and one remains silent, the one who confesses gets off with a light sentence and the silent prisoner takes the rap. If both confess they both receive moderate sentences. If both remain silent they each get off. If one prisoner uses a co-operative negotiating stance and the other party disguises their true intentions and takes an adversarial approach then the former will come off badly.

In summary, weigh up the circumstances when deciding on what approach to take in a negotiation. Don't feel that you have to stick to a particular approach but adapt as the negotiation develops. If necessary mix and match, for example, start submissive to put the other side at ease, move to co-operative to gain information and finish a negotiation competitively after the supplier has given away their position. In short, no single approach is necessarily correct, effective negotiation depends on lots of different factors which you need to read and tailor your own approach to.

Negotiation preparation and planning

"No plan survives contact with the enemy".
Helmuth von Moltke

To get the most from a face to face negotiation, prior preparation and planning are essential. Detailed below are some steps you may want to take prior to a negotiation.

Identify your broad objectives

Try to be avoid being too specific at this stage. Your objectives should be a way of guiding your research and planning but be prepared to change your objectives as you gather more knowledge.

Identify information that will help you exert influence over the other party in line with your broad objectives

The best place to start is to research the seller, their product and their competitors. Your research should focus on identifying your supplier's strengths and in particular their weaknesses. Knowing these factors can allow you to steer the meeting in a direction that favours your position and in doing so generate negotiating power.

When considering which areas of research to concentrate on, pay particular attention to information that can be quantified and that can be used to compare your supplier with their competitors or the market generally. Your main areas of research may include:

- Prices or quotations.
- Cost breakdowns of any products involved.
- Key raw material prices and their movements.
- Historic spend with the supplier and possible changes in spend.
- Supplier performance in previous contracts.
- Additional costs of dealing with a particular supplier, for example additional costs of carriage and insurance.
- Indirect benefits of dealing with a particular supplier, for example access to new markets.

- What percentage of the supplier's overall total business does the requirement represent?
- What had been the supplier's policy with other customers?
- What financial pressures may be operating on the supplier?
- What are the market conditions for the supplier's products or service?
- What is the structure of the market the supplier operates in? For example, many competitive suppliers or few.
- What approach has the supplier taken in similar negotiations?
- Why might the seller find your business particularly attractive?
- What benefits can you offer your supplier
- Is the supplier working below production capacity or otherwise, are they desperate for business or are they fully committed.

Identify missing information

If you have gaps in your research which may prevent you from fully exploiting your strengths and their weaknesses now is the time to realise it and do something about it.

The most powerful tool that you can exploit in a negotiation situation are alternative supplier quotations. The availability of credible alternative suppliers is a powerful tool to influence your suppliers. In my experience suppliers will not give something away unless they feel compelled to do so, or they receive something in return.

If research shows that this is a gap in your negotiation tool kit then it should be your number 1 priority to address it. Sourcing and bringing a supplier to the point where they are making offers can take a long time, so this should be a priority when planning a negotiation timetable.

Refine your objectives

In the light of your research, re-assess your objectives and prioritise them. Establish your walk away position or BATNA (Best Alternative To a Negotiated Agreement).

Consider choice of strategy

Your choice of strategy should reflect your objectives considering the information you have gathered at the research stage.

If your research establishes that you have a weak negotiating position, you may choose a conciliatory approach; if there are great opportunities for development, you may choose a collaborative approach; if the negotiation is a zero sum game, you may choose a adversarial approach.

Select research information that supports your chosen approach. You will want to present your information in a logical, sequential way that will hopefully develop a credible and powerful case. However, you may want to consider how you will introduce your points in a persuasive but non-confrontational way

Sometimes your most powerful information is also the most risky, for example threats to move your business to a competitor. Therefore, contrary to the usual logic, it is sometimes best to leave your strongest information until last, because it may be your final throw of the dice that you don't really want to use if possible.

Consider how the supplier may respond or counter your proposals and what your responses may be. In particular, identify what concessions you are prepared to make. In preparation try to put a value on potential concessions and identify what circumstances you will give them up.

Prepare the supplier

Some negotiators may disagree, but I believe that there should be no surprises by the time you get to the meeting. A successful agreement will be much more likely if both parties understand the negotiating position of the other side prior to the meeting. As a buyer, it is your job to make sure that the supplier arrives with an understanding of what you want from the meeting and why it would be in their interests to meet the buyer's needs.

In order to achieve this, you will want to start preparing the supplier to accept your view of how the negotiation should proceed. This conditioning process may take a variety of forms and is dealt with a little later in the book.

Set up the meeting

Draft an agenda, detailing the main issues for negotiation and the order would like to discuss them. The running order of your agenda should be compatible with your negotiation plan. My personal preference is to discuss the issues in order of importance. Alternatively you could categorize issues into themes, for example, technical issues, contract terms, timings and deal with them that way. Sometimes the order of negotiations may be dictated by a chronology of events.

If possible, keep the number of issues down to a minimum. Get agreement on as many issues as possible before the meeting, in particular try to clear as many minor issues as possible. In general, the less issues you have to resolve at the meeting the better, unless of course your strategy is to use multiple issues as a way of diversion or creating straw issues with which to bargain with.

Confirm the meeting time, date and place to the other party and include a copy of the agenda requesting them to add or amend items and confirm by return. If you do not want use an agenda at the meeting it is still useful to produce such a document to serve as an aide-memoire to keep you on track during the meeting.

Finally, remember that, you will have to respond to developments during the meeting, so prepare to be flexible.

Conditioning

"It is the absolute right of the State to supervise the formation of public opinion". Joseph Goebbels

Conditioning is the process by which one party seeks to influence the thoughts and behaviour of another, through a variety of signals and messages which work either at the conscious level or subliminally. Conditioning is most commonly used to create a positive image of a company or product and is the basis for the advertising industry and product branding.

In the context of negotiation, success can often depend upon the, aspirations and expectations of the other party. These perceptions factors can all be influenced by effective conditioning of the supplier prior to the negotiation. Conditioning methods can be used individually but are generally more effective when they are used together and in combinations that reinforce each other. Some methods are detailed below:

- Conditioning works best when it is done before the other party realise you preparing them for a negotiation. When they realise you may have a motive in your communications they will put up their defences, screening any messages you may want to plant.
- If the supplier receives a message through a third party it is more effective than received from the buyer, since they are more likely to be trusted.
- Messages received through establishment or respected sources can be particularly effective in conditioning a party. For example, some companies use by Appointment to Her Majesty the Queen on their product and sales information because some people are deferential to traditional symbols of authority. Similarly, companies will commonly refer to their achievement of ISO9000 to create the perception of quality
- Referencing authority can give legitimacy to a statement, for example, "we have been approved by the government" or "we supply Rolls Royce", will immediately create a favourable impression. Perhaps the most common way of creating legitimacy is to put something into print, 'it must be right because I read it in the newspaper' approach. Supplier's use this principle when drawing up official price lists.
- By appealing to the need to conform, for example. 'nine out of ten cats prefers brand X'. In the context of business deals, buyers who have been successfully persuaded that a particular product is the market leader will choose that product as a way

of avoiding risk or blame if things go wrong, even if it is not the most appropriate product.

- By making strong assertions about something, for example, 'we will never be beaten on price'. An assertion is an opinion made is a strongly positive way but some people will take these statements as matters of fact. This method works best when the other party is inexperienced or susceptible to moral force. However, it must be used carefully because misleading statements presented as a matter of fact during negotiations can render a contract voidable. Consequently, strong assertions are best used when there is no absolute authority on the subject that can contradict the assertion.

- It is best to start conditioning as early as possible. If you have demanding conditions it may require some time for the supplier to change their aspirations or expectations. In such circumstances, conditioning works best if the supplier has time to accept the changed landscape of the negotiation. It also gives them time to accept a poorer outcome than they originally expected, allowing them to prepare their bosses or other stakeholders within their organisation for an outcome which may be less than they expected.

- Repetition of a message, although not subtle will have a conditioning effect.

- Be careful not to overstate your position, bluffing is a high risk strategy. If you have to bluff, leave yourself an exit strategy if it all goes wrong.

Of course the supplier may set about trying to condition you to their way of thinking. The main reason suppliers want to condition buyers is to achieve a price increase. The usual ways they use are; price lists, blanket price increase letters, re-costing exercises, and raw material prices increasing.

The best way to counter another party trying to condition you is first, be aware that the process is going on. Second, do your own research. Get your own information, research the markets, reverse estimate the product. Third, cross-examine and test the other side's assertions are they real or are they bluff. Test their assumptions, test their methodology. Identify angles by which their story can be undermined. In general, if someone is bluffing and is found out, their negotiating position collapses. Finally, develop your own proactive policies which reduce the effect of or mitigate the change that your supplier proposes. The most obvious action you can do, is to reduce your dependency on that particular supplier.

SWOT analysis

"Entrepreneurs are simply those who understand that there is little difference between obstacle and opportunity and are able to turn both to their advantage."
Niccolo Machiavelli

SWOT stands for Strengths, Weaknesses, Opportunities and Threats and is a technique credited to Albert Humphrey, who originally developed it to assess stock market decisions. Today, it is often used as an analysis tool to evaluate a wide range of projects and business ventures including preparation for supplier negotiations.

Used in a negotiation planning context, SWOT analysis provides buyer's a simple structured way of identifying and critically examining factors that may be relevant in a negotiation. A typical analysis could follow the steps outlined below:

Set objective(s)

Set out your needs or objectives. These are the reference points for your SWOT analysis. For example, you need a supplier to reduce his prices or the supplier's quality needs to improve.

Identify strengths

Identify your negotiating strengths that will help you secure your objectives in the negotiation, these could include:

- Availability of suitable alternative products.

- Alternative competitive quotations.
- The prestige of dealing with your company.
- The potential for further business, 'a foot in the door'.
- The size, regularity or duration of your requirements.
- Your supplier may be desperate for orders or need quick payment.

Identify weaknesses

Identify your negotiating weaknesses, the factors that may be used against you in the negotiation. For example:

- You may have little buying power or the size of your spend may be declining.
- You may not have any alternative quotes.
- Your company may have a poor payment record.
- You may be short of time which prevents alternative suppliers being used.
- The supplier has a full order book.

Identify opportunities

Identify external conditions that may help you achieve your objectives, for example:

- Raw material prices may have fallen in price.
- Another supplier has started making the same product.
- Demand from other customers may be unusually weak.

Identify threats

Identify external conditions which could obstruct or prevent you from achieving your objectives. For example:

- Legal rights (patent, copyright) may restrict the number of suppliers for a particular product.
- Raw material markets may turn adverse.
- There may be market shortages of key components and raw materials.
- A patent challenge may be made on your production methods.

When considering external opportunities and threats, it may be useful to employ Political, Economic, Social, Technological analysis (PEST), Socio-cultural, Technological, Economic, Ecological and Regulatory factors (STEER) or Porter's Five Forces. Once you have identified and listed the various factors at play you can develop your negotiation plan, to help you in this process:

- Prioritise your strengths. Consider how you will link them up to project a convincing and persuasive argument to the supplier.
- Consider how you will exploit the supplier's weaknesses without embarrassing them, creating barriers or damaging your working relationship.
- Match up your strengths with external opportunities to identify areas of comparative advantage.
- Consider strategies for converting your weaknesses and threats into strengths and opportunities. Alternatively identify ways of avoiding, disguising or removing them so they do not play a part in the negotiation.

Team negotiations

Dr Venkman "It just seems a little pricey for a unique fixer upper opportunity, that's all. What do you think Egon?"

Dr Spengler "I think this building should be condemned. There's serious metal fatigue in all the load bearing members, the wiring is sub-standard, it's completely inadequate for our power needs and the neighbourhood is like a de-militarised zone."

Dr Stantz, arriving down a fireman's pole. "…. Wow this place is great, when can we move in. You gotta try this pole. I'm gonna get my stuff…hey, we should stay here tonight, sleep here, you know, to try it out"

Dr Venkman to the estate agent "I think we'll take it."

Extract from Ghostbuster's 1984. The ghostbusters
are negotiating the terms on their new premises with
the estate agent.

The old maxim strength in numbers is not always the case when applied to negotiations. Negotiations are difficult enough, team negotiations can be frustratingly difficult to plan and hard to control. However, in certain circumstances they can be advantageous and in some cases necessary. Detailed below are some instances where using a team could be advantageous:

- In complex negotiations, where one person cannot be expected to know all the commercial and technical details.
- Collaborative negotiations, where expanding the pie is more important than slicing the pie. Such negotiation is often based upon sharing information and drawing expertise from a wider range of expertise.
- Sometimes forming a team for a negotiation is politically expedient. Perhaps there is internal resistance to your chosen course of action, including these resistant elements within the negotiation team maybe what is needed to get their support and to get them to buy into a course of action.
- There are a wide range of interests that must be included to make the outcome of the meeting acceptable to all parties, for example pay negotiations may need to include the employer's team, several unions and third party conciliators.
- In circumstances where a team of negotiators would be expected, for example, international deals or where a team of negotiators is required to signal the importance of the meeting.

Avoid using team negotiations when:

- You need to keep your cards close to your chest. It is a common failing that when groups of people get together they sometimes start to outbid each other in terms of what they know, this is not advisable in front of your supplier.

- Including non-commercial people in negotiations can sometimes lead to red faces when commercially sensitive information is inadvertently released. Some sales people are adept at going around the buyer to get unguarded information from technical staff.

Preparation is vital to a successful team negotiation. You may want to consider taking the following steps:

Decide who will be in the team

- Combinations of skills are useful. Try to use people who have worked together previously as they will gel as a team more quickly and understand individual specialisms and characters
- In more wide ranging negotiations or project teams you may want to consider not only the organisational role of the team member but also their personalities.
- For commercial negotiations, make the team as small as possible, two person teams are sometimes the most effective, for example if the negotiation is about poor quality then the purchasing manager and the quality manager may be all that is required. If the negotiation is about poor payment, then the purchasing manager and the finance manager would be the best pairing.

Arrange a pre-meeting to decide the following:

- Identify who will open and lead the negotiation for your side and who will take the minutes.
- Identify the issues and agree your position on each.
- Decide the running order that each issue will be addressed.
- Decide who will take the lead on specific issues or topics.
- Be clear with the team what areas should not be discussed.
- Agree what concessions can be made and what cannot.
- Agree the aims of the negotiation in priority order and establish a Best Alternative To a Negotiated Agreement (BATNA).

- Discuss the circumstances when you would call for a break in the negotiations (a caucus).

Prepare the supplier

- Send your contact an agenda detailing the issues you want to discuss. Provide information they may need in advance of the meeting.
- Ask them to advise details of items they would like to discuss and find out who they will be sending for the meeting.

At the meeting

- The team leader should normally open the negotiation. It is important with team negotiations to start with introductions.
- Avoid team members going off the point or going into specialist detail that should be dealt with outside of the meeting.
- Try to recap key points, agreements and actions, at regular intervals.
- At the end of the meeting summarise the main points and any undertakings made by either side.
- Write up notes of the meeting for both parties and send them a copy, asking them to check and confirm agreement.

Conducting face to face negotiations

"I'll give you a definite maybe". Sam Goldwyn

Many simple negotiations can and should be carried out by telephone, by email or by fax. With single issue, zero sum negotiations, it is normally the most time and cost effective way of getting through your workload. In some cases, it is not only convenient but the best way of dealing with negotiations. There are times when keeping sellers at arm's length is the best policy, especially when you want to create doubt and uncertainty in the supplier's mind. Suppliers who are unsure that they have done enough to win an order are more likely to make further concessions.

However, when dealing with more complex multi-issue negotiations, or dealing with long term supply partners, face to face meetings are generally preferable. They are preferable because these negotiations often require more time for the parties to explore the options and greater subtlety in reaching an agreement. For example, it is often necessary in multi-issue negotiations to link a wide range of commitments and concessions. Only by allowing more time, can the full range of solutions be explored and hence increase the sum total of the benefits possible from collaboration.

In addition, face to face meetings help to build relationships and develop trust between the parties. Without trust, the range of possibilities for mutual benefit will always be limited. With trust both parties can concentrate on delivering their side of the bargain rather than worrying about whether the other side will keep to their commitments. This is particularly true when dealing with foreign suppliers were the hurdle of trust is often much higher.

Face to face meeting work in such circumstances because the process is more transparent and open than simple correspondence. Actually meeting the people who are responsible for managing your business, observing their body language and exchanging personal assurances is more likely to result in greater confidence all round. Parties actually meeting are more likely to foster a sense of joint enterprise and become committed to the project.

Phases of a negotiation

Despite being highly unpredictable in nature, most face to face negotiations generally follow a similar pattern, which can be typified by 3 or 4 stages: Openings, establishing negotiating positions, bargaining and the agreement. The stages generally overlap, sometimes the negotiation will yo-yo back and forth between stages and in some negotiations stages may be missed out altogether.

Openings

The opening is important because it sets the tone for the meeting. Unless you've called the meeting to dress down the supplier, it is normal to start the meeting in a friendly manner with the aim of creating a positive atmosphere, putting both parties at ease.

Following any introductions, it is normal to start the conversation with general business matters, possibly touching upon common acquaintances, customers, mutual suppliers or competitors. From a buyer's point of view you are looking to get a feel for how busy the supplier is, if there are any underlying problems and how interested they are in doing business with your company.

First time meetings with new suppliers may include presentations by both parties on their respective companies. Typically, a supplier will want to establish their company's credentials for carrying out business of the type you are interested in, and buyer will generally want to establish that their company is a reputable, trustworthy customer who offers a good prospect of sales.

The conversation should naturally move on to more specific business interests, outlining the purpose of the meeting and any prior correspondence or actions that are relevant. It is normal and preferable to have exchanged tentative enquiries and offers prior to the meeting. This correspondence will often provide guidance for negotiation planning and is sometimes used as the basis for an agenda. Prior correspondence will generally set out the highest opening offers from which the parties will negotiate from.

Establishing negotiating positions

Following on from the opening discussions, you will want to establish if and how flexible the supplier will be with respect to their offer. It is not unusual for the supplier to be reticent in indicating flexibility. Instead they will want to talk about matters other than price, such as quality, and will be trying to read your position. In particular, they will be trying to judge how much you want their product and how much you are prepared to pay. To avoid being too easy to read, you may want to disguise your priorities and mix up the order in which you raise negotiable issues. For example, if you are desperate for a quick delivery, don't make your first question, 'how quickly can you deliver it?'

On the buyer's side you may want to send signals to the seller to lower their aspirations. If you can, you may indicate that you are not entirely sold on their product or them as a supplier. You can downplay the value of their product technically, make statements about the price being too high or that you have alternative options available to you. This is the time when your research into the supplier, their product and their competitors is really valuable. If you have good information to work with, you can subtly exert pressure on the supplier and create the right conditions for driving a better deal.

In playing this game the buyer has to be careful because you need to maintain credibility. There is no point rubbishing your supplier or what they are selling, if they or their product were so bad, you wouldn't be spending valuable time meeting them. At the other extreme you don't want them to feel that they don't have to work to get your business. Where you make your pitch is down to reading the situation, and it is not a risk free decision. If you misjudge and set your demands too high, you may create the impression with the other party that it is not worth negotiating. Set the level too low and you risk giving away more than you need to. However, the consensus of opinion is that the higher you set your initial demands, the higher the likely level of the final agreement.

It is good during this stage to identify all the factors that the seller values. When it comes to putting together a bargain, you may be able to link these issues, creating value and leverage and hence obtain a better overall deal.

Bargaining

It is a point of debate amongst negotiators, whether it is better to be the first person to set a marker, or should you let the other party show their hand first. The traditional view supports the latter approach, however, at least one major negotiating consultancy suggest that the person who sets down the first marker, takes the initiative and 'anchors' the parameters of negotiation.

I suggest that if you have good research about the costs or the market price of the product then go first, and place a challenging marker. There is no point going first with a weak opening offer, it must be strong. If your market intelligence is poor and you are unsure about the market price then it is probably best to let the other side to make the first offer.

The main characteristic of the bargaining phase is movement. If you employ an overly rigid approach or fix yourself to a particular negotiating position you can end up in deadlock, so in this stage you should if necessary, be prepared to change the combination or shape of the package you offer.

Movement of negotiating position is fraught with risk; the antidote to this risk is conditionality. Conditionality is characterised by offers only provided on the basis of the other party doing something or offering a concession. For example, you may say, if the quality was improved I may be able to move on the price. Conditionality of offers is what bridges the gap between two opposed positions and allows them to move. Conditionality is typified by vagueness and hedging. Consequently, when you think that you have an agreement it is always worthwhile, re-capping each point, to ensure everyone has the same understanding.

The agreement

At the end of the negotiation, read back any agreements to avoid misunderstanding. One of the parties should agree to write-up the minutes of the meeting, any actions agreed and the agreements reached. The written up minutes, should be sent to the other party for confirmation and acceptance.

Time as a factor in negotiations

"Russia has two Generals on whom she can confide – Janvier and Fevrier". Nicholas I

Time and timing is an often overlooked factor in negotiation, but it can have profound effects on the course of a negotiation and used correctly it can be an important asset to any negotiator.

Time to research

One of the most important aspects of having time on your side is being able to research and prepare for negotiations. Return on your investment of time is particularly high if you are able to create options. A buyer with one option is severely limited in his room for manoeuvre in any subsequent negotiation, it is much better to have at least one alternative route. Alternative courses of action allow the buyer to take a more assertive approach in a negotiation and may give the opportunity to walk away from a poor deal. Perhaps the most valuable option that a buyer can take to a meeting is that of an alternative supplier. Having real competition improves buying morale and focuses the mind of the salesman like nothing else.

Constructive delays

By getting your enquiries out early you will not only keep on top of your workload but you will also allow you to sit on the quote for a while and generate some uncertainty in the seller's mind. If you delay in acting on a quotation suppliers will often progress their quotation with you allowing the buyer a perfect opportunity to negotiate lower prices or improve the terms. For example a supplier telephones you to ask if everything is ok with their quote and whether they will be receiving the order. The seller is clearly concerned that the delay means they may have lost the order. In circumstances like these the buyer can bring up reasons why he has not been back in touch; maybe another supplier has made you a particularly good offer and you were considering placing the order with them, or maybe you have a budgetary constraint holding you back. In any case, the seller's response is likely to be, 'is it too late to improve upon my offer', which of course is what you want.

Deadlock

Deadlock occurs when you reach an impasse in the course of negotiation. It is an extreme form of delay because it is not quite clear that it will eventually be broken. It is a very uncomfortable stance to take especially for people who normally value being positive. However, it can be a valuable negotiating tactic if you believe it will benefit your position and you are in a position to withstand a delay. Possible benefits of deadlock may be to open up divisions in your opponent's camp, leading them to make concessions and lower their expectations.

However, deadlock is a high risk strategy that I would not recommend, especially when dealing with long term business partners where building trust is important. Firstly, it comes across as being bloody minded and secondly, it could be turned around by the supplier. Remember delays for buyers are generally much more painful than delays for suppliers.

Deadlines

Deadlines are used by both buyers and sellers to put pressure on their opponents. Generally they put constraints on the party subject to them, for this reason it is best to hide your deadlines and try to discover what deadlines your opponent is subject to.

Deadlines that put pressure on the buyer may include short quotation validity, buy by dates, kitting dates, stock subject to prior sale, long lead times, time limited offers, and order now before the price goes up. The best way of dealing with deadlines is to provide you with plenty of time and develop alternative options. Similarly, buyers can place their own time limits on suppliers including: deadlines for the receipt of quotations, production schedules that must be met, and making delivery on time of the essence in a contract.

Timing of negotiation

Most buyers have little leeway in choosing when they have to place orders, but if you can, there are certain times of the month and times of the year when salesmen are more likely to do a deal. Month and financial year ends are sensitive time for companies and salesmen alike, because most salesmen are rewarded based on sales rather than profit.

Long-term versus short-term

Sellers tend to be more powerful in the short run but generally in the longer term balance of power shifts to the buyer as alternative options are opened up. Sellers considering a short term win should be reminded of this fact and even if the salesman's horizons don't stretch longer than the current financial year, you may at least take the satisfaction in knowing that your day will come.

Plumber's time

Avoid negotiating when you are in a crisis especially if this is known by your supplier. So with the plumber analogy, it is more cost effective to have a plumber service your boiler in the hotter months of the year when they are short of work, than have to call one out to repair it in the middle of winter.

Be patient

Some nationalities deal with slow paced negotiation better than others, Americans in particular tend to be impatient in reaching agreement. By contrast some eastern cultures are more patient and accept delays and slow negotiations as a matter of course.

It is widely believed that a slower paced negotiation is more likely to result in a successful final agreement. This is because both sides have time to fully understand and appreciate all the elements of a negotiation. Extended negotiations also allow the parties to accept that their original expectations may not be realisable. In essence, the parties need time to accept a change in their expectations, a process sometimes called conditioning.

Negotiating with sole suppliers

"You can get much farther with a kind word and a gun than you can with a kind word alone. " Al Capone

Fortunately for buyers, most markets are characterised by a large number of competing suppliers offering broadly similar products. In a competitive market, as long as the buyer is prepared to do the basic leg work and receives offers from a number of compliant suppliers, the buyer can play them off against each other to arrive at the best deal. In this type of environment the buyer most definitely has the upper hand.

However, when a competitive market for a product doesn't exist, buyers are placed in the relatively unusual position of having to negotiate without the most powerful tool in the buyer's armoury, the option of using another supplier. Some buyer's find this a very uncomfortable position to be in, but don't despair, there are a number of ways of evening the odds and coming out with a good result.

First of all, check your own assumptions. For a time, I worked for a boss who told me many times that I should never 'assume', because it makes an ASS of U and Me, he was right (if not a little patronizing). Just because you have no alternatives and you know that the supplier is a sole source, doesn't mean that the supplier also knows this. The supplier may be blissfully unaware of the powerful position he is in. If the supplier is unaware of this, do your utmost to avoid them discovering their bargaining strength.

Suppliers can become single sources through a variety of reasons, the most common being through market domination, patent rights, product design or customer specification. There is very little a buyer can do in the two former cases, but can try to stop unnecessary specification of proprietary parts by colleagues. The best way of achieving this is to educate members of the engineering department to specify generic parts and avoid designing branded items into your product. Similarly, the sales force should be made aware of the risks of accepting customer orders requiring the use of specified brands or named suppliers.

If a supplier has become a single source because of customer spec-ification or nomination and it is proving difficult to obtain the parts competitively, advise the supplier that you intend to go back to the customer with a suggested alternative. The risk to the supplier of not only losing your custom but having the customer specify alternative suppliers in the future may prove persuasive. Of course actually referring the matter to your customer is not something you would want to do and should be used very much as a last resort.

In the case of nominated suppliers, it is not uncommon for the end customer to have a negotiated pricing agreement with the sup-plier, called 'framework agreements'. If this is the case you need to know about it, so make it a standing agreement with your sales, estimators, and contracts people to investigate such matters before committing a price

When a supplier knows they are the sole source of supply you may have to work a little harder and different tactics may be necessary. One approach may be to find out what the supplier values, this may not necessarily be a higher price and could be something that you can accommodate at little cost. Maybe you can find negotiation leverage through: the offer of longer contracts, higher minimum quantities, earlier payment, and recommendation to other potential customers or some other commercial term.

Find a way of shaming your supplier into lower prices. For exam-ple, deconstruct the supplier's prices into its constituent parts. Most companies build up their prices in a predictable way, materials and labour plus fixed proportions for overhead cost and profit. In negotia-tions regarding price it is not unreasonable to ask a salesman what proportion of the selling price is made up of materials. Armed with this information it is then not hard to estimate the cost of the material content and from that draw reasonable assessments on the labour, overhead and profit elements. This information can then be used to question the seller's position on prices or price increases.

Similarly, build up records of the supplier's historical prices. If there is a pattern of increases which bear little relationship to the changes in the cost of labour, raw materials or improvements in efficiency, they can be used to challenges prices or price increases.

You could point out that their high prices are making your product uncompetitive and so you are both losing market share.

Realistically, such negotiations will often have little impact on a supplier who knows that the buyer is in a corner. Most businesses have a mixture of products, some are dogs and some stars; you can bet that most companies will try to milk a star product for all its worth. When you come up against this approach you may have to employ a more direct approach.

Threaten to change your specification. Justify your position on the basis that although it is costly to perform an engineering change, that option is not as costly as paying the supplier's exorbitant prices. Viewed over a period of several years, costs of changing can be reasonably justified.

Stress the long term value of your business to the supplier which is jeopardized by the supplier's short term pricing policy. Point out that in the short term you may have little room to manoeuvre but in the long term your options could be much wider.

When dealing with a single source OEM, I have on occasion and without notice to the OEM bought their product through distribution. The OEM may draw the conclusion that you have found an alternative product especially if you do not contradict this point. This may create the desired leverage. Similarly, you can covertly build up stocks of a product and then stop buying without explanation.

If no competition exists for the product, you can create or threaten to create it. If the item amounts to a significant spend it could be feasible either start production yourself or partner a specialist in a similar line of business.

If the single source supplier also sells you non-monopoly products, you can create leverage by including these into a bigger package. If the supplier refuses you could threaten to resource the competitive items to compensate for the highly priced monopoly items or simply out of bloody mindedness.

Auction tactics

"Never interrupt your enemy when he's making a mistake".
Napoleon I

Public auctions normally work on an ascending bid basis. Bids are placed until there are no more increases in bids and the fall of the gabble forms the contract. Sellers may put lots up for sale without reserve, may post a reserve price or may keep the reserve secret.

To be successful at auctions, do you homework first and stick to some basic rules:

- What price would you pay on the high street? This should be your limit less any premium you would be prepared to pay for the benefit of dealing with a business with after sales.
- Position yourself so you can see the whole room, and you can judge when your opponents are getting to their limits.
- Try to spot dummy bidders. Dummy bidders are used to push the price higher and to create an impression of demand. They normally fall out of the bidding after the reserve price has been met.
- Let other people bid first, try to enter the bidding process as late as possible.
- If you have to start the bidding, start low. The lower the starting price the more likely that the end bid will be lower. High bids tend to indicate to other bidders a high common value.
- Avoid bidding wars.
- Keep to your limit.

The usual method of bidding is called the English method; the bidder bids just above the last highest bid up to his limit. Alternatively, proxy English bidding is where the bidder bids his limit price and awaits the outcome.

Bidders generally fall into one of two categories, those who have formed a private valuation for the lot based upon personal reasons and those who are looking to re-sell the item at a profit. In the former case the bidders limit is likely to be independent of market valuation and in the latter case the bidders will set their limit by what they estimate to be the common market value of the lot. If demand appears strong the perception of the common value could rise and add a dynamic to bidder's original limits.

Dutch auctions

This type of auction got its name from 17th century tulip auctions in Holland. Sometimes known as descending price auctions, the price of an item is lowered until it gets a bid, which is the winning bid and results in the sale.

A form of Dutch auction is used today to set the prices of some initial public offerings (IPO) of shares. The company reveals the maximum number of shares it will sell and the potential investors then state how many shares they want to buy and the price they are prepared to pay. All the bids are assessed and a price is established at which all the shares will be taken up (the clearing price). Bidders are then allocated shares on the basis of the highest bidders first, but all bidders pay the same 'clearing price'.

Online auctions

The market maker on behalf of the buyer issues a request for quotations (RFQs) for a designated work package from suppliers. At a time designated in the RFQ, suppliers log onto the auction site and over a period of time are able to submit one or more quotations for the work. Bidding is in real time and dynamic, i.e. suppliers respond to competitors online bids. In effect, it is like all the suppliers sitting in the same room bidding against each other.

The buyer is not usually bound to use the lowest bidder, they can proceed to place the contract based on some other factor, such as technical ability or reliability. Although online reverse auctions like this gained popularity in the 90s they have been criticised and are generally unpopular with sellers and as a result have been in decline.

Body language in negotiation

"Information is a negotiators greatest weapon". Victor
Kiam

Non-verbal communication is an interesting, if not attractive subject to many negotiators. It suggests that we can gain an insight into what the other side are thinking simply from their body movements and facial expressions.

Without doubt, we all use non-verbal communication in our daily lives to consciously and sometimes unconsciously pass information to others about how we feel. So too in negotiation, we send non-verbal signals but whilst we are in negotiation, it is fair to say that skilled negotiators will control the non-verbal signals they send. So be careful and view people's body language with a degree of scepticism. Some of the most commonly recognised non-verbal signs are detailed below:

Eyes

- Good eye contact in most western countries is seen as a sign of honesty and straight-forward dealing, avoiding eye contact indicates the opposite.
- Gazing or looking around the room indicates lack of interest or boredom.
- Staring is usually taken to be aggressive or prying behaviour. On the positive side, holding eye contact slightly longer than usual after making a statement can be used to reinforce what has been said.
- When blinking the eyes stay closed longer, this may indicate that the speaker feels superior or believes they are an authority in what they are saying. In some cases it may indicate that the person is simply disinterested. Eye blocking may be forgivable when speaking to an audience but not on a one to one basis.
- Notwithstanding rapid changes in the brightness of the light, the change in size of pupils is something which even a trained actor finds hard to control. Pupils opening wider are normally an indication of interest or excitement. People instinctively

know this which is why people consider talking to someone with sunglasses on is impolite and exactly why card players wear glasses.

- More frequent blinking is normally linked with pupil dilation but in this case it indicates an interest in the subject.
- When maintaining eye contact, the ideal area to fix your gaze is the area between the eyes and the eyebrows. Don't look at the bigger triangle between the person's eyes and their chest as this may indicate you fancy your contact. Generally looking below the level of the eyes indicates a more social gaze.
- Avoid sideways glances as these generally indicate suspicion or hostility.

Hand to face gestures

- Hand to mouth gestures can be an indication someone is lying or evasive, particularly when the hand covers the mouth. People sometimes disguise this move by coughing to suggest another purpose. Be careful interpreting this movement negatively, it could just be that the person has a bad cold and is being polite. If you are talking to a supplier and they cover their mouth, this may indicate that they do not believe you.
- Hands to nose gestures are similar to hand to mouth gestures but less obvious. Indeed it may be a hand to mouth gesture which is deflected to the nose. It has even been suggested that when lying the nerves in the nose tingle.
- Hand to eye rubbing can indicate that the person does not want to witness a lie.
- Hand to ear gestures may indicate that the listener either doesn't believe what he is hearing or is ready to speak themselves.
- A speaker loosening a collar may indicate that they are lying and don't feel convinced the other party believes what they are saying.
- Neck scratching on the part of the listener may indicate that the person is uncertain about what has been said.

- Fingers in the mouth and nail biting may indicate insecurity.
- Hand to chin and stroking the chin usually indicates that the listener is thinking about what you have said and evaluating it. If the gesture moves to the hand supporting the chin this probably indicates that the person has decided against the proposal.
- Hand to the forehead, generally indicates the person realises they have made a mistake.

Hand and finger gestures

- Forming a cup with the palms may indicate that the person is asking for a favour.
- Pinching fingers as if holding a small object may indicate the speaker is trying to get across an idea.
- Rubbing palms together indicates that the person anticipates or believes they have struck a good deal. Or it could be they are cold and you should turn the heating up.
- Fidgety or drumming fingers indicate boredom.
- Thumbs in pockets can be seen as a sign of confidence or authority.
- Hands made into fists indicate anger or aggressiveness.
- Open palms are an obvious gesture of honesty, but may be disingenuous.
- Hands clasp is generally negative and may indicate frustration.
- An upward steeple (prayer position), is often used when a person is giving an opinion. It can also indicate the person is confident or feels superior. Another interpretation of the prayer position is that the person is hoping for good news.
- A lowered steeple (inverted prayer), normally indicates that the person is listening and weighing up what is being said.

Handshakes

- The double hand grip, sometimes called the 'politician's' grip because it is meant to convey sincerity but can often create the opposite effect.

- Handshakes with arm, shoulder or wrist grasps are normally only used by close friends.
- The knuckle grind, suggests I'm in charge.
- The wet fish handshake is universally disliked and suggests lack of commitment from the person.

Arms

- Crossed arms are defensive, crossed arms with fists are even more defensive and possible aggressive. Arms crossed with hands clasping upper arms, indicates a negative position has been taken. One arm crossed indicates partly negative position but willing to be persuaded otherwise.
- Hands across genitals indicates nervousness, hands touching cuffs indicates nervousness or unsure what to do next.
- Hands and arms behind the head generally indicates confidence. A negotiator may do this when they think they have made a strong case or they are in a strong position.

Legs

- Leg crosses are used as defensive barriers. The degree of leg cross generally indicates the level of negativity. A person holding a crossed leg in place may be particularly stubborn. Crossing legs whilst standing may indicate a degree of reserve or a need to go to the toilet.
- Ankles locked together normally indicate that the other person is holding back information or is making an effort to control their emotions.

Seated posture

- Leaning forward in a chair, open armed, is an indication of willingness.
- Leaning back, the person has not bought into your proposal.

Other Gestures

- Picking small or imaginary specs off themselves may indicate the person disapproves but doesn't feel they can broach the subject.
- Looking down the nose, generally indicates disapproval.

Negotiation terms and tactics

"When you say that you agree to a thing in principle, you mean that you have not the slightest intention of carrying it out". Otto von Bismarck

Anchoring

Making the first offer and thereby setting it as a reference point for later negotiations.

Authority

The need to check with a higher authority can be used to stall for time or get you out of a tight situation. I used it all the time in domestic situations, "I need to check with the wife first".

Bait and switch

Attract interest with a low offer which is not actually available and then offer a similar product at a much higher price.

Bluffing

This is when a negotiating party leads the other side to believe that their negotiating position is stronger than it actually is.

Broken record

Repeat the same phrase over and over again, for example "It's too much". Margaret Thatcher was renowned for using this tactic, typically "No, no, no, no." The emphasis serves to fix the message in the mind of the other side and reinforces your own self-determination.

The budget limit

"I like your product but I don't have the budget, the most I can afford is…" The budget constraint may be real or imaginary but it must be believable. There are counter-measures the most common is to offer you a lower specification product which usually is unsuitable.

Imply a bundled purchase

Use near to the end of a negotiation to reveal any missed concession. "What if I took two of them?" Lock in the price and then drop any bundled items you really do not want. Some suppliers don't back out.

Cherry picking

Selecting only certain items from a supplier's quotation and buying the other parts from another supplier. Seller's dislike this practice and will put clauses into quotes to allow them to re-quote if the quotation is not accepted in full.

Concessions

Always trade concessions, never give concessions without getting something in return, even if it is only an obligation.

Delaying tactics

If a supplier is pushing for a price increase and you have no options, putting back the time of implementation can buy you time to find alternatives.

Deliberate mistakes

Sometimes artificially low prices are presented by the seller with the intention of distracting the buyer. The buyer might think that they need to close the deal quickly before the mistake is discovered and they do not negotiate properly. Toward the end of the negotiation the seller admits to a mistake and changes the price to the correct level.

Denigration

Denigrating the other side's offer works by lowering their expectations by pointing out their faults. This tactic is commonly used by car salesmen undermining the value of your cherished trade-in vehicle. It is not a tactic I would recommend for building long term relationships.

Escalation 1

If you're not getting anywhere with a negotiation, threaten to take the matter to the other party's boss. You can bet they will in the very least try harder and in all likelihood come up with an acceptable solution. Salespeople will usually do anything to avoid the interference of their boss.

Escalation 2

The seller increases the price during the negotiation or after apparent agreement, with spurious justification. In the end the frustrated buyer can end up paying more just to put the deal to bed.

Final offer

A final offer doesn't necessarily mean that the supplier will not negotiate further. Maybe they just won't improve upon their price but maybe they will improve other elements of the deal.

Fishing expedition

When a party is short of hard facts and are consequently unable to create leverage they will go fishing for useful information. Sometimes this may include making provocative statements to gain a response from a tight-lipped party.

Hostage tactic

The psychological basis of this tactic is that the buyer has sunk time money or prestige into the project. The supplier then introduces additional demands and refuses to proceed until you agree to the demand. A variation on this theme is that one party seizes property or claims a lien on property until the other party agrees to their demands.

Avoiding this situation is about anticipation and thorough evaluation before you commit. If you can negotiate your own hostage at the start of the project then this will improve your bargaining position. If a supplier pulls this trick, you need to find another supplier. A classic example of hostage tactics is children's card collection offers. Some cards just never seem to come up encouraging further purchases.

Impasse

If you reach an impasse in negotiations, call a break. Giving people time out, allows people to re-assess and get use to an idea. A break also allows time to devise a revised offer to avoid the point of impasse.

Karrass krunch

Named after Chester L Karrass, "You've got to do better than that" is a straightforward way of stripping out any padding in the price. The technique simply requires unselfconsciousness from the buyer, directness and maybe a bit of bluff. On the downside, suppliers get use to this approach from some buyer's and purposeful build padding into the price.

Monkey on the back

Put the burden of reaching agreement on the other party e.g. 'you come up with the money and you've got a deal.'

Nibbling

This is the practice, usually at the end of the negotiation process, of asking for small incremental improvements to seal the deal. For example, asking for the car dealer to throw in car mats to close the deal. Common sales nibbles are carriage, small order, certification and packaging charges.

Nit picking

This is picking fault with trivia. Most people subject to such a tactic are likely to become impatient and either become annoyed or make concessions to end the negotiation.

Nuisance pricing

The supplier doesn't really want the work and puts in an unrealistic offer.

Padding

Building up a quote and thus allowing it to be reduced in negotiation.

Poker face

This is hiding your emotions or interest during negotiation. Try to stay emotionally detached and objective. Showing overt interest or excitement about a product or deal could encourage the other party to raise their aspirations and hold out for more.

Pre-conditions

Setting pre-conditions before agreeing to a meeting. For example, "there's no point in holding a meeting unless you can offer the full price". Pre-conditions seek to make certain terms non-negotiable.

Price breakdowns

Avoid lump sum prices, by getting a supplier to break down a price will expose them to scrutiny. Additionally it will allow you to learn about their pricing process.

Reasonable price

Appeals to our sense of fair play but these words should put all good buyers on red alert. Yes, the offer may be reasonable, but then again it could be a smokescreen.

Russian front

Present two unpleasant options, one of which is so unattractive that the other party feels compelled to choose the lesser of the two evils.

Salami technique

Take the negotiation slice by slice rather than as a whole. Sometimes used when dealing with a particularly complex issue or where a party is unsure about committing fully. It can also be used by a buyer when it is advantageous to break up a quotation. Stalin is often accredited with using Salami tactics to gradually take over Eastern Europe despite widespread opposition.

Silence 1

If you have enough time, send out enquiries, receive quotations and then sit on them. When suppliers follow up their quotes it is a perfect position to get them to improve their offers.

Silence 2

Most people are generally uncomfortable with silence, so it can be used to get the other party to come up with a suggestion or an offer.

Scope creep

This is the practice of adding demands after the project has started. If anticipated in the seller's contract terms it can prove a boon for the seller, if mismanaged by the supplier it can eat away at their profit and create free value for the buyer.

Pencil sharpening

A polite phrase used to ask suppliers to improve their offer. Like the Karrass Krunch but more subtle.

Split the difference

This is an appealing tactic for both parties. Just make sure that by the time you reach this stage, the middle is well within your target range of preferred outcomes.

Stonewalling

This tactic is named after General "Stonewall" Jackson who was renowned for putting up impenetrable defences. The essence of this tactic is refusing to budge on a point driving the other party to make concessions.

Straw issues

Unimportant issues sometimes played up prior to trading as a concession.

Too big to fail

If you allow your supplier or customer to become too important to your business, you can become a hostage to their survival. In 2009, Focus DIY, were able to force a one sided deal on its landlords simply because they could not afford for Focus to go into administration.

The walk away

Effectively tell the supplier their offer is not good enough and close discussions. High risk, but if you know the supplier must do a deal, something is usually forthcoming

Trial balloon

Put a hypothetical question forward to elicit a response from the other party without committing yourself. Questions like, "what if…" for example, "what if the quantity was increased", "what if I could place the order now?"

Value

Value is completely different to the price. The price is generally publically available information whereas value is something personal to an individual or group and is private. Often the value placed on an item by an individual is much higher than the market price. If you can establish what this value is, it will give you an edge in negotiation.

Vanishing man

Become unavailable to negotiate. This tactic works on the basis that the other side will eventually give up trying to negotiate.

Sales Tactics and Countermeasures

Sales tactics

"A reasonable man gets nowhere in negotiations" attributed
to Willie Walsh, although denied

Typical approaches a sales man may choose:

- "What do I have to beat?" or "what's the best offer you have?" If you tell them this, then you are only going to get a slightly better offer than you already have. Of course you may choose to exaggerate the offers you have. If you play along with the salesman, you prefer one supplier over the others who have quoted, which is not good practice.
- "Come back to me if my price is not competitive". Two things follow from this statement. First, if the salesman thinks he will get a second chance he will not give his best offer. Secondly, ask yourself why the salesman believes he can get away with not giving you his best offer from the start.
- "What price are you looking for?" The salesman is looking for a marker. If you play along with this ploy, make sure your marker will be unacceptable to him and force a counter-offer.
- "What's your budget?" Again, if you play along with this, be sure your budget is too low.
- Offering an unsuitable alternative at a lower price is an attempt to distract you. Stick to what you want.
- Salesmen will want to talk about quality not price. Quality should be a given.
- Freebies. People like to reciprocate. Remember, the person offering you the freebie is not paying personally. As a general rule, don't accept freebies if you are acting on behalf of another person. Freebies can create obligations, moral or otherwise.

- The salesman may appeal to the 'herd mentality' because people generally like to fit in. My advice, don't be a sheep.
- Limited offers and time pressures are designed to distract you from making a rational decision. Ask yourself, why does the salesman want to distract me?

Builders and tradesmen

- Use tradesmen who have a valuable reputation to lose if they foul up or behave badly. Ideally, use tradesmen who belong to a recognised trade association. Ask to see examples of workmanship and or references.
- If the job requires the input of several trades, pick someone who can quote for the whole job and sub-contract out the parts. Never use people who turn up at your door without a prior invitation. Avoid cash in hand tradesmen. Avoid tradesmen without a recognised trading or home address.
- Get at least 3 quotes for a reasonably sized job. Always let the tradesman survey the job. Make sure quotations are itemized and check them to ensure they cover all elements of the work.
- Be clear about what you want the tradesman to do. Actively question them on the extent of the job to build up a detailed specification of what you want. Some tradesmen are adept at discovering additional work, after the job has started, which has not been quoted for. Be particularly careful about estimates for earthworks, for example, foundations. Remove all uncertainty before work commences. Agree how long the job will take to complete. Determine what delays could occur and who would pay what, in the event of a delay(s).
- Insist upon a fixed price and do not accept 'estimates'. The tradesman should be an expert in the field and capable of accurately pricing simple domestic jobs. Do not accept quotations based on hourly or daily rates. Don't let the tradesman start work until the specification and price have been agreed in writing. Agree to make payment only when the job is completed.

- It is sometimes reasonable for tradesman to ask for upfront payments to purchase materials or fixtures. To avoid this, you could agree to purchase these privately and leave them off the quotation. Any materials bought privately should be of a quality agreed with the tradesman. Do not pay any labour costs up front.

- If work is not going as planned, record progress by taking photographs (when the tradesman isn't around). Point out any concerns you have and allow the tradesman reasonable opportunity to put matters right. If matters don't improve, put your concerns in writing and again allow the tradesman reasonable opportunity to put matters right. If you are still not satisfied don't pay, if they think they have a case, let them take the matter to a solicitor or threaten court action. If you have already paid the tradesman and you can find him, take him to court. Failing that, report the matter to Trading Standards and if they think it is serious enough to represent fraud, report the matter to the police.

Car dealers

- "If I could do you a special offer, would you do a deal today?" The purpose is to get you to commit and this may be used against you later.

- Keys to your car are taken to assess it as a trade-in. Now you are stuck. Some car salesmen work on the basis that the longer you are there the more likely you are to buy a car.

- Scale of authority. Sales staff continually seeking approval from their manager for special deals. The tactic is designed to stop you backing out. A salesman should have all the authority necessary to make a sale, so don't be drawn in.

- They change the shape of the money by breaking down the cost to match what you think you can afford. Deposits are kept low monthly payments are kept low by extending the credit period. Final payments are used to keep principal sum down but unless you come up with a large lump sum at the end of the loan period, ownership is not transferred to you.

Supermarkets

- Un-announced price increases allow supermarkets to then make advertised price reductions.
- Changing the packaging format. Now doubly concentrated but effectively half the volume. It is very likely you will not get double the active ingredients per ml. This is usually followed by a cycle of promotions when greater quantities are offered... and then the whole cycle begins again.
- Buy one get one free, but the price for one is usually higher than the original unit price.
- Price reductions on specific goods, encourages switching and habit formation. Incremental price increases to the original price follow after 3 or 4 weeks.
- Limited offers, for example only 3 purchases per customer, appeals to people's greed and usually guarantees a high selling rate.
- Price points, £0.99 sounds much better than £1.
- Complimentary products are placed side by side.
- Environment; absence of clocks inside the store, slow music encourages people to spend more time in the store and more money on goods, shopping trolleys with wonky wheels to slow you down (a degree of cynicism is required of a good buyer).
- Low prices on staples and price point goods to increase footfall in shops but higher margins on other goods.
- Shelf psychology. Lowest priced items are placed either very high or very low. Most profitable products are placed at eye level.
- End of aisles are key selling points known as high traffic areas. Supermarkets know you have to slow down to go round them and they attract impulse purchases. Supermarket designers always ensure there are lots of isles and gaps in aisles.

- Staples like milk or bread, known as 'destination goods', are placed usually at the back of the store to draw you past other offers.

Timeshares

- Pressure is put on the client to sign on the day, and great play will be made of a cooling off period during which you can change your mind. This is an attractive proposition to people who just want to leave but who don't want to say 'no' to the salesperson who has been so nice to them. Of course many people later forget to act, are too lazy to act, or take action too late.
- If you do sign on the day, make sure you have the full contract details before you leave, this can be missing and when you chase it up it takes longer than the cooling off period to arrive.
- You must re-sell through them or their agent (it is explained to maintain standards) and of course they will charge a large commission or transfer fee.
- Annual service fees can often amount to what you would normally spend on a holiday. Check what annual increases they allow themselves on service fees.
- Non-payment of annual service fees (maybe they haven't invoiced you) can lead to them taking action for repossession or costs.
- Collateral contract. Two contracts are signed, the main contract which is all above board and a second contract for a shorter period (not given the protection afforded to people entering long period timeshares) for something such as club fees for the site. You find that you cannot back out of the second contract without repudiating the main agreement.
- Points in lieu which you can use on other holidays organized by them, if you don't want to use your week(s) or you want to go somewhere different. Translate the points into currency and do a comparison to see what you would get if you paid cash. Often you would be better off doing the latter.

Supplier cheats

"Course it's cheating, nobody ever got rich being honest."
Harry Wormwood. Matilda (1996)

Some sharper than sharp practices I have known suppliers use.

- The use of multiple suppliers to maximise credit. When one account goes on credit stop because of non-payment, they move to the next and so on.
- Phantom shortages. Claiming shortages in deliveries that cannot be proven.
- Reducing the quality of supplies without informing the buyer.
- Short deliveries. This is particularly common when charged by weight. It is legal and not unusual to be supplied product at the bottom end of specification but some suppliers go further.
- Using sub-contractors to perform work when the buyer believes the work is being performed by the company itself.
- Premature invoicing particularly at financial period ends.
- Evergreen contracts that only allow limited periods for cancellation or termination of contract, termimation at other times result in financial penalties.
- Service agreements that allow charges to escalate at an unjustifiable rate.

Outright scams

"There's a sucker born every minute" David Hannum but
often attributed to P T Barnum

Scams are often based on exploiting one or more of the seven deadly sins: greed, lust, gluttony, sloth, envy, pride and wrath. If you are virtuous, you are more difficult to scam, leading to the truism, 'you can't con an honest man'.

- Advanced fee frauds – The most common version of this in recent times has been the large lottery win in a foreign country, requiring an upfront payment to be made in order to claim the prize.
- Badger game - The victim, often a married man, is enticed or coerced into a compromising situation with another woman. The man is then blackmailed.
- Boiler room fraud – cold callers, usually based overseas, sell non-existent or worthless securities with the promise of high rewards.
- Embarrassing cheque - The gist of this is that a company with an embarrassing name takes orders for goods which don't exist. The company sends refunds by cheque, bearing the company's embarrassing name. The hope being that people are too embarrassed to cash the cheques.
- Goldbricking – selling an item for more than its worth under false pretences. Greed prevents the victim from properly investigating the offer. If it seems too good to be true, it probably is.
- Flesh pot or clip joint – money is paid to enter an illicit area. Those entering receive little or no service or are ejected. They cannot complain because their entering into the establishment is either illegal or immoral.
- Melon drop – somebody bumps into you, dropping what they claim is a valuable item, which is broken. They go on to claim compensation.
- Mock auction – normally performed where a crowd will gather. Typically, members of the scam team pose as customers and purchase high value items for low prices. Having excited the greed of the crowd they then put up for sale a worthless item, at say £10, with the promise that those that buy will have the chance of bidding on a 50" plasma tv at a knockdown price. 50 people stump up £10 each, the 50" telly is bought by one of the gang, who then walk away with £500.
- Pyramid selling – A scheme were people buy into the right to sell the same right to new recruits in order to receive a share of the new recruits fees. Your position in the pyramid is important

because eventually there are no new gullible recruits joining the scheme. Those at the top of the scheme can make a lot of money but typically 90% will lose out.

- Pig in a poke – Somebody buys something on faith without knowing what they are actually buying.
- Phoenix company fraud – A company goes bankrupt only for a second company with the same ownership to appear overnight.
- Ponzi scheme - Money from new investors is used to pay high returns to existing investors. The high returns attract new investors until the scheme eventually collapses. See Bernard Madoff.
- Pump and dump - Influential investors act in concert by buying shares, using their influence to promote the shares, before selling at the top of the market.
- Romance fraud – Can occur on internet dating were the new 'partner' becomes stuck in their home country and requests money to travel to meet the victim. Another version, a member of the partner's family needs money for urgent medical care without which the partner remains stuck, looking after the relative.
- A shill or plant - Someone paid by the conman to play a third party, maybe another customer or an enthusiastic bystander.
- Spanish prisoner – The principle of this scam is that a valuable item is being held and the victim puts up money to free the valuable item in the expectation of a large reward.
- Thai gem and jewellery scam – At one time prevalent in Bangkok, this scam involves a native 'guide' taking you to a shop which has special deals for tourists. A number of people are usually involved including a local driver and sometimes westerners to add credibility. Once in the shop high pressure sales tactics follow and the victim ends up buying essential worthless 'gems'.
- West African letter or 419 fraud – A type of advanced fee fraud. Victims are asked to help transfer money to another country in return for a percentage of the money you helped transfer.

Legal Aspects

Forming a valid contract

"A verbal contract isn't worth the paper it's written on"
Sam Goldwyn

One of the basic skills someone working in purchasing should master is creating legally valid contracts. Not only should contracts be legally valid, but they should also be effective as instruments of communication between the parties.

The main tool buyers use to create consistently valid and effective contracts is the purchase order (P.O.). Purchase orders are company standardized contracts, strictly controlled by administrative procedures and levels of authority. The benefit of using purchase orders is that they are recognised by suppliers and the courts alike as authority to create contracts on behalf of the company.

To use this tool effectively and responsibly, purchasing staff need to understand the administrative procedures which govern the use of purchase orders and the contract law that is the basis of their legal authority. Company procedures will normally set out the following basic steps to ensure that purchase orders are used in a controlled and responsible way:

- Procedures for the selection and approval of suppliers such that only suppliers capable of performing are allowed to bid for work.
- An enquiry process, in which the technical and commercial requirements of the company are spelled out.
- A system for reviewing supplier offers to ensure technical compliance and commercial suitability.
- Negotiation, to test the offer and in doing so identify and iron out potential problems before they occur.

- Raising the official order, on standard forms, checked for accuracy and relevant to a particular offer.
- Checking and signing off the purchase order, according to an agreed level of authorisation.
- Checking the supplier's acknowledgement to ensure it is consistent with the purchase order.

The second element buyers need to understand are the legal requirements necessary to form a legally binding contract, these are set out below:

- There is a current offer and an unconditional acceptance.
- Consideration must be given. This is normally the promise to supply or the promise to pay.
- The details of the contract must be sufficiently complete and certain.
- The parties have the legal capacity to enter into the contract.
- The subject matter is legal. For example, you cannot form a legally enforceable contract to perform a crime.
- There is an intention to create legal relations. Consent must be genuine. There mustn't be duress on either of the parties
- Performance must be possible. For example a seller must be able to give good title (ownership) summed up by the latin phrase nemo dat quod non habet (no one can give that they do not have).
- Some contracts require special legal procedures or forms, for example, the sale of land must be made in writing or under seal.

Failure to meet these requirements may result in the contract being void or voidable. A void agreement is one that cannot be enforced because one or more of the above pre-requisites are missing for example the agreement is for an illegal act. Void agreements are said to be void ab initio (from the start). A voidable contract is one that may be valid but one of the parties may not be bound by the contract and able to repudiate the contract. For example, a contract between a child and an adult may be repudiated by the child. The right to repudiate a contract may be lost if the unbound party unnecessarily delays repudiating, or affirms the contract. The right to repudiate may also be lost if third party rights have been acquired (goods sold on to a third party), or if irreversible steps had already been taken to fulfil the contract.

It is important to get all aspects of contract formation right because the cost of getting them wrong can be very expensive in terms of commercial loss, including, the loss of goodwill if you fall out with your suppliers.

Finally, remember, that purchasing procedures and knowledge of the law will not protect you from entering commercially bad contracts. To prevent that you need to rely on other skills, 'caveat emptor', let the buyer beware.

Offer, invitation to treat and acceptance

"For every promise there is a price to pay". Jim Rohn

Agreement is the essence of forming a contract and fundamental to this is an offer by one party and an acceptance by the other.

Creating an offer

An offer can be any statement, if when looked at objectively, can be understood to be an unequivocal willingness of a party to be legally bound if certain conditions are met.

When deciding whether or not a statement amounts to a clear indication to be legally bound, the courts will look at the facts of each case. In particular, they will look for certain essential terms and whether they have been expressed clearly enough. From a buyer's point of view, dealing with the purchase of goods, even a simple statement identifying the goods and the price could be sufficiently clear and show intent to be legally bound.

There are some business communications that are generally not construed to be offers, such as; price lists, advertisements and catalogues. This is because such communications made to a wide audience, if taken up by a sufficiently large number of people could result in an inability to supply and consequently a breach of contract. In the interests of practicality, the law created another condition called an invitation to treat. An invitation to treat is not considered to be a direct offer but merely encouragement for parties to make an offer. The classic case in this respect was Fisher v Bell, in which it was held by the court that the presence of a flick knife in a shop window was not an offer but an invitation to treat. So at the supermarket, it is presenting your basket of goods at the checkout which is the offer, not the displays of goods on the shelves.

However, it often depends on the facts of the case and there can be exceptions to the general rule. In Carlill v Carbolic Smoke Ball Co. it was held that an advertisement could be construed as an offer to the world. In this case, the court considered that the depositing of £1000 with a third party showed an intention to be bound.

Estimates can be construed as offers and can be legally binding again it will depend on the existence of essential terms and clarity of expression.

An invitation to tender (ITT) is generally an invitation to treat. Sending out ITTs is simply saying to your supplier that you will accept offers for the work(s) you have detailed.

Termination of an offer

Offers may be terminated by revocation at any time prior to acceptance by the offeree. To be effective revocation of the offer must be communicated, if an offeror changes their mind and it is not communicated, this is not sufficient. An offer may be revoked even if the offer states it is open to acceptance for a specific period. The logic behind this is that the offer to keep it open is part and parcel of the original offer that can be revoked.

An offer may be terminated by lapse of time. If an offer states it is only open for acceptance for a particular period, any acceptance outside of this period will be ineffective. It is possible that offers can lapse through the passing of a reasonable time. What amounts to a reasonable time will depend on the circumstances of the individual case.

Death generally revokes an offer; this is most definitely the case when the offeree has notice of the death prior to the purported acceptance. In the instance where the offeree has no notice of the death then it is possible that the deceased estate may be responsible for the contract.

Acceptance

To create a contract an acceptance must be unconditional, that is, it doesn't introduce new terms. If new terms are introduced then it is not an acceptance but it is a counter-offer which effectively destroys the original offer.

As stated earlier, the general rule is that an acceptance is effective when it is communicated to the offeror. The original offer may state a particular method for acceptance. In the absence of a stated method any reasonable method of communication can be used. Silence alone cannot amount to acceptance but conduct can indicate acceptance, such as taking receipt of goods.

When an acceptance is posted, it is effective from the time of posting even if delivery is delayed. With regard to electronic communication, delivery is effective when received. This rule will determine the place a contract was formed, which in turn can have implications on the country of jurisdiction when dealing with international suppliers.

Incorporated and implied contract terms

"The one great principle of the English law is to make business for itself. There is no other principle distinctly, certainly, and consistently maintained through all its narrow turnings". Bleak House, Charles Dickens

Terms can be implied into contracts either by reference, by representations made prior to the contract, by custom and practice, by the common law or by statute.

Incorporation by reference

Terms can be incorporated into a contract by reference. They are usually incorporated through the pre-contract and contractual communications between the parties.

The terms most frequently incorporated into contracts by reference are standard terms and conditions of contract. In order to incorporate standard terms and conditions, the party wishing to rely upon them must do everything reasonably possible to bring them to the attention of the other party. This would include clearly referring to them in pre-contract documents and making them freely available to the other party. If the party wishing to rely on standard terms and conditions discourages the other party from reading them, then the courts are likely to decide that they have not been incorporated into the contract. One exception to this rule is when the party wishing to avoid incorporation of terms has physically signed the document referring to them. Provided there was no fraud or misrepresentation then the party signing the document will be binding.

Other terms and documents regularly incorporated into contracts by reference include: specifications, national standards and drawings. All will be validly incorporated if they are clearly identified in pre-contract documentation and brought to the attention of the other party, who then is able to assess them, object to them or put in a counter offer.

It is not uncommon to detail on correspondence all of the documents that you wish to incorporate into the contract in an enclosures list. When two or more documents cover similar subjects, it is necessary to indicate the order of precedence the documents should be read.

Representations

A representation is a statement of fact made during negotiations, before a contract is formed, that is relied upon when the contract is subsequently made. In simple terms, it is a statement that induces a party to enter the contract. Normally, representations are verbal assurances from one party to the other, for example, "we have not had any quality problems with this type of machine".

Statements of opinion are not representations. If one party says, "in my opinion this is a reliable type of machine", that is unlikely to be classed as a representation.

In general, the law does not make a distinction between whether the representation was the main inducement or only part of the inducement to enter the contract.

To be actionable, a representation must have become a term of the contract. A representation will be viewed as a term of the contract, if, when viewed objectively, it was made with the intention of it becoming a binding promise. When considering whether this intention existed, the courts will look at; the relative knowledge of the parties, the importance of the statement to the parties, the time it was made during negotiations and whether it was recorded. Some standard terms and conditions explicitly attempt to exclude representations through 'whole agreement' clauses which seek to exclude any statements not included in the final contract.

If a representation turns out to be factually incorrect, it is a misrepresentation. A party who enters a contract on the basis of a misrepresentation may rescind (cancel) the contract and possibly claim damages. Rescission will seek to return the parties to the pre-contract position. If this is not possible because the goods have been sold on or incorporated into another product, the courts have discretion to award damages in lieu of rescission, even if the misrepresentation was made innocently.

If the misrepresentation was made fraudulently or negligently, damages can be claimed. In the former case, all damages however remote can be claimed but if the misrepresentation was only negligently made, a narrower assessment of damages is used.

The failure of a party to disclose a fact is generally not regarded as a misrepresentation, although this is not the case in insurance contracts or contracts of utmost good faith.

Custom and practice

Where trading partners have a history of regularly dealing with each other on the same terms, in the absence of express agreement, the courts may imply terms based on the previous course of dealing.

Terms implied by common law

If the express terms of a contract are vague or lacking in detail the courts may imply terms to fill in the gaps in order to give the contract business efficacy. For example, if the contract is silent about payment, the courts will imply a term that payment should be made within a reasonable time from receipt of the goods. In some cases, the courts will use trade customs and practices to inform their decisions.

Terms implied by statute

Statutory laws are usually enacted to protect the public good or where history has shown that abuses can occur. This is contrary to a general principle of English Law that parties can agree to whatever terms they choose, 'freedom of contract'. The main source of statutory implied terms relating to purchasing are found in the Sale of Goods Acts and the Unfair Contract Terms Act 1977. These Acts protect first and foremost the general public when dealing with business but can also be applied in business to business dealings.

Standard terms and conditions of contract

"Law is a bottomless pit". John Arbuthnot

It is a key principle of English law that parties can agree whatever terms and conditions they choose, so called 'freedom of contract'. However, drafting express terms and conditions of contract is both slow and expensive. The solution has been to create standard terms and contract (often called standard conditions of purchase or standard conditions of sale depending on the party wishing to use them).

However, to be effective, standard terms and conditions must be properly incorporated into the contract. To ensure this, the party wishing to rely upon the standard terms must take reasonable steps to bring them to the attention of the other party, prior to the creation of the contract. Ideally, this should include referring to your standard terms on any enquiry or tender documentation and any subsequent purchase order documentation. If possible, your enquiries or purchase orders should include an opportunity for the supplier to sign an acknowledgement that they accept your terms of trading. When designing hardcopy purchase orders, it is a good idea to have the standard terms and conditions printed on the back of the printed order. A clear reference to the terms and conditions should be made on the face of the order, such as, 'we acknowledge receipt of this order and agree to the terms and conditions set out overleaf. Ideally there should be a box for the supplier to sign. If the supplier signs and returns an acceptance of such a document, this will normally be enough proof that the terms and conditions have been accepted and incorporated into the contract.

'Battle of the forms'

A contract is formed as soon as an offer by one party is unconditionally accepted by the other, but what happens when both parties never actually unconditionally accept the other party's offer. This problem often occurs when each party responds to the other party's communications but reference their own terms and conditions of contract. For example:

- The buyer sends an enquiry referencing the buyer's terms and conditions of purchase.
- The supplier responds with a quote which references the seller's terms and conditions of sale.
- The buyer sends an order including the purchaser's terms and conditions of purchase.
- The suppler acknowledges the order on documentation which refers to the seller's terms and conditions of sale.

- The delivery is made and the delivery note refers to the seller's terms and conditions of sale.
- The buyer stamps the delivery note 'accepted under the buyer's terms and conditions of purchase.

In these circumstances, whose terms and conditions apply? The usual method applied by the courts is to adopt an analysis based upon identifying each stage as an offer, counter offer or acceptance. In the above case, at any point, either party may be deemed to accept the others offer by his actions or by failing to respond with a counter offer. In general, it is the person who fires the last shot who wins the battle. This process is known as the battle of the forms, a classic case of which was Re Bond Worth (1979). In this case the buyers Bond Worth ordered fibre from Monsanto Ltd, the purchase order included reference to Bond Worth's conditions of purchase. Monsanto Ltd raised a series of acknowledgements as the material became available, these acknowledgements referred to the conditions of sale of Monsanto Ltd. Deliveries where made following each of the acknowledgments. Bond Worth didn't respond to the acknowledgements and accepted the deliveries. Bond Worth then went into receivership, owing Monsanto Ltd a lot of money. Monsanto sought to rely on a 'retention of title' clause in their conditions of sale. The court held that a contract existed and was governed by Monsanto's conditions of sale. The rationale behind the decision was that Monsanto's acknowledgements amounted to a counter-offer which was accepted by the conduct of Bond Worth, who did not respond to the acknowledgements and accepted delivery.

Sometimes companies try to include a knockout blow in their terms and conditions. In Butler Machine Tool Company Ltd v Ex-Cell-O Ltd (1978), the sellers, Butler Machine Tool Company, included in their conditions of sale the clause that their conditions 'shall prevail over any terms and conditions in the buyer's order'. Ex-Cell-O sent an order on their conditions of purchase which included a tear off acknowledgement which included the words, 'we accept your order on the terms and conditions thereon. Butler Machine Tool Company signed and returned the acknowledgement slip and sent a covering letter stating the order was accepted on the terms and conditions of the original offer. On appeal, it was held that the return of the tear off slip amounted to acceptance of the buyer's order on their terms and conditions, the knockout blow failed.

Interpreting standard terms and conditions

"Take nothing on its looks; take everything on evidence. There's no better rule". Great Expectations, Charles Dickens

Unless you work in a particularly contentious or litigious area of purchasing, you will seldom have need to refer to the detail in your standard terms and conditions of purchase. Typically, contracting parties only reach for the small print when something goes wrong and they want to know who is liable to pay for the foul up.

Listed below are some of the most commonly used clauses in standard terms and conditions of purchase, a brief explanation of what they are and their purpose:

Definitions

Defines the key terms found in the agreement that may be open to interpretation, these definitions would normally include the participants in the contract and the main terms.

Sometimes what amounts to a 'condition' of contract will be defined. This definition will usually mirror S11 Sale of Goods Act (SoGA). Note. If a requirement is classified as a condition, more serious consequences can follow if it is breached, for example, it may give the right to terminate the contract.

Application of terms

This clause seeks to establish the primacy of the buyer's terms in any 'battle of the forms'. Typical sub-clauses may:

- Seek to confirm that the conduct of the supplier, for example, through the delivery of goods, will serve as evidence of agreement to the buyer's terms and conditions.
- State that any changes to the buyer's terms and conditions, are only binding if made in writing by a specified person.
- Attempt to establish the primacy of the terms and conditions over any other terms and conditions, a so called knockout punch.

Price and payment

- This clause may define price if not already covered in the 'definitions clause', it will usually make it clear whether duties and taxes are inclusive.
- The clause will usually allow for a credit period prior to payment, for example, 'the price is payable 30 days after delivery of the goods'.
- Sub-clauses may be included setting out any settlement discounts applicable.
- Express provision is made for the common law right to set-off payments against sums due from the supplier.

Quality

This clause will set out the nature and quality of goods to be supplied and will tend to follow the Sale of Goods Act. Sub-clauses will cover:

- 'Specification' (s13 SoGA).
- 'Description' (s13 SoGA).
- 'Sale by reference to samples (s15 SoGA).
- 'Quality and fitness for purpose' (s14 SoGA).

Quantity

This clause will set out to describe what discrepancies in delivery quantities are not acceptable and what remedies will be available to the buyer in such instances. This clause will mirror s30 SoGA.

Delivery

This clause will set out the time, place and method of delivery. Sub-clauses may deal with:

- What amounts to a breach and the consequences of the breach? It is not uncommon for purchasing terms and conditions to make the time of delivery 'of the essence' to the contract, which in the event of a late delivery would allow the buyer to terminate the contract rather than just claim damages.
- The provision of liquidated damages for late delivery.
- The method of transport and who pays for it.
- Delivery by instalment.

Title to Goods

This clause usually seeks to establish the right of the seller to sell the goods and give good title, mirroring s12 SoGA.

Confidentiality

If the buyer is supplying drawings, know how or special tooling, they may want to ensure that the details are kept secret. An express confidentiality clause will normally confirm that:

- Any intellectual property or tooling provided by the buyer, are and remain the property of the buyer.
- That the property should not be given away, shared or sold to another party without the express agreement of the buyer.
- The seller should make available the buyer's property at the request of the buyer.

Inspection

This clause gives the right to inspect goods, possibly at the supplier's or their sub-contractor's premises, prior to the passing of property to the buyer. This express provisions mirror s34 and s35 of the Sale of Goods Act.

Right to rejection

This clause will set out the grounds for acceptance and rejection, in particular:

- It may seek to contradict the presumption that receipt of the goods amounts to acceptance and instead allow the buyer reasonable time to inspect the goods.
- Set out the buyer's rights to reject the goods if they do not comply with the contract.
- Detail the remedies available to the buyer including rejection, the right to demand replacement goods.

Passing of property and risk

This clause sets out when property in the goods shall pass to the buyer, which will normally be at the earliest time possible, usually at the point when the goods are ascertained. The passing of risk is usually delayed as long as possible, normally to the point when the goods are delivered to the buyer. Sub-clauses will:

- Make it clear that passing of property will not affect the buyer's rights to reject the goods if they later prove defective.

Warranty or guarantee

This clause normally spells out what the seller will or will not accept in respect to the liability for the performance of the goods. Typically such a clause will cover:

- What is considered a defect under the contract and what is not?
- The time period covered by the warranty, for example, 12 months from receipt of goods.
- The extent of the warranty. Is the seller obliged to replace defective goods or just repair them?
- Whether the buyer seeks to be covered for consequential loss, for example, profits from the loss of production?
- What time limits are there for the seller to make good any faults?

- Whether repairs cover both parts and labour? Does the seller pay for incidental costs like shipping which may be high if the replacement parts are being sent overseas?
- What is excluded from the warranty, for example, fair wear and tear?
- Conditions necessary for the maintenance of the warranty for example, regular servicing.

Right to indemnity

The buyer will normally want an express indemnity from liability caused by any breaches of contract by the supplier. It is common for the buyer to list as sub-clauses the potential liabilities he wants to be indemnified against these may include:

- Royalty's payable by the supplier in respect of the goods.
- Indemnity against the infringement of patents.
- Claims in contract or tort relating to damages to people or property.
- Consequential losses incurred because of the seller's or its sub-contractor's actions.

Force majeure

This clause seeks to excuse a party from its liability under the contract if some unforeseen event, beyond the control of that party, prevents it from carrying out its obligations under the contract. Force majeure clauses are normally used to excuse acts of God and acts of war but could be used to limit liability in a whole range of circumstances.

Sub-contracting and assignment

This clause restricts the right of the supplier to sub-contract all or part of the work. By having a measure of control over the ultimate source of goods, the buyer can be better assured of the goods quality. This may be of particular importance where environmental or ethical considerations are important to the buyer. Such a clause will usually require the supplier to seek written consent from the buyer before sub-contracting the work. If permission is given by the buyer, the clause will usually make it clear that it is the supplier's responsibility to assure the suitability of the sub-contractor. There is usually a sub-clause which expressly allows the supplier to use suppliers of minor parts without the buyer's permission.

Waiver

The buyer may wish to waiver a right under the contract but not wish to prejudice his other rights under the contract. This clause allows the buyer to give some leeway on specific issues but at the same time avoid compromising the rest of the terms and conditions.

Variation and cancellation

Once agreed, a contract is normally binding on both parties. However, because circumstances may change in the period after the contract has been formed, the buyer may seek the right to vary the contract. Without an express clause in the contract to allow this right, the contract may be at risk of becoming frustrated (performance becomes impossible).

Such clauses normally provide that the buyer will pay the supplier reasonable costs for the change in work, usually with the proviso that the supplier is not in breach of the contract.

Similarly, the buyer may want the right to cancel all or part of the contract. Without a variation or cancellation clause, this would probably amount to a breach of contract, actionable for damages. So the purchaser's terms and conditions usually expressly allow for cancellation and limit the amount of damages payable.

Insolvency

The terms and conditions may make specific arrangements in case the supplier becomes insolvent or some other form of financial difficulty. These arrangements will normally include the right to cancel the order and the right to enter the supplier's premises to take possession of goods, materials or other property which had passed or vested with the buyer.

Disputes

This clause sets out the method of resolving disputes usually through a named independent arbitrator. It may go further in confirming that any decision made by the arbitrator is binding on the parties.

Contract law

This is a statement identifying the law applicable to the contract and the Court of jurisdiction. Every contract will have one of these clauses hence the name 'boiler plate' clause.

Title and passing of property and risk

"Possession isn't nine-tenths of the law. It's nine-tenths of the problem". John Lennon

The basic rule in English law is that property passes (vests) when the parties intend it to pass. If the contract makes no express provisions for vesting, property will usually pass to the buyer when the goods have been appropriated to the contract. Appropriation of goods to the contract usually occurs when the seller does something which irrevocably assigns the goods to the contract.

Generally, property in general goods will not be appropriated to the contract on the formation of the contract. This is the case even if a deposit is paid. Consequently, if the supplier becomes insolvent, the buyer will not normally be able to claim the goods. Similarly, if goods are to be manufactured to order, in the absence of an express term to the contrary, property does not normally pass when the goods are completed unless the seller takes further steps to appropriate the goods to the contract. The exceptions to this rule are contracts for the sale of specific goods that are in a deliverable state. In this instance, it is likely that property in the goods will pass to the buyer on the formation of an unconditional binding contract.

So the key question becomes what is necessary to appropriate goods to a contract. A pre-requisite of goods being appropriated to the contract is that they can be ascertained, which means they are identified or assigned to a contract. It is a rule in English law and covered by s16 of the Sale of Goods Act, that no property in goods can be transferred to the buyer unless the goods are ascertained. Ascertainment may occur if the seller in some way specifically earmarks the goods for the contract, for example, by marking them with the buyer's name or segregating goods on behalf of the buyer. Generally, this is only fully effective if the act of identifying the goods is communicated to the buyer. The only guaranteed way of confirming the goods have been appropriated to the contract, is delivery. In the case of Carlos Federspeil and Co S.A. v Twigg and Co Ltd (1957), the seller became insolvent. The goods (bicycles), which had been paid for by the buyer and were ready for export, were held to be the property of the receiver, not the buyer. So, when considering title or passing of property clauses:

- Make the passing of property an express provision.
- Make it a condition of the contract that the goods and any materials bought for the manufacture of the goods are appropriated to the contract and marked up as property of your company including your order number.

These steps are particularly important where you make payments upfront prior to delivery to you.

Suppliers will sometimes seek to reserve the title in the goods until payment has been made in full. This is called a 'retention of title' clause (ROT) or Romalpa clause. This follows a famous case in 1976 when the sellers, Aluminium Vaasen, were able to claim unsold goods from the buyer, Romalpa, when the latter became insolvent. Not all ROT clauses are effective, some fail because the goods are irreversibly changed by the buyer's manufacturing process or embodied in the structure of a building or similar.

Buyers working for companies acting as sub-contractors should be aware that prime contractors will often make it a provision of their order that the sub-contractors should not agree to ROT clauses with their suppliers. Buyers should therefore check the terms and conditions of the head contract before agreeing terms and conditions with their suppliers.

In international buying, the incoterms normally make it clear when property is intended to pass.

Risk

The basic rule in English law is that the owner of the property bears the risk of damage, deterioration or loss. So risk passes when ownership passes not when possession changes. Buyers should consider this when they are buying specific, deliverable goods that they do not immediately take possession of. For example, a buyer makes an unconditional contract to buy a second hand car that is immediately available but agrees to leave it with the seller until the following day. In this instance, the ownership and property in the car, is likely to pass to the buyer when the contract is formed. If the car is stolen from the car dealer overnight, it is the buyer's loss.

Terms about quality

"The quality, not the longevity, of one's life is what is important."
Martin Luther King, Jr.

The parties to a contract can make express provision with respect to the specification and quality of goods. In addition, certain terms will be implied by statute into all contracts for the sale of goods and the supply of services.

The two principle statutes are The Sale of Goods Act 1979 amended in 1994 and the Supply of Goods and Services Act 1982. Both these statutes imply terms as to the nature and quality of goods supplied.

By section 13 of the Act, goods should correspond with the description.

By section 14 of the Act, goods should be of 'satisfactory' quality, previous to the 1994 Act the words were, 'merchantable' quality. What amounts to 'satisfactory' is based upon the standard that a reasonable person would regard as satisfactory, taking into account all the circumstances. The Act makes specific allowances for defects brought to the attention of the buyer prior to the sale.

By the same section of the Act, it is implied that goods should be reasonably fit for the purpose for which they are being bought, but only when the buyer makes the particular purpose for which the goods are being bought known to the seller and the buyer relied upon the seller's skill and judgment. For this reason, it is good practice for buyers to make it clear to the seller prior to the contract the specific purpose of the goods.

One of the leading cases on this point is Aswan Engineering v Lupine Ltd (Thurgar Bolle Ltd, third party) [1986]. In this case Thurgar Bolle Ltd supplied pails to Lupine Ltd for the purpose of holding materials. The pails failed under extreme conditions and Lupine Ltd sued Thurgar Bolle Ltd for damages. One of the claims made by Lupine was that the pails were not fit for purpose however it was shown that Lupine had relied upon their own judgment in deciding what type of pail to use and their claim failed.

Section 15 SoGA, implies a condition that in the case of a sale by sample, the goods supplied will correspond with the sample quality.

The right to inspect

By SoGA s34, the buyer is not deemed to have accepted the goods until he has been given reasonable opportunity to examine them and confirm they conform to the contract. This rule applies even if the buyer signs for the goods. However, the best policy is to ensure that when goods are signed for the delivery note is marked-up 'unchecked'.

The seller may attempt to restrict the right of the buyer to inspect the goods through the use of standard terms or other express agreement. In a business to business contract such a clause could be effective depending upon whether the term was considered reasonable in accordance of the rules set out in the Unfair Contract Terms Act 1977.

Acceptance

In general, goods are regarded as being accepted when they are delivered to the buyer, SoGA s35 (except where s34 provides otherwise). Other indications that the goods have been accepted include; doing something to the goods inconsistent with the ownership of the seller such as re-selling the goods, or the buyer retains the goods for a reasonable period of time without advising the seller that he has rejected them.

Latent defects

Goods should be of a satisfactory quality when risk passes from the seller to the buyer (usually at the time of delivery). However, in the case of latent defects, the goods will still be regarded as unsatisfactory as long as it can be shown that the latent defect was present when the passing of risk occurred.

Remedies for breach

Rejection of goods

Terms relating to the quality of goods are generally drafted or implied as contract conditions, the breach of which normally allows the buyer the right to reject the goods, terminate the contract and claim damages.

In the event of a breach of contract, the buyer can reject the goods without the need to terminate the contract. However, it is normal for the buyer to allow the seller to supply replacement goods. The buyer cannot reject the goods if the breach is so minor that it would be unreasonable to reject the goods. These rules do not affect the buyer's right to claim damages, if he can prove the breach caused loss.

In a business to business contract, if some goods in a batch are faulty then the buyer usually has the right to reject the entire lot as long as it is not unreasonable to do so. The buyer may accept those goods unaffected by the breach and reject the rest. However, the buyer cannot accept some of the affected goods and not others.

In order to be effective, a rejection of goods should be a clear unequivocal communication that the buyer intends to reject the goods. The buyer can lose the right to reject goods if it is deemed the goods have been accepted, as described above.

If the buyer rejects the seller's goods because they are unsatisfactory or unfit, the supplier is probably entitled to send a replacement delivery, if it is within the contract period. Failure by the buyer to receive replacement goods of an acceptable quality could breach the contract for non-acceptance and the seller could possibly claim damages.

Severable contracts

When goods are planned to be delivered in several instalments and paid for individually the contract is described as severable. In such contractual circumstances, the delivery of a defective consignment does not automatically allow the buyer to reject other consignments or terminate the contract. Each consignment would be viewed on its own merits. Whether the buyer would be allowed to terminate the whole contract would depend upon all the circumstances including the wording of the contract. Factors taken into consideration would include the proportion of the defective consignments to the whole and the likelihood of further breaches.

Damages

Under the common law, the buyer can claim any loss caused by the breach of contract. In order to succeed the buyer needs to show that his losses were caused as a natural consequence of the breach and that the losses were a reasonably foreseeable consequence of the breach. Finally, the injured party must take reasonable steps to mitigate the loss.

Bonds and guarantees

"Scargills in pinstripes" Vince Cable, on bankers

Surety bonds and letters of guarantee

The purpose of most surety bonds is to ensure that one party is safeguarded from the default of the other party. Bonds are normally issued by a bank or insurance company and are payable in the event of the default specified in the bond.

Surety bonds and letters of guarantee are often used in the construction industry because of:

- The uncertain nature of construction work.
- The common use of advanced payments to contractors.
- The long duration of contracts.

The financial institution issuing the guarantee will charge a premium for the service and may insist upon the contractor lodging cash or assets as security. Some of the main surety bonds are listed below:

Bid bonds / tender guarantees

Bidders for a contract are required to put up a bid bond that guarantees that if they win the bid the will proceed with the contract. If the bidder fails to proceed with the contract the customer will be able to present the bond to the guarantor (usually a bank or insurance company) to cover the difference in cost between the winning bid and the next lowest bid. In some instances the customer may require that the bid bond provided by the winning bidder is transformed into a performance bond when the contract is placed.

Performance bonds

Suppliers may be required by the buyer to provide security in case the supplier does not complete their side of the agreement; this is called a performance bond. Performance bonds are most frequently found in construction contracts and provide that should the seller fail to complete the work then the buyer will receive a sum of money to ensure the work is completed.

Maintenance bonds

Normally these bonds are required by the buyer to guarantee performance after delivery or completion.

Advance payment guarantee

This is use to guarantee that any payments made up front by the customer will be used in accordance with terms of the contract. If the contractor fails to perform their obligations, this type of guarantee will allow the customer to recover his advance money.

Fidelity bond

This is essentially an insurance policy to cover the risk of a contractor's employees causing loss through negligence or fraudulence.

Memorandum of understanding (MOU)

"The whole duty of government is to prevent crime and to preserve contracts". Lord Melbourne

This is a document often used to indicate a joint understanding or goal between two or more companies. MOUs are often written in more general terms than a contract, often preferring to set out the aims of the parties rather than set out the obligations of the parties.

The legal status of a memorandum of understanding is similar to that of a letter of intent. Whether or not it is legally enforceable depends upon the drafting, the intention and the actions of the parties.

Sometimes, MOUs are regarded as standing agreements between companies. However, an MOU would have to be properly incorporated into each contract to be effective.

Letters of comfort

"A false hope only gives false comfort". Gene Brewer

A letter of comfort is a written promise, from a third party that it will provide support or stand behind the company which is the subject of the promise. Normally, this promise is given by the parent company in relation to a debt or extension of credit to the company. A typical letter of comfort will normally include:

- A statement confirming the debt and or the proposed advances to the subsidiary.
- A promise to stand behind the subsidiary and not sell or reduce control in it.
- Details of how the parent company would support the subsidiary in the instance of difficulties.

Normally letters of comfort will only carry moral force and do not create any binding contractual obligations upon the person or company making the promise. In Kleinwort Benson Ltd v Malaysia Mining Corp. Ltd [1989], a loan was agreed after the parent company raised a letter of comfort which stated that "It is our policy to ensure that the business of the subsidiary is at all times in a position to meet its liabilities to you under the loan agreement". The subsidiary subsequently went into liquidation and the creditors sought repayment from the parent company. The court held that the letter of comfort was not intended to create a contractual binding promise by the parent company and the action failed. However, in some circumstances a letter of comfort may be effective when:

- There is an explicit intention to create binding contractual relations.
- An intention to create legally binding relations can be implied, perhaps by the provision of consideration.
- The agreement is made under seal.

Late delivery

"I am extraordinarily patient, provided I get my own way in the end". Margaret Thatcher

Contractual terms are classed as either 'warranties' or 'conditions' the distinction is important because the law regards the breach of a condition as more serious than the breach of a warranty and consequently the methods of redress are stronger.

Normally the time of delivery is classed as a warranty, the breach of which could lead to a claim for damages if the buyer can prove he has suffered loss. However, breach of a warranty will not normally allow the buyer to terminate the contract. Time of delivery can be made a condition of the contract if:

- The parties expressly agree that delivery dates are to be strictly to be complied with.
- The nature of the subject matter or the surrounding circumstances show that time should be considered of the essence.
- The buyer subjected to the delay gives notice to the seller.

It is common for standard conditions of purchase to make 'time of the essence' but buyers should be aware that including this clause alone may not always be sufficient to be effective.

'Best endeavours'

Buyer's should be wary of suppliers who want to include a 'best endeavours' clause. Normally this is simply an attempt to avoid an absolute obligation to achieve something. Whether the party in default has actually used best endeavours will be judged on the reasonableness of their efforts in the circumstances.

A seller insisting upon a 'reasonable endeavours' should if possible be avoided. The standard of effort required to achieve 'reasonable endeavours' is even lower still. A contract offering 'reasonable' endeavours may provide so little weight as to be almost worthless.

If possible, the buyer should employ other incentives for ensuring on time deliveries. This may include bonus payments or liquidated damages clauses. Liquidated damages are pre-determined sum of money one party agrees to pay the other in the event of a default, usually late delivery.

It is not unusual for sellers subject to liquidated damages clauses to insist upon their own clauses allowing them either additional time or justifiable reasons for late delivery. Such clauses are called, 'extension of time' or 'force majeure' clauses. Both these clauses seek to avoid the termination of the contract or the imposition of damages due to delays outside the control of the supplier.

One final note, if the contract is silent on the matter of delivery, the general rule is that delivery must be made within a reasonable period of time.

Unfair contract terms

"Unless both sides win, no agreement can be permanent".
Jimmy Carter

The basic law is that parties are free to negotiate whatever deal they want to, even terms and conditions that are unreasonable. However, because sellers often abused consumers by unfairly limiting liability when problems arose, the Unfair Contract Terms Act 1977 (UCTA) was enacted.

Application of the act

UCTA applies to contract terms that attempt to exclude or restrict liability that arise out of a breach of contractual or civil obligations. In the case of contractual obligations, the Act applies either where the customer is dealing as a consumer or where the party seeking to exclude liability is relying upon standard written terms.

Under UCTA certain contract terms which seek to restrict or avoid liability following a breach of contractual or civil obligations (tort) can be held to be ineffective. In particular, clauses will be struck down that attempt to:

- Exclude or limit liability for death or personal injury caused by negligence.
- Exclude or limit the rights of consumers.
- Exclude the implied right to title given by the seller.

There are a second group of clauses that are not automatically rendered ineffective but are only effective insofar as they satisfy a test of reasonableness. In this second group are contracts that attempt to:

- Exclude or limit liability for negligence to property.
- Exclude or limit the statutory rights of businesses.
- Use standard conditions to exclude or limit liability generally, or to avoid performing the contract in part or in full.

The test of reasonableness

The reasonableness test is applied by considering all the circumstances of the case. Schedule 2 of the Act sets out the guidelines for application of the reasonableness test, these include:

- Whether the customer received inducements to agree to the term.
- The degree to which the clause has been negotiated, in particular, whether the customer knew or ought to have known of the existence of the clause and its extent.
- Whether the exclusion was subject to a condition not being complied with, for example, a new car warranty is normally subject to a regular servicing clause.
- Whether the clause was practically possible.
- Special modification of the product for the customer.
- Previous course of dealings between the parties.
- The relative bargaining strengths of the parties, taking into account the alternative means by which the customer's requirements could have been met.

In addition, s.11 the act allows consideration of the resources of the parties to meet any subsequent liability and the availability of insurance. Case history has also shown that the courts will consider:

- The degree of exclusion.
- The extent of the limitation claimed.
- The duration of its operation.

The onus of proof is placed on the party that wants to rely upon the clause, to prove it is reasonable in the circumstances.

The courts will consider the clause as a whole they cannot sever the reasonable from the unreasonable parts. So it is important when drafting or considering a clause to bear this in mind, don't draft a string of conditions from patently reasonable to outright unreasonable because they all will fail.

Some contracts are not covered by the Act including, international supply contracts, contracts for insurance or contracts that relate to the land, intellectual property rights, securities and the constitution of companies which each have their own special legal arrangements.

Letters of intent

"Make no mistake about it: once a band has signed a letter of intent, they will either eventually sign a contract that suits the label or they will be destroyed". Steve Albini

A letter of intent is a document issued by an intending purchaser of goods or services in the pre-contract stage of negotiations. The purpose of such a arrangement is to indicate to the seller that the buyer intends to award the contract to the seller when the final details of the contract have been negotiated.

A buyer may consider using a letter of intent when time is limited and delays in finalising the contract could jeopardise the project timetable. Letters of intent may also be used by buyers to reserve limited stock which if not secured could lead to delays. Often letters of intent are issued at the request of the seller who is under pressure from the buyer to start work prior to the formal issuing of a contract. The purpose being to provide some security for the costs incurred. Letters of intent are most regularly used in the construction industry.

The traditional view is that in most circumstances letters of intent do not have any contractual effect. Lord Denning MR put it this way, "If the law does not recognise a contract to enter into a contract (when there is a fundamental term to be agreed) it seems to me it cannot recognise a contract to negotiate. The reason is because it is too uncertain to have any binding force".

However, in certain cases the courts have found that, in the actions of the parties, the construction of the letter and the overall circumstances, a letter of intent can create rights and obligations.

In Wilson Smithnett and Cape (Sugar) Ltd v Bangladesh Sugar and Food Industries Corporation, a letter of intent was sent from the purchasers requiring the suppliers to enter into a performance bond, which they did. The judge in this case found that the letter of intent contained all the necessary terms to constitute an offer and the sellers by entering into a performance bond were deemed to have accepted the offer.

In CJ Sims Ltd v Shaftesbury Plc [1991], Shaftesbury raised a letter of intent asking Sims to commence work which they did and incurred costs, some of which were met by Shaftesbury. Further, Sims claimed reasonable costs including profit and overhead. The judge held that assuming Shaftesbury's quantity surveyor was reasonably satisfied, Sims were entitled under the letter of intent to reasonable costs in the event the negotiations failed to reach a conclusion. The key words in Shaftesbury's letter of intent read 'In the unlikely event of the contract not proceeding, (the contractors) will be reimbursed their reasonable costs, all of which must be substantiated in full to the reasonable satisfaction of our quantity surveyor'.

More recently in Mowlem Plc v Stena Line Ports Ltd [2004], a letter of intent was given by Stena which limited Mowlem's entitlement to a maximum of £10 million, Mowlem exceeded this sum but it was held that their relationship was governed by the letter of intent and that they could only claim up to the £10 million limit.

However, even if it is held that the letter of intent is not valid and a contract was never entered into, the seller may claim a quantum meruit payment on the basis that no party may unjustly enrich himself at the expense of another simply because a contract has not been found to exist. An example of this was British Steel Corporation v Cleveland Bridge Engineering [1982].

If work commences under a letter of intent and a subsequent contract is agreed, it is normally the terms of the final agreement that apply to the entire period and the seller cannot normally claim a quantum meruit for the work performed prior to the agreement. See Trollope and Colls Ltd and Holland and Hannen and Cubitts Ltd trading as Nuclear Civil Constructors (a firm) v Atomic Power Construction Ltd (1962).

Subject to contract

"Only free men can negotiate; prisoners cannot enter into contracts. Your freedom and mine cannot be separated." Nelson Mandela

An alternative way that parties try to avoid or delay the creation of a legally binding contract is by using the term 'subject to contract' or similar wording. This phrase is correctly used in contracts for the sale of land to denote that a document isn't the final sale document. However, the phrase appears to have migrated to other commercial matters were its effect is less certain. In general, using 'subject to contract' will not prevent the creation of a legally binding contract. The courts will look objectively at all the facts and if everything points to the intention to create a legally binding agreement, a contract will be recognised.

Notwithstanding these cases, from a buyer's point of view it is best to avoid creating letters of intent because they are simply poor buying for the following reasons.

- It ties the buyer to the seller and as a result in most circumstances will reduce the buyer's room for manoeuvre and probably weaken the buyer's negotiation position.
- The need to complete negotiations and sign a formal contract may be put on the back burner.
- If work commences without a completed contract and problems arise it will invariably be more difficult and more costly to resolve.
- Either party may default on the contract resulting in serious consequences for the other party.
- Other informal arrangements and commitments may be made. The resulting lack of contract control could prove expensive for the buyer.
- In the absence of contractual clarity, expensive litigation to resolve disputes is more likely.

Conclusion, allow yourself enough time to conclude negotiations properly and raise a detailed contract.

Confidentiality agreement

"A man is not finished when he is defeated. He is finished when he quits". Richard M. Nixon

Confidentiality is protected on a number of levels by the law:

- When parties are in a contractual relationship, the matter of confidentiality may be expressly provided for or may be implied into the contract by the common law.
- When the confider and the confidee are not in a contractual relationship, the law may impose a duty of confidentiality on the parties through equitable principles.
- Information and trade secrets can be formally protected by patent and copyright laws.

Not all information will be treated as confidential and attract protection. The information must have the 'necessary quality of confidence', so, for example, information in the public domain will not be protected. Secondly, the confider must emphasise to the receiver that the information is to be kept confidential.

Confidential information may come in a variety of forms; it may be commercial, technical, financial or personal information. With respect to purchasing, the confidential information normally relates to technical information such as processes or designs that are detailed on drawings or specification sheets.

The best policy for a buyer is to adopt a multi-layered approach to protecting confidential information.

- Be careful who you share confidential information with. You should avoid sending confidential information to direct or indirect competitors. You should avoid sending confidential information to close suppliers of competitors. You should avoid sending confidential information to suppliers who have a poor reputation for maintaining confidentiality. You should avoid sending information to countries where there is a poor regard for maintaining confidential information.

- Need to know. Remove any confidential information not required by the supplier from documents.
- Ask the supplier to sign a confidentiality clause and include a statement regarding confidentiality of information in purchasing paperwork including: tenders, enquiries and purchase orders.
- Documents holding confidential information should be marked confidential. Documents containing original pieces of work, designs or drawings should include a copyright statement.
- Inventions capable of being patented should be patented and any documents should refer to this.

It is particularly important to agree a confidentiality agreement with companies you have outsourced business functions to. These companies and their staff often have access to your offices, your staff and sometimes your business systems.

All company employees have an implied duty of confidentiality to their employer, both during and sometimes after the period of employment. Remedies for breach or anticipated breach of confidentiality may include:

- Injunction issued by the courts to restrain publication.
- An order to deliver up confidential documents.
- An award of damages.

Defective goods

"Discourage litigation. Persuade your neighbours to compromise whenever you can. As a peacemaker the lawyer has superior opportunity of being a good man. There will still be business enough." Abraham Lincoln

Liability for defective products will usually be fall in one of three ways.

Contractual liability

The usual legal remedy for a buyer of defective goods is an action for breach of contract. The supply of defective goods will normally breach the express or implied condition that goods should be of a satisfactory quality.

The advantages of pursuing a contractual claim is that liability is strict (no culpability is necessary for a party to be legally responsible for their acts), the supplier's ability to limit liability is constrained by the Unfair Contract Terms Act and compensation can be awarded for a wide range of losses including economic loss. However, a buyer can normally only claim against his immediate supplier under the rules of privity of contract. If the claimant was not directly supplied by the original supplier of the product, he must claim against his immediate supplier who in turn has a claim against his supplier and so on. In this way liability is passed up the supply chain.

Tortious liability

Under the rule established in Donoghue v Stevenson, a manufacturer of a product owes a duty of care to the ultimate customer to take reasonable care in in its manufacture.

To be successful a buyer doesn't need to have a contract with a supplier, he simply needs to show that the manufacturer owed a duty of care, there was a breach of that duty and the breach had a direct causal link to the claimant's loss. However, no claim for economic loss can follow from this sort of action and damages considered too remote from the negligence will not be supported.

Consumer Protection Act 1987

The Act applies to; the manufacturer, processor or abstractor of a product. It can also apply to the importer into the EC, own-brander or anybody who supplied the product unless on request by the injured party they can identify their supplier or the producer. The Act doesn't cover losses to business property or economic loss.

Unlike the first two there is no need to prove the existence of a contract or negligence. Under the Act, anyone injured by a defective product can sue if they suffer physical injury or damaged to property.

Product liability claims usually arise because of one or more of the following reasons:

- Design faults. The product has inherent design flaws which make it dangerous.
- Manufacturing faults. The product was made incorrectly or poorly which make it dangerous.
- Poor or inadequate instructions on the safe use of the product.
- Poor management of faults. For example, failure to warn customers of known faults or failure to instigate an effective recall of dangerous products.

A product is considered defective if its safety is not such as the general public are entitled to expect. When deciding whether a product is defective the courts will consider matters such as misuse, state of scientific knowledge when the product was introduced and age of the product. To succeed in a claim the plaintiff must prove the injury or loss was caused by the product. There is a minimum level for claiming loss under the CPA 1987 which is currently set at £275).

Risk Management

Risk management in purchasing

"Risk comes from not knowing what you are doing".
Warren Buffet

Risk is the effect of uncertainty upon objectives, costs, quality or timings. Risk management is concerned with the identification, analysis and control of uncertainty. There are three stages to a risk management:

- Identifying the potential risks.
- Assessing the degree of risk and prioritization.
- Taking steps to avoid the risks and making plans to mitigate the damage should the risk event occur.

Identifying the risks

The first thing to acknowledge is that identifying risks is not a straight forward task. Donald Rumsfeld put it this way.

> *"Reports that say that something hasn't happened are always interesting to me, because as we know, there are known knowns; there are things we know we know. We also know there are known unknowns; that is to say we know there are some things we do not know. But there are also unknown unknowns -- the ones we don't know we don't know."*

In practice, we will never be able to identify all the risks all of the time, however, we know from experience that there are perennial risks we can plan for. The main purchasing related risks normally fall within one of the following categories:

Global supply risks

These are risks that may affect the whole market or economy. The most common supply risks are material and energy shortages caused by natural disasters, wars, strikes, trade embargoes and financial crises. The oil crisis in 1973 triggered the 3 day week in the UK and in more recent times California had electricity blackouts due to lack of generating capacity (a situation that could well affect the UK in the coming years). In recent years, the rapid economic growth of China has created scarcity of some materials. Another side effect of Chinese economic growth has to the decline of domestic industrial capacity and support networks. It has now become almost impossible to find domestic suppliers for some industrial products.

Supplier risks

This covers the acts or omissions of individual companies. More specifically, risks arising from poor supplier performance, such as: late delivery, faulty goods, prices increases and insolvency.

Intellectual property loss

This is unlikely to lead to immediate losses or disruption and will probably not directly affect the purchasing department. However, in the longer term, the loss of intellectual property could result in the loss of customers, markets or result in costly litigation.

High risk purchasing strategies

High risk purchasing strategies could include: outsourcing, off shoring, sub-contracting and single sourcing. Introducing new materials, processes and suppliers tend to be more risky than existing methods. Basically any circumstance involving novelty or loss of control will create a risk.

Compliance failure

Failing an external audit can result in a loss of confidence by customers, loss of key contracts, and maybe increased costs of doing business, for example through higher insurance costs.

Failure of technology

Most purchasing and stock control systems are heavily dependent upon technology. If computer systems, data storage or communication systems fail, this can have serious effects on the purchasing department and the business generally.

Loss of key staff

Losing an important member of staff can be a major risk especially if they have specific skills or knowledge. The loss of sales staff to competitors is often viewed as a serious risk, mainly due to the risk to pricing information or loss of customers.

Purchasing fraud

The main frauds are stealing company stock or buyers taking kick-backs from suppliers.

Assessing the risk

Identified risks should be assessed and prioritised. In assessing the nature of risk there a two main concerns:

- What is the probability of the risk occurring?
- What would be the magnitude of the consequences?

The first issue is by far the most difficult to answer because departments seldom keep records of failures. In some instances you may be able to rely upon actuarial tables and official statistics but in most instances you will be left to best guesses based on your own historic data or experience.

The second question is much easier to assess. The easiest way is to think of all the negative impacts and grade them. When grading the seriousness of the potential consequences consider the following:

- The reach of the event. Would it only affect purchasing or would it affect other departments?
- The degree of impact the event would have on operations.
- Could the event trigger additional problems?

- Would any customers be affected, if so, how many and to what extent?
- What would be the duration of the event?
- Would the event have any long term consequences for the business such as loss of goodwill, prestige, or income flow?

According to your company's circumstances you may want to set up a weighting for the different categories of risk you identify and if it helps draw up a matrix as below:

	High probability	Moderate probability	Low probability
Serious damage	Top priority	High priority	Medium priority
Moderate damage	High priority	Medium priority	Low priority
Low damage	Medium priority	Low priority	Lowest priority

Considering the major categories of problems referred to above.

Global supply problems

Global commodity markets are defined by risk but in most instances problems tend to be minor and are quickly corrected by market forces. Serious global supply problems are fortunately quite rare but when they occur the present a high risk to businesses. An equitable characteristic of global supply crises is that they tend to affect all competitors the same, with scarce resources being allocated through the price mechanism. Often the issue is not an absolute shortage of supplies but vastly inflated prices. Those who can pay higher prices will still get the goods but at a cost.

Supplier risk

Perhaps the greatest supplier related risk, is the complete failure of a key supplier with little or no notice. Not only can it cause severe interruptions to the flow of materials into a business but it is also quite common. It is not easy to identify suppliers in financial difficulty because they will hide their problems from customers to avoid further loss of sales which would invariably undermine their business further. Other supplier risks include the failure to supply sufficient quantities on time or the technical failure of a supplier's product. The risk of supplier failure is particularly high for new suppliers or new products. Even manufacturing giants like Toyota, recognised as employing best practices in supply chain methodology can have serious failures, as witnessed recently with their brake system problems and previously in 1997 when their solve brake valve supplier burnt down. The modern trend of partnership sourcing and sole suppliers probably makes the risk should a supplier fail, even greater.

Intellectual property loss

Loss of intellectual property can have serious long term consequences for the business but are often overlooked because the financial impact doesn't tend to be immediate or immediately apparent. However, the overall risk is probably low because it is rare for a buyer to be in a possession of valuable intellectual property that has not been legally protected by the company prior to being made available to the buyer.

High risk purchasing strategies

Outsourcing and off shoring may pose a particularly high risk because they involve the loss of internal capacity and skills. Outsourcing cleaning or catering may be low risk but if the function is an integral business service like IT or production capacity, the risk will be high. In most cases, the outsourced company becomes the sole supplier of the service or product.

A failure of business systems

This is unlikely to have serious company-wide repercussions unless your business trading in real time. Most system interruptions tend to be repaired quickly and most companies have back-up files. With respect to purchasing, the most likely consequence will be the late placement of orders and a lot of extra work as alternative 'manual systems' are employed.

Losing a member of staff

This event is quite common but generally presents a low level of risk. Buyers tend to be generalists and are to a degree interchangeable (unfortunately few of us are indispensable). We have what recruitment consultants describe as 'transferable skills'. It is therefore unlikely that the loss of one person would create a high risk.

Compliance failure

This should not normally be the source of high risk because there are few if any external factors at play. If systems and records are maintained there should be a low probability of occurrence. The risk is created by not being prepared. However, purchasing managers often consider non-compliance a high priority risk. This is because non-compliance can be damaging to the manager's own reputation. This is what some commentator's call the risk disconnect.

Purchasing fraud

The probability of purchasing fraud may be quite high but in most companies the level of financial risk is low. However, the consequences for the fraudster, any supplier's involved and the fraudster's line manager may be serious. The most long lasting and damaging effect will not be to the business as a whole but to the perceived integrity of the purchasing department.

Steps to avoid or mitigate risk

Once risks have been identified and prioritised, buying staff can take steps to avoid or reduce them. The best defences are often those that are layered, flexible and do not rely solely on once source of protection.

Anticipating market failure

The first line of defence is being well informed. Research the markets, research your suppliers and review your historic data. Use the knowledge gained to remove weaknesses before they become real problems.

It is essential to monitor supplier performance and keep records. Changing patterns of performance or behaviour indicate something may be wrong and prompt further investigations. Financial reports from Companies House, credit rating agencies or online sources may be of value but will often not be sufficiently up to date to be useful since there is usually a 12 to 18 month delay in the publication of financial data. If you are dealing with a smaller company the amount of data is very limited in any case. The best information is often gleaned from conversations with your supplier's staff, reports from delivery drivers or mutual contacts. Watch out for tell-tale signs of suppliers in difficulty, such as redundancies, delays due to shortages of materials, reduction in credit terms, requests for early payment and changes in senior management.

Prepare contingency plans and alternative purchasing options at your leisure rather than scramble around for solutions when a problem occurs. Time is your greatest asset when things go wrong so allow yourself time to respond to unexpected or changing circumstances. I have known purchasing managers who thrived on crisis management it seemed to give them a purpose and power. However, the reality is that when your back is against the wall, you negotiate from a position of weakness. Costs mount, staff plans are disrupted and you have to call in favours.

Some specific measures you can take to cover the major risks from suppliers are detailed below:

- If there is a real risk of your supplier failing, spend time re-sourcing your purchases and accept that for a period of time you may have to dual source.
- Some short term protection can be gained by increasing stock levels of critical items supplied by them. Alternatively, reserve supply capacity or arrange a consignment stock of goods.
- If you are concerned about a supplier's financial situation, avoid up-front payments. If the supplier is bidding on a major contract, consider requesting a performance bond.
- If the supplier is simply unreliable, consider agreeing service levels with them and maybe linking incentives to performance. Liquidated damages are perhaps the most common form of delivery incentive although they can often be difficult to apply. An alternative approach with a persistently poor supplier is to

agree a two price structure, with a low basic price which can be enhanced if delivery is made on time. Investigate the root cause of the supplier's delivery problems, maybe it is lack of planning or capacity.

Spreading and transferring risk

There are ways of spreading and transferring risk, the most obvious method being an insurance policy. With insurance, high individual risk is passed to a large 'insurance pool' of people who each share a small part of the risk. In the public sector, civil servants transfer risk by hiring consultants to carry out risky tasks. Private Finance Initiatives are another form of public risk avoidance.

Purchasing managers are principally concerned with the distribution of risk between the buyer and the supplier. Our principal tools for distributing risk are contractual. Look at any standard terms and conditions of contract and identify the risk that the parties are attempting to shift. Consider the following:

- Warranty clauses cover the risk of defective goods. The buyer wants the supplier to be responsible for as wide a range of defects for as long as possible, the seller tries to limit responsibility.
- Indemnity clauses cover the risk of litigation by third parties. The buyer wants the seller to cover this risk whereas the seller may want to share this risk with the buyer.
- Variation clauses seek to apportion the risk of unforeseen work or conditions.
- Property and risk in goods will often be separated. Buyers will often seek property ownership as soon as the contract is made but want to defer the risk in the goods until they have been delivered.
- Force majeure clauses seek to avoid risk for acts beyond the control of the parties.

Portfolio approach

When making investment decisions about your personal savings or pension, a good financial advisor will recommend that you spread your investments widely such that if one market or product performs badly it will not have too great an impact on your wealth. The principle of portfolio investment can be applied to purchasing decisions. For example, it may be unwise to source a critical item from only one region of the world because trade agreements may change, natural disasters may occur, exchange rates may move adversely or there may be disruption of shipping. This principle would suggest that you spread your purchases over a diverse range of sources to reduce risk.

This approach is at odds with the current practice of single sourcing supplies. In a world of global low cost sourcing, it would suggest that there is still value in maintaining local domestic production on the grounds of reducing risk.

As a final word on risk management, don't become paralysed by obsessive risk avoidance. Remember that due to the very nature of uncertainty you will never be able to identify and prevent all the potential risks. Risk management is an insurance policy, nobody in their right mind spend more time and money on their insurance policy than the potential loss.

Currency fluctuations

"The best way to destroy the capitalist system is to debauch the currency. By a continuing process of inflation, governments can confiscate, secretly and unobserved, an important part of the wealth of their citizens". John Maynard Keynes

Currency fluctuations can pose a risk to business profitability if not properly managed. The two main areas of risk the company are:

- When the currency in which you are paid, is different to the currency your main costs are incurred.

- When the value of the currency you are paid in changes from the time you set your sales price to the time you are due for payment.

It is the purchasing manager's role to identify risks relating to the supply chain and put in place measures to avoid or mitigate any potential losses. It is not the purchasing manager's role to speculate.

Identify the areas of risk

- Identify high value foreign currency expenditures.
- Identify contracts with long periods between the quotation and the commitment to pay for raw materials.
- Identify contracts made in highly volatile currencies.
- Identify contracts were a large proportion of the raw material budget is paid for in a different currency than that which you receive payment.

Minimizing foreign exchange risk

In order of priority:

- Agree a firm price (not subject to variation) in sterling.
- Agree a firm price (not subject to variation) in the currency which your customer will pay you. Buy forward this currency.
- Agree a firm price (not subject to variation) in another currency. Try to avoid currencies with a record for volatile movements. Buy forward this currency.
- Agree a price which is subject to an exchange rate variation formula.

Exchange rate variation

If the supplier is unwilling to offer a firm price (not subject to variation) in either sterling or a foreign currency due to the risk of exchange rate fluctuation, then you may have to negotiate a exchange rate variation formula. This is a mechanism by which the price is subject to an agreed variation based upon movements of the exchange rate about a base rate.

This does not have to be complex clause, in fact the simpler the better but there are some key features to include:

- Identify and agree the market to be used for reference for example London.
- Agree the price in the foreign currency
- Set the base rate of the payment currency against sterling. Example, £1:€1.50
- Set the date at which the currencies will be re-assessed, usually the date the payment is contractually due.
- To avoid trivial change, set a minimum exchange rate variation below which no contract price variation is triggered, for example 2%.

Example A machine costs €150,000. The EU supplier agrees a sterling price of £100,000. The exchange rate is set at a base rate of €1.50 to the £.

It is agreed to apply an exchange rate variation formula at the time the machine is due for delivery. The terms of the formula are that if the exchange rate is either 2% higher or lower than the base rate, then the price will be varied in direct proportion to the increase or decrease in the exchange rate.

If at the contract due date the exchange rate is €1.4 (the £ has depreciated) the revised price will be: 150,000 /1.4 = £107,143

If at the contract due date the exchange rate is €1.6 (the £ has appreciated) the revised price will be: £150,000 / 1.6 = £93,750.

Buying forward

If you know that you are going to have large outlays in a foreign currency you may be advised to forward buy that currency when you agree your purchases. There are a number of ways of buying forward currency:

- Buy immediately at the spot rate and let it sit in your foreign currency account.
- Enter a foreign currency contract to buy currency at an agreed rate for delivery and payment at a specified time in the future. There is an obligation to take the currency at the contract rate.
- A foreign currency option. Similar to a foreign currency contract but more flexible since there is no obligation to buy the currency, however you will pay a premium for this privilege.

Financial analysis

"Gold and silver, like other commodities, have an intrinsic value, which is not arbitrary, but is dependent on their scarcity, the quantity of labour bestowed in procuring them, and the value of the capital employed in the mines which produce them." David Ricardo

The financial probity of your suppliers may not appear as important as your customer's ability to pay, but a supplier who gets into financial difficulty and ceases to trade, can have serious consequences for your company. Apart from the obvious risk to supply you might suffer the loss of free issue material or up-front payments. If the supplier is a single source then you will have the additional headache of finding a new supplier possibly at little or no notice. It is therefore good practice to regularly review the financial stability of your key suppliers.

The two types of financial measures you may want to check are the supplier's liquidity (their ability to meet their immediate financial obligations) and secondly their profitability (their ability to continue trading in the medium term).

The most important indication of a company's liquidity is by measuring its current assets against its current liabilities, called the current ratio.

Current Ratio = Current Assets / Current Liabilities

Where current assets = cash + cash equivalents + accounts receivable + inventory and current liabilities are accounts payable + notes payable + accruals.

The current ratio indicates a company's ability to meet its short term obligations. Generally a ratio of 1.5:1 or over is healthy. The weakness of this measure is that inventory can take a while to turn into cash. The quick ratio, sometimes called the acid test takes account of this by excluding inventory. One problem relying upon measures of liquidity is that cash flow problems can often emerge very quickly whilst company financial information is usually over a year old.

Perhaps a better indication of company health is profitability. If a company has made a series of losses then the likelihood it will make a good long term supplier is doubtful. Even better is to look at the supplier's profit margins, as this may indicate whether the supplier will continue to have a stable investor / ownership base.

Profit Margin = Profit before Tax / Sales Turnover x 100

However, profit margins will vary markedly between different industries, so be careful, a good profit margin for a food retailer may be considered poor for the clothing firm. From a buyer's point of view, a company with good profit margins also indicates an opportunity to reduce some of those profits by lower prices or better service.

Another financial measure that should be considered in certain circumstances is the supplier's gearing ratio (the level of borrowings to shareholder equity). Generally, the higher the gearing the higher the risk, particularly if borrowing is mainly short term debt. When gearing is high, the risk of change of ownership is particularly high. Other warning signals buyers should watch for in suppliers are:

- A decline in the company's share price.
- Suppliers want to reduce payment terms, they offer generous settlement discounts or they want to be paid up-front.
- Credit insurance companies will not provide cover.
- The supplier is late filing their accounts.
- The supplier is making staff redundant.

- There are delays in supply blamed on the lack of materials.
- Senior staff leave, particularly the Finance Director.

Suppliers with financial problems

"I think business is very simple, profit, loss. Take the sales
subtract the costs, you get this big positive number. The math
is quite straight forward". Bill Gates

Insolvency means that a company cannot meet its legally due debts and either the shareholders have decided to act voluntarily to settle their debts or creditors have taken legal steps to recover their money.

Sometimes financial problems develop very quickly, (the company may be hit by bad debt) and sometimes the decline is more gradual. When the decline is gradual, you may be able anticipate the difficulties and start to take actions to safeguard your position. This may include: preparing alternative sources of supply options, avoid up-front payments, prepare to remove tooling if necessary, arrange a parent company guarantee and avoid up-front payments.

However, if the decline is rapid, supplier insolvency can result in the failure of the supply chain, especially in these days of single source 'strategic' buying. It is therefore important to quickly establish what type of insolvency your supplier is in and what steps can be taken to reduce the possible damage to your company.

Types of insolvency

Informal arrangements with creditors

The company will contact some or all of its creditors in the attempt to reach an agreement on rearranging the debt.

A company voluntary agreement (CVA)

This is similar to informal arrangements but any agreements reached are formalised by the court. An insolvency practitioner (IP) would be appointed to guide the company through the process.

Administration

The company applies to the courts to suspend the requirement to pay creditors. During this breathing space the company is run by an insolvency practitioner whose job it is to restructure its debt, sell off assets, find a new owner or raise new equity. It is not unusual for the company to emerge from administration almost intact. Depending on the depth of the company's problems it may continue to trade as normal during the period of administration.

Receivership

A receiver is appointed to sell off the company's assets and pay off its creditors. Once this is complete any remaining value is returned to the original owners.

Liquidation

The company ceases trading and its assets are sold off to pay creditors. Liquidation can take various forms:

- Compulsory liquidation. One or more creditors can apply to the court for a winding up order which directs the company to cease trading and sell its assets.
- A member's voluntary liquidation. The company can still pay its debts but the owners decide to close the business and sell the company's assets.
- Creditor's voluntary liquidation. The owners decide to put the company into liquidation with the likelihood that the sale of assets will not be sufficient to pay all creditors.

When a company becomes insolvent it can become very difficult to enforce your contractual rights. However, there are some practical steps that can be taken by the buyer:

- Maintaining continuity of supply whilst finding alternative arrangements is perhaps the highest priority of any buyer. Contact the insolvency practitioner as soon as practical and if possible arrange a meeting. Find out his plans for the company, whether he intends for the company to continue to supply and for how long. There may be stock you can secure or it may even be possible to buy part of the business or process. If you have property at the suppliers, make a point of locating it, make sure it is marked up as your property and make the IP aware of this. If necessary agree with the IP a plan to remove the property. Remember that it is often in the insolvency practitioner's interest to maintain the goodwill of customers as this may form part of the value of the company if it is sold as a going concern.

- Recovering your company's property is also an important concern. Typically this may include tooling, free issue materials, part complete work, or drawings / technical instructions. It is an important aspect of any plan to recover property that any property sent to a supplier is clearly marked up as your property.

Ethical purchasing

Purchasing fraud

"When the President does it, that means that it is not illegal". Richard Nixon

The vast majority of professional buyers are honest but occasionally some are not. As a purchasing manager you should be aware of the possibility of fraud and build checks into the purchasing system to monitor and identify transactions and behaviour which may indicate fraud.

Examples of purchasing fraud

- The buyer knowingly agrees prices over the market rate for goods with a view to being paid off by the supplier.
- The buyer signs for goods not received with a view to being paid off by the supplier.
- The buyer signs off invoices at higher values than agreed with a view to being paid off by the supplier.
- The buyer purchases goods or services from companies they have a personal interest in or own outright.

Specific signs or knowledge

- Buyer fails to use competitive enquiries and keeps no records of quote analysis.
- Buyer uses the same small pool of suppliers for enquiries.
- The buyer frequent updates prices particularly with off the system amendments.
- Missing purchase orders from files.
- Invoices not supported by system purchase orders.
- Incorrect or excessive use of informal orders.
- Tip offs from suppliers or previous acquaintances.

General signs

- Extravagant personal spending.
- Pay-offs by suppliers, are not always paid directly. Maybe the pay-off is made to someone close to the fraudster.
- Excessive secrecy and lack of auditable records.
- Phone calls taken outside of the office.
- Higher than expected levels of purchasing relative to overall business activity.
- Suppliers are used who are located close to the buyer's home.
- Suppliers are used with family connections.
- A new buyer introduces a supplier they have worked with previously.
- Over familiarity with suppliers.

Preventative actions

Working on the basis that prevention is better than cure:
- Separate duties. Do not allow buyer's control the full purchasing cycle. In particular, to not allow the buyer to raise new supplier accounts, place the purchase order, sign for the goods and sign off invoices.
- Check references from previous employers.
- Change buyer commodities regularly.
- Require supervisory approval of transactions such as signing off orders.

Options available on discovering fraud

Obtaining proof of fraud is very difficult and given the seriousness of any accusations, dealing with fraudulent buyers is not easy to tackle. However, following an investigation into the matter, if you have reasonable belief that the employee has been fraudulent the only course of action should be to dismiss the employee without notice on grounds of dishonesty. In any claim for wrongful dismissal by the employee, the employer will normally have to justify his decision by reference to the employment record but can also rely upon evidence discovered after the dismissal.

Finally, a word of warning!

Failure to report knowledge of fraudulent dealings by your subordinates is gross negligence and you can be dismissed if you do report such behaviour. However, don't be surprised if reporting a colleague for fraud, damages your own career. Sometimes management don't like embarrassments, or whistle blowers on other employees, however correct and truthful the disclosure. Sometimes your boss may be in on the act. The best solution is to prevent it happening in the first place.

The Bribery Act 2010

"Those are my principles. If you don't like them I have others".
Groucho Marx

This Act was given Royal Assent in April 2010 and is due to come into force April 2011. In brief summary, the Act makes it an offence:

- To offer, promise or give advantage in the expectation of inducing improper performance (S1).
- To take, request or agree to accept an advantage, intending to alter performance in an activity (S2).
- To bribe a foreign official (S6)
- Failure of a corporation to prevent bribery by persons acting for it.

The Act applies to:

- Those performing in a public function.
- Those engaged in a business activity.
- Those acting in the course of employment.
- Those performing an activity on behalf of a body of persons.

Where the person performing the activity:

- Should act in good faith.
- Should behave impartially.
- Is in a position of trust.

When considering what performance can be expected the test is what a reasonable UK person would expect. The Act makes it clear that cultural relativism should not be considered when determining proper behaviour (S5). Note. Cultural relativism is the principle that peoples' individual behaviour can only be viewed in the light of their own cultural background.

The penalties for breach of the law are harsh, up to 10 years imprisonment and unlimited fine for individuals and unlimited, debarment from EU contracts and confiscation of any gains for companies. It is a defence for a company to show that it had an adequate policy to prevent bribery.

The Act has been criticised on the basis that it will disadvantage UK business when they are tendering for contracts in parts of the world were bribery is deeply engrained culturally. At the time of writing the Act is being reviewed by the new government.

Sarbanes Oxley (SOX)

"Fraud is the homage that force pays to reason." Charles
Curtis

If you work for a publically listed American company you will probably have to comply with Sarbanes Oxley Act 2002. This Act was the US response to the Enron and other corporate accounting scandals. Even though the Sarbanes Oxley Act was targeted at poor and fraudulent financial auditing of companies there are elements of the audit process which require a degree of supply chain compliance. The main issues that relate to supply chain management:

- Is stock valued correctly?
- How are stock write-offs treated?
- How are stock transactions recorded in the accounting system?
- Are stock transactions recorded in a timely manner?
- How are requirements requisitioned, purchase orders authorised and records kept?

- How are duties separated? In particular, the functions of ordering, receiving and paying for goods must be separated.
- Off balance sheet obligations must be recognised. Typically long term contractual obligations with damages clauses.

Ethical trading

"Criminals are never very amusing. It's because they're failures. Those who make real money aren't counted as criminals. This is a class distinction, not an ethical problem."
Orson Welles

The objects of ethical trading are summarised in the UN Global Compact's ten principles. Under these principles businesses should:

- Support and respect the protection of internationally proclaimed human rights.
- Ensure they are not complicit with human rights abuses.
- Uphold the freedom of association and recognition of collective bargaining rights.
- Eliminate all forms of forced and compulsory labour.
- Abolish child labour.
- Eliminate discrimination in employment
- Take a precautionary approach to environmental challenges.
- Undertake initiatives to promote greater environmental responsibility
- Encourage the development and diffusion of environmentally friendly technologies.
- Work against corruption in all forms including extortion and bribery.

Leaving aside the morals, businesses are interested in developing ethically sourced products because it allows them marketing opportunities and perhaps more importantly avoid damage to their brand image. It is an uncomfortable mix and in some cases not free of corporate and public hypocrisy.

Code of professional ethics (reviewed March 2009)

All members sign up to the code of ethics when they join CIPS. As a member of the Chartered Institute of Purchasing and Supply, I will:

- maintain the highest standard of integrity in all my business relationships
- reject any business practice which might reasonably be deemed improper
- never use my authority or position for my own personal gain
- enhance the proficiency and stature of the profession by acquiring and applying knowledge in the most appropriate way
- foster the highest standards of professional competence amongst those for whom I am responsible
- optimise the use of resources which I have influence over for the benefit of my organisation
- comply with both the letter and the intent of:
  - the law of countries in which I practice
  - agreed contractual obligations
- CIPS guidance on professional practice
- declare any personal interest that might affect, or be seen by others to affect, my impartiality or decision making
- ensure that the information I give in the course of my work is accurate
- respect the confidentiality of information I receive and never use it for personal gain
- strive for genuine, fair and transparent competition
- not accept inducements or gifts, other than items of small value such as business diaries or calendars
- always to declare the offer or acceptance of hospitality and never allow hospitality to influence a business decision
- remain impartial in all business dealing and not be influenced by those with vested interests

Reproduced with thanks to the CIPS (Trudy).

Overseas Purchasing

Global sourcing

"The internet is becoming the town square for the global village of tomorrow". Bill Gates

Companies seek foreign sources of supply either, because the goods sought are not available domestically, or can be bought overseas at a lower cost. In recent years, the overwhelming reason for sourcing overseas has been to take advantage of low cost labour, found in some developing countries. Historically, goods sourced in these countries have had a high labour content, typically: clothes, shoes and low value / high volume consumer goods.

However, as the UK and the West in general, have de-industrialised it has become increasingly difficult for buyers to source some goods domestically. Many domestic industries have disappeared and others have shrunk to such an extent that they have lost the critical mass required to maintain the key skills, ancillary services and sources of raw materials necessary to maintain economic viability.

At the same time, developing countries, once only considered suitable for supplying low skill, low cost items, have invested in technology and equipment and are now supplying precision engineered and manufactured goods. Not only are these products less expensive than domestic production but the quality is often superior.

Sometimes the policy of low cost country sourcing has been thought of as 'strategic' purchasing. However, truly strategic purchasing takes a long term view of supply. In the long term, it is reasonable to expect that costs in low cost countries, even China, will eventually increase as workers demand a greater share of the wealth created. As and when this happens, what shall we do if there are very few domestic suppliers left? If we lose options, we become less effective buyers. For this reason, I would suggest that if economics and bosses allow, there is a long term strategic case for sourcing a proportion of your critical items domestically.

Risks of sourcing overseas

Buying goods overseas can carry additional costs and risks. For this reason, it is necessary to pay particular attention to the overall unit costs when considering the benefits of overseas purchases. When calculating the overall unit cost you may wish to consider:

- Minimum order quantities (MOQs). These tend to be higher not least to reduce the unit cost of shipping. Ceteris paribus, expect higher stocking and obsolescence costs.
- Lead times. These tend to be longer, not least due to shipping times. Consider adding 4-6 weeks shipping time from China or India and up to a week from the date of arrival at the UK port to delivery at your works.
- The vagaries of sea freight may increase the risk of stocking out. You may need to review the level of your safety stocks. In one case, my UK distributor of a Chinese made handle ran out of stock despite being supplied with accurate forecasts and timely orders. Although assurances were given that the handles were on the way, they arrived too late, it stopped the production line and that of our customer. Quality. If the quality of the goods is poor, then it can be difficult to resolve. The supplier may not have agents in the UK to verify the poor quality and the process of rejecting the goods can be difficult. Payment cannot normally be withheld because in most circumstances payment will have already been made to the supplier.
- Currency fluctuations. Depreciation of your home currency can leave you exposed. I bought some castings from Japan in the summer of 2008 at a fixed sterling price. The exchange rate was 216 yen to the £. When the castings were invoiced in November, the £ had fallen to 135 yen. My Japanese supplier received about 38% less Yen. It could easily have been the other way round.

- Payment terms. These tend to be shorter than for domestic suppliers. In some countries it is normal to pay for the goods prior to shipment or release of the bill of lading. Alternatively, your supplier may insist on you arranging a letter of credit, which will create an additional cost.
- Unavailability of certain materials overseas may require an expensive engineering change or the free issue of materials and the high cost of shipping.
- Costs of ensuring intellectual property rights are protected and the risk that designs may be copied.
- Costs of agent's fees.
- Your local sources may go out of business due to lack of demand and leave you dependent on overseas suppliers.

Shipping costs and timings

Shipping a 20' container CIF to a UK destination will probably incur the following costs.

Your Chinese supplier will have included in the price either expressly or as part of the price about £1100 for shipping a 20' container or a 40' £1800. In addition there may be document and insurance costs of £100. So if the container carries 10 pallets that is £120 per 4' pallet.

UK costs will include: haulage from the port at perhaps £500 - £750, landing charges of £130, customs inspection and clearance £100. So, all in all it could cost about £220 per pallet delivered excluding any duty to pay or if you work by weight about £0.11 / kg (20 tonne load).

Additional costs

When directly importing products you must be very careful to avoid delays in customs clearance and delivery because this can result in demurrage charges. Normally, shipping lines allow a number of days 'free time', usually 1 to 4 days, but after this period expires the charges can make your eyes water.

For calculating loads (dimensions internal)

- 20' container = 5870 x 2330 x 2350mm height
- 40' container = 12000 x 2330 x 2350mm height
- Height 2890mm for high cube containers
- 20' load = 11 euro pallets or 9 / 10 standard pallets 1 tier
- 40' load = 23 / 24 euro pallets or 20 / 21 standard pallets 1 tier
- Standard pallet size 1200 x 1000mm
- Euro pallet size 1200 x 800mm

Typical shipping costs for a 20' container from China port to a UK destination (Jan 2011)

Sea-freight	£1100
Insurance	£40
Fumigation	£60
Documents	£10
Haulage UK	£500 - £750
Landing fee	£130
Customs exam	£40
Customs entry	£45
Documents	£20
Agency fee	£20

Typical shipping times to the UK.

Murmansk, Russia	5 days	Naples, Italy	7 days
New York, USA	10 days	Lagos, Nigeria	12 days
Rio De Jan, Brazil	16 days	Cape Town, SA	18 days
Mombasa, Kenya	19 days	Bombay, India	20 days
Chennai, India	22 days	Jakarta, Indonesia	25 days
Bangkok, Thailand	27 days	Hong Kong, China	28 days
Tianjin, China	32 days	Pusan, South Korea	32 days
Tokyo, Japan	33 days	Sydney, Australia	34 days

The Decline of the pound

"A weak currency is the sign of a weak economy, and a weak economy leads to a weak nation." Ross Perot

The cost of imports has risen steeply since 2008 following the collapse in the value of the pound. In 2007 you would receive over 15 Yuan to the pound; at the start of 2011 you will receive about 10. The pound has fallen markedly against the currencies of most of our trading partners.

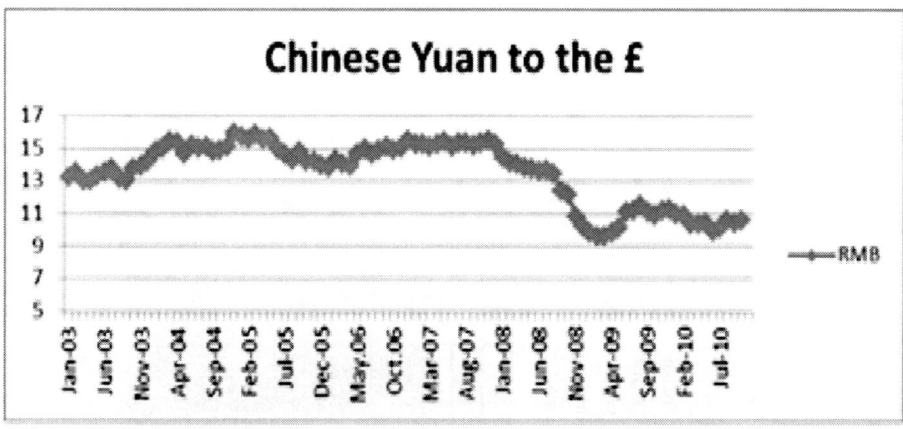

The main reasons for the recent decline in the value of the pound are:

- A lack of confidence in the pound caused by the weakness of the economy and high borrowing by UK government and consumers.
- Low interest rates. Rates of return on investments for international investors are lower.
- Long term balance of payments deficit, which results in less pounds being demanded to buy our goods.
- Printing money. The government's 'quantitative easing' policies increase the money supply which tend to devalue the currency. Investors will avoid holding pounds in anticipation of inflation.

Incoterms

	Load to truck	Export duty payment	Transport to exporters port	Unload from truck at the origin's port	Landing charges at the origins port	Transport to importer's port	Landing charges at importer's port	Unload onto truck at importer's port	Transport to named destination	Insurance	Entry customs clearance	Entry duties and taxes
EXW	No	No	No	No	No	No	No	No	No	No	No	No
FCA	Yes	Yes	Yes	No	No	No	No	No	No	No	No	No
FAS	Yes	Yes	Yes	Yes	No	No	No	No	No	No	No	No
FOB	Yes	Yes	Yes	Yes	Yes	No	No	No	No	No	No	No
CFR	Yes	Yes	Yes	Yes	Yes	Yes	No	No	No	No	No	No
CIF	Yes	Yes	Yes	Yes	Yes	Yes	No	No	No	Yes	No	No
CPT	Yes	Yes	Yes	Yes	Yes	Yes	No	No	No	No	No	No
CIP	Yes	Yes	Yes	Yes	Yes	Yes	No	No	No	Yes	No	No
DAF	Yes	Yes	Yes	Yes	Yes	Yes	No	No	No	No	No	No
DES	Yes	Yes	Yes	Yes	Yes	Yes	No	No	No	Yes	No	No
DEQ	Yes	Yes	Yes	Yes	Yes	Yes	Yes	No	No	Yes	No	No
DDU	Yes	Yes	Yes	Yes	Yes	Yes	Yes	Yes	Yes	Yes	No	No
DDP	Yes	Yes	Yes	Yes	Yes	Yes	Yes	Yes	Yes	Yes	Yes	Yes

International Commercial Terms (INCOTERMS)

"This is the moment when we must build on the wealth that open markets have created, and share its benefits more equitably. Trade has been a cornerstone of our growth and global development. But we will not be able to sustain this growth if it favours the few, and not the many." Barack Obama

These are internationally recognised standards for sales terms.

Ex Works (named place)

FCA	Free Carrier (named place)
FAS	Free Alongside Ship (named port of shipment)
FOB	Free On Board (named port of shipment)
CFR	Cost and Freight (named port of destination)
CIF	Cost Insurance and Freight (named port of destination)
CPT	Carriage Paid To (named place of destination)
CIP	Carriage and Insurance Paid (named placed of destination)
DAF	Delivered At Frontier (named place)
DES	Delivered Ex Ship (named port of destination)
DEQ	Delivered Ex Quay (named port of destination)
DDU	Delivered Duty Unpaid (named place of destination)
DDP	Delivered Duty Paid (named place of destination)

The above is a guide to Incoterms 2000.

The full rules are available from the International Chambers of Commerce (ICC) 14/15 Belgrave Square, London.

Note in the latest 2010 edition which come into effect in April 2011, DAF, DES, DEQ, DDU have been superseded by two new terms:

DAT	Delivered At Terminal
DAP	Delivered At Place

Letters of credit

"Each country can gain by specializing in the good where it has comparative advantage and trading that good for the other." David Ricardo. The law of comparative advantage

When purchasing goods from overseas suppliers, they may require the buyer to open a letter of credit in their favour to guarantee the security of payment. Indeed, the exporter's credit insurers may insist that this happens.

In some cases, the letter of credit is the actual method of payment and in other it is just a fall-back position if the buyer refuses or cannot pay. Letters of credit work like this:

- The buyer or applicant asks his bank (issuing bank) to open a letter of credit in favour of the seller or beneficiary. The issuing bank may require the applicant to provide collateral for what is in effect an extension of credit.
- The issuing bank sends a copy of the LC to the exporter's bank (advising bank). who check the letter of credit for authenticity
- When the goods are dispatched or made available as per the terms of the agreement, the advising bank send the issuing bank, documentary evidence that the goods have been despatched in the correct time, place and method as required in the terms of the letter.
- If the documents are in order. the issuing bank transfers the agreed sum to the advising bank who credit the seller's account.

The importer will normally pay for opening the letter of credit. Banks will normally charge in the region of 1 to 10% of the value of the LC. The exporter will normally be liable for the advising banks fees. Letters of credit have developed a number of variations:

Revocable letter of credit

This form of letter of credit can be amended or cancelled by the issuing bank without the agreement of the beneficiary. Consequently it is not popular with exporters since their risk is increased.

Irrevocable letter of credit

This letter of credit cannot be cancelled or amended without all the parties agreeing. This is the most commonly used letter of credit.

Standby or non-performing letter of credit

If the beneficiary does not get paid from its customer it can then demand payment from the bank by forwarding the copy of the unpaid invoice and supporting documentation.

Revolving letter of credit

This is used when there are regular shipments of the same commodity between supplier and customer. It eliminates the need to issue an LC for each individual transaction.

Sight letter of credit

This is payable as soon as the correct documents have been presented by the advising bank to the issuing bank.

Confirmed letter of credit

Under this type of letter of credit, both the issuing and the advising bank take responsibility. If the issuing bank fails to comply, then the beneficiary can seek payment from the advising bank as long as the terms of the letter have been met.

Transferable letter of credit

This allows the beneficiary to assign part or all of the benefit to another party. Transferable letters of credit can be either revocable or irrevocable.

Shipping terms

"I'm nobody's messenger boy, all right? I'm a delivery boy!"
Shrek (2001)

Airway bill (AWB)

This is a bill of lading covering the transport of goods on domestic and international flights. The AWB serves as a receipt for the shipper and the carrier agrees to deliver to a specific destination. Unlike a bill of lading, it is not a negotiable document.

Bill of lading (B/L)

A bill of lading serves several purposes. It is the contract between the exporter and the ocean carrier, it is the receipt for goods given by the ocean carrier and it is also a document of title. Production of an original bill of lading is normally required for release of goods to your agent. A 'clean' bill of lading is a receipt given by the carrier indicating that the goods were received in apparent good order and there were no irregularities.

Booking reference number

This is a number issued by the carrier or his agent and used as a method of control prior to the completion of the B/L.

Break bulk (B/B)

Consolidated cargo usually on a master airway bill (MAWB) broken down into its parts prior to customs clearance.

Carnet

A document issued by customs allowing the holder to ship goods to a foreign country for display or exhibition purposes, without incurring duty.

Certificate of origin

This is required by certain countries to identify the origin of a product.

Commercial invoice

This is the bill from the seller to the buyer. It is often used by authorities to determine the value of goods when working out duties. Some countries require a specific customs invoice for the same purpose.

Commodity Code

A 10 digit number used to identify and set duty rate.

Customs clearance

This is the process of getting the shipment released by the customs authorities by presenting the correct documents and payment of duties or fees.

Customs procedure code (CPC)

Describes the purpose of the shipment and how and when the duty will be collected.

Demurrage

Additional fees payable by the shippers or consignees to the carriers for delaying their equipment or vessel. Normally, the shipper will have several days 'free time' to arrange clearance without incurring charges. Demurrage fees are normally charged by the day, by cubic meter and are extortionate.

Dock receipt (D/R)

Used by shipper and carrier to verify shipment details and act as a receipt from the carrier.

Freight forwarder

The freight forwarder usually works on behalf of the shipper, making arrangements with the carriers on behalf of the shipper. The forwarder normally handles the creation of shipping documentation on behalf of the shipper, arranges insurance and advises the shipper on matters such as packing and labelling.

General System of Preferences (GSP)

This is a system, giving certain countries preferential access to the EU market. Since it currently covers about 176 countries it is arguable just how preferential treatment is.

Import certificate

This is a document sometimes required by the authorities in the destination country, to control specific commodities.

Insurance certificate

Used to assure the consignee goods are covered if the consignment is damaged or lost whilst in transit.

Intermediate consignee

This is an organization such as a bank or carrier, who either acts for the purchaser, the exporter or the consignee, ensuring the ultimate delivery of the product.

Landed costs

The total costs of a product delivered to the buyer's premises including all transport, documentation, duty and charges.

Master airway bill (MAWB)

The freight forwarder may consolidate shipments from a number of shippers for the same destination, under one airway bill, known as the master airway bill. The freight forwarder will normally pass each shipper its own airway bill known as the house airway bill (HAWB)

Packing list

This document is supplied by the shipper to the carrier, detailing the type of package and what is in each individual package or container. The packing list also includes net weights.

Sea waybill

Like the bill of lading, this document serves a number of purposes. It is evidence of a contract of carriage and it also acts as a receipt. However, the sea waybill is not proof of title, so goods cannot be sold whilst in transit. The main advantage of the sea waybill is that there is no need for the consignee to produce the sea waybill to obtain delivery.

Customs duty

"I have never smuggled anything in my life. Why, then, do I feel an uneasy sense of guilt on approaching a customs barrier?" John Steinbeck

Between EU member states no customs duties apply. The current members of the EU are: Austria, Belgium, Bulgaria, Republic of Cyprus, The Czech Republic, Denmark, Estonia, Finland, France, Germany, Greece, Hungary, The Irish Republic (Eire), Italy, Latvia, Lithuania, Luxembourg, Malta, The Netherlands, Poland, Portugal, Romania, Slovenia, Slovakia, Spain, Sweden and The United Kingdom.

When importing goods into the EU all member countries apply common rules and duty rates. In the UK these rules are contained in 'The Integrated Tarif of the United Kingdom' generally referred to as the 'The Tarif.'. The basics of paying duty are detailed below:

- For customs purposes the value of an import is based upon the CIF price but may also include others costs incurred in purchasing the goods, this is called the 'transaction value'.
- Products are categorised into groups using Commodity Codes. A commodity code is a 10 digit number. The first digits determining the broad product heading and later digits increasingly narrow down the product by its use and its components.
- Different types of goods are subject to different rates of duty as determined by the authorities. The levels of duty can be checked by looking up the commodity code.
- There are about 16,000 different commodity codes and they are contained in volume 2 of The Tariff, which is available by subscription or through the HRMC help service.

- In addition to the Commodity Code, importers need to know the Customs Procedure Code. This code describes the purpose of the shipment and determines when and how duty is collected.
- Import declarations are normally made on a 'Single Administrative Document (SAD), in the UK it is form C88. For most importers this document will be prepared and submitted by your import agent.
- For frequent importers the best way to pay is through a deferment account by applying for a 'duty account number' (DAN). To qualify for such an account, security has to be provided to cover your monthly maximum liabilities and payment and payment is by direct debit. On the positive side you will receive about 30 day's credit.

Inward processing relief (IPR)

"Government's view of the economy could be summed up in a few short phrases: If it moves, tax it. If it keeps moving, regulate it. And if it stops moving, subsidize it". Ronald Reagan

This allows UK businesses to claim relief on import duties and VAT, paid on goods from outside the EU, that are to be re-exported outside of the EU. There are 2 ways of claiming relief:

Suspension

Customs duties are suspended when the goods are first entered into the IPR system. This method is suitable for importers who will be re-exporting all of the imported goods after processing.

IPR drawback

Duties and charges are paid when you first enter the parts into the IPR system and then claimed back after they have been processed and re-exported. The drawback method is suitable when not all the imports are destined for re-export. Import VAT cannot be claimed back under this system.

Authorisation

In order to be eligible for relief under the IPR system you must be authorised. Authorisation can be achieved in one of the following ways:

Simplified authorisation

This route is best used for those companies who want to use IPR occasionally and who do all the processing in the UK. The time it takes to process the goods and re-export (the throughput period), should normally be 6 months or less.

Local authorisation

This is suitable for regular users of IPR, particularly traders using 'Customs Freight Simplified Procedures'. At least one month's notice of importing is required.

Specific authorisation

Imports of some goods, particularly agricultural produce are restricted into the EU, because of this the importer must show why you cannot use goods produced in the EU.

Single community authorisation

This is suitable for importers who are processing goods in more than one EU country prior to re-export.

Retrospective authorisation

Normally issued only in exceptional circumstances where abnormal conditions prevent prior seeking of approval.

Conditions

Claiming IPR is subject to a number of conditions:

- The throughput period should not normally be more than 1 year.

- Compensating products are the final processed products for re-export. Any by-products of processing are regarded as secondary compensatory products and are treated as waste or scrap.
- You must specify your rate of yield of processed products from IPR imports in your application.
- Economic test. This applies to certain goods, particularly agricultural products. Evidence is required why you cannot use EU produce.
- You must keep extensive records of goods you enter into IPR for 4 years from export or disposal.

Cultural differences (take with a pinch of salt)

"I worry that we are approaching a time when that which is shocking is squeezed out by the Stalinism of political correctness". Joe Eszterhas

The Arab world

"This creed of the desert seemed inexpressible in words, and indeed in thought". T. E. Lawrence

The culture is dominated by Islam. Arabs expect to be told what to do by decree. Society is highly ordered and there is little uncertainty because of laws and regulations which control most aspects of life including business. Society is relatively unequal in wealth distribution and power. Caste systems in this region stop upward social mobility. People are loyal to family and extended family. There is little room for individualism.

Personal etiquette

Dress code is very strict certain parts of the body must be covered. Visitors must keep to local dress code but dressing as a local may offend! Shoes must be removed entering some buildings, follow the lead of your host. Do not point with the left hand or use it to gesture or eat with. Do not show the bottom of your feet as it is insulting, similarly the thumbs up gesture is offensive. If offered a gift it is impolite to refuse. Women in some Arab countries are not allowed to drive.

Business

Negotiations generally move at a slow pace. The most senior person at a meeting is the one who often says the least. Often the person doing most of the talking is the least important. Meetings may be interrupted by breaks for prayers. Do not discuss women or enquire after the female members of your host's family. Yes can mean 'possibly'.

China

> *"I believe that if you treat China as an enemy, then it is likely to become one".* Peter Mandelson

There is a very strong collectivist culture in China. Individualism is not as highly thought of as in the west. Most Chinese are atheist.

Personal etiquette

Dress conservatively in neutral colours, businesswomen should avoid high heels and revealing clothing. Avoid excessive hand waving and gesticulation. Avoid finger pointing, if you have to indicate use your open palm.

Bowing, nodding or a hand shake are normal forms of greeting. Applause is not uncommon when meeting a larger group of people. Do not start to eat before the host and try everything you are offered. Chop sticks should not be placed upright in a dish as it is unlucky. Don't feel it necessary to finish everything on your plate as it may be taken as an indication you have not had enough.

Personal gift giving should be in private. A good gift would be a quality pen or to a group of people a banquet. Avoid giving black, white or blue gifts as they are unlucky, as are handkerchiefs and clocks.

Be punctual or early if you are the guest. Business is generally not discussed during meals. There isn't a culture of tipping in China and it may even be taken as offensive.

Business etiquette

The Chinese will not rush a negotiation. Culturally the Chinese have a very long term perspective in securing their aims. The use of middlemen, to make introductions and appointments is important. Face to face meetings are important, trust based upon personal relationships and friendship is more important than in the UK.

Formality is more important than in the west and punctuality is important at meetings. Titles should be used reflecting the importance of rank and seniority. Business cards are exchanged with both hands. Do not write on business cards or openly put in your pocket or wallet. The most senior person in the party normally opens negotiations.

Chinese are less direct than western negotiators. They will often avoid saying no or being negative, so reading subtle signals that a proposal has been rejected are more important. Equally be careful about taking 'yes' to be a positive agreement, it may simply mean the proposal has not been rejected.

Avoid embarrassing the Chinese. Asians generally have a more developed consciousness of saving face. Allow Chinese to leave a meeting first. Do not expect quick business decisions, the Chinese may be prepared to wait for the right moment to make a decision.

India

> *"But nothing in India is identifiable, the mere asking of a question causes it to disappear or to merge in something else".*
> E. M. Forster

Indian culture is in a period of change. There are still high levels of inequality but the traditional caste system has been outlawed. Indians generally take a longer term view than Westerners. Indians tend to be less risk averse than some other Asian countries. Frugality is a cultural norm.

Personal etiquette

Suit and tie for business are normally expected. It is rude to touch people's heads. Don't point your feet at a person, or touch someone else with your feet. Wagging a finger at someone is insulting. Whistling is impolite. Thanking your host for a meal may be impolite as it may be regarded as payment.

Business

Using correct titles is important to Indians. Indians are notorious for haggling, it is almost a ritual. It is expected that you will challenge the price. Indians will avoid saying no, if an Indian is evasive it probably means no. Try to avoid point blank refusals as they can be insulting.

Indonesia

Indonesians tend to be deferential to people in authority or high status. They tend to be risk averse and uncertainty is reduced through the use of rules and regulations. Individualism is very weak in Indonesia. Family and extended relationships are important. People tend to be more subjective than objective.

Japan

"In Japan, I was immensely impressed by the politeness, industrious nature and conscientiousness of the Japanese people." Paul Getty

Japanese business like Japanese society is very hierarchical but they are hierarchies based on consensus rather than western top down styles. The Japanese can be a little introverted and a little suspicious of foreigners. Despite this they are very polite people. The Japanese work very well in groups and individual rights are not highly valued. Japanese management emphasises a bottom up approach to decision making. Japanese are quite ritualistic and social and business rules are important to them. They like order and tend to be risk averse.

Personal etiquette

Ideally, dress conservatively, wear a suit. Casual is not suitable in a business setting. Women should not wear trousers. Don't point at people and don't blow your nose in public. Respect for other people is important particularly older people. The Japanese generally use last names followed by san (Mr, Sir). Handshakes are fine but you may be greeted with a bow which you should reciprocate. The higher the status of the person you are meeting, the longer to hold the bow. Palms should face your thighs. Avoid excessive gesticulation and facial movements. The Japanese use of body language is minimal. Avoid the OK sign, in Japan it mean money. Avoid passing money in public. Drinking is an important business relaxation. Never fill your own glass. The host should order and pay for a business meal. Slurping shows you have enjoyed your food. Tipping is unnecessary. Gifts are important, but remember to wrap and give them at the end of the visit. Gifts should be given or received with both hands. Try to avoid surprise gifts. Avoid giving sharp objects or gifting number 4 or 9 which are unlucky. Modesty is highly valued in Japan so avoid being brash or too forward.

Business

Business cards are important to the Japanese business people. Always exchange cards after the initial greeting and prior to commencing business, always give and receive with both hands. Do not write on business cards as it could be seen as disrespectful and do not openly put them in your pocket or wallet but place them in front of you during the meeting.

The Japanese will try to avoid conflict in meetings and will aim for a consensus. Like some other Asian cultures, they will avoid giving a negative. Yes can sometimes mean no.

Communication with the Japanese can be difficult due to the subtleties of the Japanese language. The use of body language is limited so be prepared to spend time getting the correct understanding. Avoid strong eye contact. Concessions are important as they create obligations which the Japanese feel must be repaid. Japanese are very conscious of saving face, hence the value of making concessions.

Japanese don't like to ask for money, they are a Finance Director's dream. Don't try humour during negotiation; the Japanese don't normally mix humour and business.

'Western' business culture

When dealing with foreigners, it is useful to understand how other people perceive 'westerners'. Despite our distinct national identities those living in the West do share quite distinct characteristics when compared with Asians, Africans and Arabs. Some of our most common shared characteristics are detailed below.

We tend to value individualism far more than other cultures. We have a strong sense of equality and opportunity for each person.

We tend to have short time horizons. Time is a commodity in short supply. Our approach to business is more direct and confrontational.

The differences between 'Western' countries are less obvious than with some more distant parts of the world, however differences do exist.

France

"I have had some problems because the French don't like people to have success, they don't like the number one". Alain Prost

The French can come across as overly concerned about rules and regulations. Management structures are rigidly hierarchical in short they can be a little bureaucratic. The French take a good deal of pride in their personal appearance and dress. Rules of punctuality are not as important to the French as some other Westerners. Lunchtimes can be extended and often mixed with business. The French are quite private people, so do not pry into personal matters. The French consider themselves an intellectual nation, so gifts should reflect this. Most French business people speak English but if you can speak some French this is appreciated as the French are very proud of their language. The French can appear a little superior when dealing with each other but particularly when dealing with foreigners. The French are naturally suspicious of other Europeans and particularly suspicious of Americans and Anglo Saxons.

Germany

"I'd rather have a German division in front of me than have a French brigade behind me". George Patton

German businesses often have strict functional hierarchies. Germans highly value technical competence; this is reflected in the seniority of staff. Germans follow rules methodically and planning is meticulous, however, this can lead to a degree of inflexibility which makes it difficult to change plans. Germans tend to be more direct and objective than some other westerners, they are uncomfortable with ambiguity.

They do not self-deprecate so may come across as arrogant. Germans rarely mix humour with business, however I have noticed that some Germans have recognised this trait and try to be witty. Meetings in Germany tend to be reviewing affairs. Much of the serious work has often been done before the meeting. Don't expect the Germans to rush anything but they will reliably keep to commitments.

Italy

"Men are nearly always willing to believe what they wish."
Julius Caesar

Family companies proliferate. Management decisions tend to be quite paternalistic with a strong leader directing. Long term planning has not historically been a strong point. Italians speak a lot, it's important to listen but get agreements in writing. Emotional outbursts are more likely than in other Western countries. Job descriptions may be flexible; one person may pick up a variety of roles. Meetings may be unstructured and like open forums. People may come and go from meetings without ceremony and may be interrupted by phone calls. The decision of the meeting may not be the one implemented. Personal relationships may be more important than other western countries.

Spain

"Bullfighting is the only art in which the artist is in danger of
death and in which the degree of brilliance in the performance
is left to the fighter's honor." Ernest Hemingway

Spanish managers can be quite autocratic. Seeking consensus from subordinates may be seen as a sign of weakness. Meetings are used to provide information and instructions rather than open debate. Long term planning is not a national strength. Rules and regulations are not over emphasised. Personal relations are often more important in establishing business than some other western countries. Body language is used by the Spanish more than Northern Europeans, eye contact is important.

Russia

"If what you have done yesterday still looks big to you, you haven't done much
today." Mikhail Gorbachev

Russian management is autocratic and authority is rarely delegated. Intermediaries and local contacts may be important. Expect to lubricate the channels of business. Meetings are usually for giving out orders the real decisions are often made in private sub-meetings. Russians generally don't rush negotiations, they may be frustratingly patient. They will often say little and will show little body language. Don't expect a win-win agreement; compromise is not a national strong point. Russians can appear rude and brusque. Punctuality is not as important as in some countries and don't expect apologies. Russians can be a little melancholy (no surprise given their recent history) and partial to a drink.

Although Russia is a signatory to the United Nations Conventions against Corruption and numerous pieces of legislation, corruption and extortion are endemic.

UK

"The British nation is unique in this respect. They are the only people who like to be told how bad things are, who like to be told the worst". Winston Churchill

Communication and relationships are generally less formal than with some other western countries. Company management structures tend to be flat and there is often blurring with respect to responsibilities. Sometimes, even employees are unclear about their place in the management scheme. Experience is valued more highly than education and generalists more than specialists, which is often quite the opposite of continental Europe.

The British are sometimes unclear in their instructions particularly amongst themselves. Meetings are common and are often used as forums for debating options or potential courses of action. The only result guaranteed from a British meeting is the time for the next meeting. In meetings, the British will generally try to avoid conflict and will use euphemisms to describe unpalatable issues, in this respect they are similar to Asian negotiators; consequently Britons may appear evasive. Diplomatic language pervades. The British will use humour in most business circumstances and are often self-deprecating but be careful not to agree as this will offend. Self-promotion will be viewed with scepticism. There is a degree of blame culture in the British psyche which is probably why they seek agreement in meetings to share the responsibility. The term systemic failure is a euphemism commonly used in the public sector to avoid direct accountability.

USA

"Everybody in America is so money hungry. It's like a rat race and even when you win you're still a freaking rat".
Mike Tyson

American business style is direct and to the point. Short-termism pervades. Americans may look for quick wins rather than long term results. Americans tend to be more enthusiastic than other westerners, which may come across as insincere. Or looking at it another way Americans are generally not as pessimistic or cynical as some other western countries. Achievement is valued higher than experience. Americans don't get irony as quickly as some other westerners. In particular they don't understand self-deprecation. Americans are likely to ask personal questions more than some other westerners. Americans are more likely to accept new ideas than other westerners. Americans are generally not as cynical as some other western countries.

Bribery and corruption in foreign lands

When conducting business overseas it is useful to know which countries have a reputation for informal business practices.

The developed economies are largely free of corruption, the best examples being Scandinavia, Canada, Australia, New Zealand and Japan. Exceptions to the rule are Italy and Greece.

In most other countries bribery is not unusual including central and South America (with the exception of Chile, Uruguay and Costa Rica), most of Africa (Southern Africa not being as bad), most of Asia (including China but not Hong Hong), the Middle East (UAE and Qatar being exceptions), the Balkans, Russia and its former Republics. In some countries like Somalia, Sudan, Iraq and Afghanistan bribery is a way of life. Regular updates on the perceptions of global corruption are produced by Transparency International, for a full list visit http://www.transparency.org.

Project Buying

Project management methodologies

"I love deadlines, I love the whooshing noise they make as they go by". Douglas Adams

What is project management?

The Office of Government and Commerce (OGC) described a project as "a unique set of coordinated activities, with definite starting and finishing points, undertaken by an individual or team to meet specific objectives within defined time, cost and performance parameters". I would only add, that most projects are a combination of both unique and routine work and that normally only one person is ultimately accountable for the project, the project manager.

Project management is the method by which we go about planning the work, organizing the resources and managing the stakeholders. Project managers normally have to work within the so called 'triple constraints' or sometimes called the 'iron triangle' of project management, namely: time, resources and quality. The argument goes that at any one time you cannot maximise all three parameters, the best that can be achieved is two of the three. So:

- If you want a high quality product in a short time, you will need to commit a lot of resources.
- If you want a high quality product but only have limited resources it will take a long time.
- If you want something quickly and with few resources it will be poor quality.

Purchasing and project management

Traditionally, purchasing staff have been concerned with managing suppliers and the supply of materials and services into a company. In some cases this may have involved elements of project management. However, with the emergence of supply chain management as the dominant philosophy in the field of purchasing and supply, the role of the purchasing manager / supply chain manager, has had to evolve to meet a much wider range of responsibilities including project management.

Since project management can be a very complex task, a wide range of project management theories and systems have been developed to provide assistance. Some popular methods are detailed below:

- Generic stages approach.
- Critical Chain Project Management (CCPM).
- Critical Path Analysis (CPA).
- PRINCE2 (Projects IN Controlled Environments)

A generic, stages method

- Project initiation.
- A planning and design stage.
- An implementation stage.
- A monitoring and control stage.
- Project completion.

Each stage is normally comprised of several activities examples of which are detailed below:

The project initiation stage

Creation of a project charter

These are the ground rules of the project and will typically include:

- The title of the project.
- Its basic organisation including the name of the project leader.
- The authority for the project and terms of reference.
- The broad scope of the project, for example, to reduce the costs of managing the supply chain. The scope will usually set out the projects objectives which should be 'specific', 'measurable', 'achievable', 'realistic' and 'time limited' (SMART). It may also deal with the size, extent or duration of the project.

The planning and design stage

Preliminary organisation

- Identify the key stakeholders in the project. Use techniques like stakeholder analysis (SA), to identify the people who can influence the success of the project.
- Using the information from the SA, sell the project to the stakeholders and win their support.
- If the project requires a team effort, identify your team members. Typically the team will have a mix of skills related to the task, however, sometimes the team maybe very narrowly focused.
- Agree with stakeholders and team members' clear objectives for the project.

Create a list of identifiable activities

- Break down the project into clearly defined, manageable work packages. Work packages should be logical, self-contained and realistic.
- Breaking down the work into small packages to allow better management of the project. In particular it allows for specialist teams to be assigned, allowing easier monitoring of progress, better budgeting and cost tracking.
- Sometimes work packages are sufficiently complex that they can be broken down a further level.
- Try to put time limits on tasks.

Set-out a timetable for completion of each activity

- The time table should be in a logical and chronological sequence of events. Major events in the projects life should be marked up as milestones warranting a group review to take stock and update the plan if necessary.
- Consider items dependent upon the completion of other activities and independent tasks that can be completed concurrently.
- Take advice from experienced personnel on duration of tasks.
- Try to fit in with team members everyday duties.

- Hold regular meetings to update the project team and stake-holders.
- Consider using tools like Gantt charts or proprietary software.

Agree responsibility matrix

- A good plan will make it clear who is responsible for achieving each of the tasks within the plan.
- Responsibilities can be shown as a simple matrix with tasks along the vertical axis and the various actionees along the horizontal axis. The matrix can be filled out with the actual level of responsibility or involvement of each of the actionees, for example, 'S' indicates sign off, 'A' accountable, 'P' participant, I input.
- The responsibility matrix should be widely distributed and agreed to ensure that people buy in to their responsibilities.

Risk management

- Identify the potential risks involved in the project.
- Assess the degree of risk and prioritise them.
- Agree ways of mitigating or insuring against the risks should they occur.

Implementation stage

Communication and reviews

Co-ordination and control is the most important aspect of this stage, elements of which will include:

- Regular reviews should be held with the project team and details widely distributed.
- At review meetings assess progress. Try to use objective and quantitative measures of progress.
- Significant changes in objectives, activities, budgets and timings should be reported and documented.
- If changes arise from revised customer or technical specification, this should be documented and if necessary identified by an issue number, for example the original issue 1.0 would be

superseded by issue 1.1. There should be a control procedure for issuing revisions which normally include an agreed method of approval which sets out the change, who approved it and when it was approved.

- Use spread sheets to measure the progress of activities, resources used, estimated costs and actual costs.

Project completion stage

Closing out a project

It is important to close out a project:

- This avoids the project from drifting and brings a degree of finality.
- It allows the project leader to showcase the results of the project to the stakeholders and team members. At the meeting, team members can see the results of the project and be recognised for their efforts.
- Identify where the project succeeded and where it was less successful. This information can be used in any future projects.

Critical path analysis (CPA)

"You will launch many projects, but have time to finish only a few. So think, plan, develop, launch and tap good people to be responsible. Give them authority and hold them accountable. Trying to do too much yourself creates a bottleneck". Donald Rumsfeld

Sometimes called CPM (Critical Path Method), CPA is a project planning tool suitable for projects made up of a series of individual activities, whose duration can be estimated and which have identifiable links with other activities.

CPA is a useful tool because it:

- Identifies the minimum time to complete a project.

- Identifies the sequence of activities that must be completed on time to achieve the minimum project time.
- Identifies those activities that are not on the critical path and have 'float' (free time).
- Identifies those tasks that are sequentially 'dependent' and those that are 'independent' (do not rely upon other activities). Independent activities do not rely upon completion of a preceding activity and can be performed in 'parallel' with other activities.

This allows project managers to take the following actions if necessary:

- If the projected needs to be accelerated, it allows management to target the correct activities (those activities on the critical path).
- By identifying activities with 'float' allows resources to be transferred to critical path activities.
- Be mindful that if you switch resources around another a different critical path may arise.

Steps involved in critical path analysis

1   List all activities, duration and sequence

An activity is a task that gets something done. Identify any prerequisite tasks and the duration of the activity. For example:

Task	Activity	Prerequisite	Duration	Type
A	Plan & run mrp	None	1	Sequential
B	Order receive steel	A	2	Sequential
C	Order receive castings	A	6	Sequential
D	Order receive motors	A	6	Sequential
E	Fabricate steel	B	4	Sequential
F	Machine castings	C	2	Sequential
G	Assembly	D,E,F	1	Sequential
H	Test	G	1	Sequential

2   Plot the activities using nodes and arrows as detailed

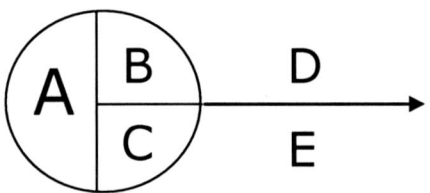

Where: A = node reference, B = earliest start time (EST) of activities that immediately follow the node, C= latest finish time of immediately preceding activities (LFT), D = the activity reference and E = the duration. Sometimes on the EST is shown.

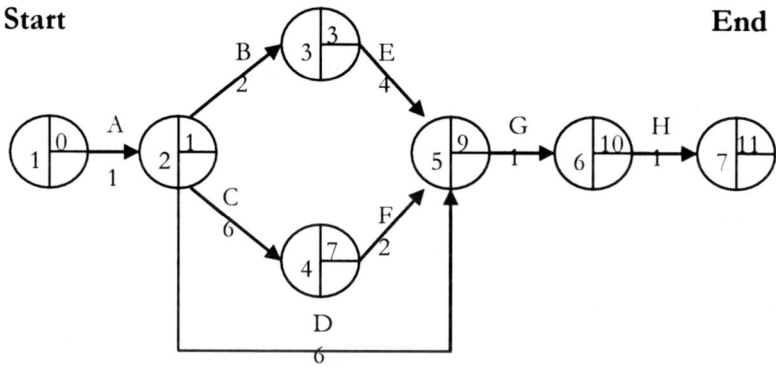

Start   **End**

3   Create a spread sheet, that depicts the map and calculates the critical path as follows:

Activity	A	B	C	D	E	F	G	H	
Start	0	1	1	1	3	7	9	10	
End	1	3	7	7	7	9	10	11	
Duration	1	2	6	6	4	2	1	1	
Potential paths									Duration of path
ABCGH	1	1	0	0	1	0	1	1	9
ACFGH	**1**	**0**	**1**	**0**	**0**	**1**	**1**	**1**	**11**
ADGH	1	0	0	1	0	0	1	1	9

To calculate the total duration of a path add together duration for every activity on a particular path. On a spreadsheet this can be done by multiplying duration by either 1 or 0 and summing the total. If an activity occurs on a path indicate this by using 1, if it is not use 0.

Analyse the result

The critical path is the route with the longest lead time, in this case ACFGH (shown in bold).

Critical chain project management (CCPM)

"Of all the things I've done, the most vital is coordinating the talents of those who work for us and pointing them towards a certain goal". Walt Disney

This methodology was developed by Eliyahu M Goldratt in the late 1990s. In his book, 'Critical Chain', he takes critical path analysis and turns some of its core principles upside down.

The essence of critical chain project management is that the traditional focus of CPA on completing tasks against estimated completion dates is flawed. There are 2 principle effects:

1   Task duration times are exaggerated to provide a cushion of safety.

2   Tasks are rarely completed prior to the scheduled completion date.

In the first instance, planners will actively pad out estimates to give protection against unforeseen events such as; rush jobs, parallel projects overload capacity, third party delays. In effect, they will create hidden safety margins.

In the second case, task completion dates create inefficient and wasteful behaviour. According to Parkinson's Law, work expands to fill the time available and this is exactly what happens when using completion dates. People will put off work until it is absolutely necessary to do it.

Critical chain project management takes a different approach, it:

- Removes the focus on task completion dates, accepting that the only completion dates that matter are the final due dates.
- Strips out false data and padding from estimated task times. Aggressive targets are set for completing the task which only has a 50% likelihood of success.
- Focuses resources on the critical task. Resources need to be available as soon as the previous task is complete. This is achieved by determining how quickly resources working on non-critical work can be re-employed onto work on the critical

path. Secondly, resources regularly provide updates on progress and status. When the projected finish time of task A matches the advanced notice requirement of the resource for task B this is communicated so there is no delay in the sequence of tasks.

- Any safety cushion removed from tasks is consolidated at the end of the project as a 'project buffer'. This principle is applied to non-critical paths; again safety times are stripped out of each task and accumulated at the end, the 'feeding buffer'.

What this achieves:

- It removes the waste caused by the comfort factor of built in slack time.
- It removes the safety cushion of time by setting task duration at 50% of original time.
- Resources are released from tasks completed early.

Control is maintained by:

- Resources regularly feeding back information on their progress.
- If tasks are completed early the time is accumulated in the project buffer.
- If tasks run over then the project buffer is reduced. If the project buffer falls below a certain level, remedial action can be considered.

Critical chain project management may require a cultural change in an organization since there are often deep rooted practices which seek to:

- Protect reputations by building in safety margins.
- Make the job fill the time available.
- Ignore the competition for resources and capacity.
- Continuous updating of priorities for resources ensures optimum use of capacity.

PRINCE 2

This system is often used to control large public sector projects. This was developed by the Central Computer and Telecommunications Agency (CTTA) in the late 1980s as a standard of managing government IT projects. It was later developed to fit a wider range of applications. Prince is a registered trademark of CCTA. Further details of PRINCE2 can be found from the OGC.

Gantt chart

"Organization charts and fancy titles count for next to nothing". Colin Powell

This is project scheduling tool, named after Henry Gantt, an American mechanical engineer who devised the chart around 1910. The chart illustrates how the work package breaks down into its elements, the duration of each element with the start and finish times. Different variations of Gantt chart exist, which show progress and or dependencies between elements. Gantt charts concentrate on management scheduling and ignores the cost elements of a project.

Gantt charts have been readily adapted for software applications; one of the most regularly used packages is Microsoft Project (MSP), which also incorporates critical path analysis.

Stakeholder management

"Don't fight a battle if you don't gain anything by winning".
Erwin Rommel

This topic could easily be renamed 'office politics' because it deals with the subject of people, power and influence and how they can affect the success of new policies, projects or management.

In your daily life, you make choices and do things that affect other people. How you go about making choices and how you put them into practice, will often draw a reaction from other people and make the difference between success and failure.

Stakeholder management is a method of analysis used in business, politics and public policy contexts to formalise and quantify the personal standpoints, interests and reactions of the various personalities involved.

The first step is to identify the parties that have an interest or have influence in what you propose to do; these people are called 'stakeholders'. Probably the best way of identifying all stakeholders is to have a brainstorming session. With respect to a complex project like building a new airport terminal, there may be hundreds of different interested parties including: local residents, airlines, airport employees, government, conservation groups, construction companies etc. The main point at this stage is to have as wide an appreciation as possible, hence why brainstorming is the ideal tool.

Having identified the possible stakeholders, they then need to be organised and prioritised according to their level of interest, their power and their influence. To do this, analysts sometimes use a 4 quadrant matrix, with power along one axis and interest along the other. Stakeholders are then mapped according to their relative power and interest.

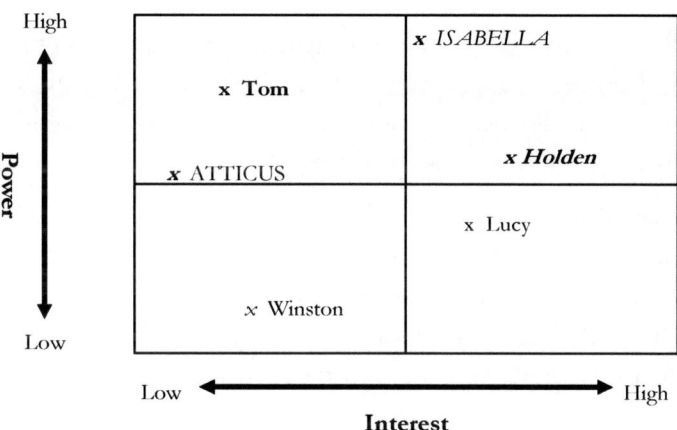

In a typical business scenario, the quadrants may be populated as follows:

- The high power, high interest quadrant is likely to be occupied by your direct boss, directors of the business and other business managers who are directly affected by the project.

- The high power, less interested quadrant, may include people who have great influence over the success of a project but are not necessarily that interested in its outcome. Such a group may include finance, engineers or IT professionals without whose technical input the project will fail. The low power, low interest quadrant is occupied by those people who are neither directly affected by or have any influence over the project.
- The low power, low interest quadrant is occupied by those people who are neither directly affected by or have any influence over the project.
- The low power high interest quadrant, will be occupied by those people who are directly impacted the project but who may have very little status or influence in the company. For example, the office cleaner may be very interested in proposals to outsource the cleaning contract but with little influence on the matter. Such people can normally raise their power by forming a larger group or by forming coalitions with other people or groups.

Once you have identified the key stakeholders, and mapped their interest and power, the next step is to understand their attitude to the project or policy. To help elucidate the stance of a stakeholder, you can ask yourself the following questions:

- What is their goal or motivation?
- What is their emotional involvement?
- What has been their position on similar matters?
- What is their attitude towards you?
- What is their stated position on the issue?

Some stakeholders will be supporters, some blockers and some neutral. To help the stakeholder map can be colour coded, or in this case, BLOCK caps are supporters, bold are blockers and normal text are neutral.

Having identified the main stakeholders, their attitude and their relative importance to the project it is possible to tailor your stakeholder management efforts. In the example, we have supporters in Atticus and

Isabella, both will be important allies in the project particularly the latter and these people should be kept informed and called upon for advice. We have problems with Tom and Holden, both of whom need persuading of the project's benefits. If they can't be persuaded, you may need to consider strategies to minimize the damage they can cause to the project. People like Lucy, shouldn't be ignored, their interest is high and they could forge alliances which would increase their power, this group need regular monitoring. Winston, can largely be ignored, having little interest or power to influence.

Value engineering (VE) / Value analysis (VA)

"Engineers like solving problems. If there are no problems handily available, they will create their own problems". Scott Adams

At first sight it may seem that value engineering should be a matter for the company's production and design engineers. However, because bought-out materials are such a high proportion of sales revenue, purchasing managers are often called upon to lead or at least contribute to value engineering projects.

The essence of VE is an examination of a product's functionality relative to its costs, with the aim of increasing value. Improved value is achieved by either:

- Increasing functionality whilst maintaining costs.
- Maintaining functionality but reducing costs.
- Increasing functionality and reducing costs.

The starting point of any VE exercise is to identify the basic functions of a product. Particular attention should be paid to what your customer's value. VE analysis should recognise these functions are a basic minimum and seek to preserve them. Having identified the basic necessary functions of a product, the aim is to eliminate unnecessary costs, whilst maintaining these functions. A simple VE project may take the following steps:

Perform a function analysis

To establish the basic functions of the product by asking:

- What does the product do?
- What does it need to do?
- What does it do that is unnecessary?

When analyzing function, try to put yourself in the shoes of the customer.

Perform a method analysis

This stage seeks to identify how the product is made, by asking questions like:

- What types of materials are used? How much material is used? How many components are used? How many different types of components are used?
- What processes are used in manufacture? Why are particular processes used? What technology is used?
- Who manufactures the goods? How many people are involved in the manufacture? What skills do staff have? How are staff organized?

To aid this process try breaking down the function into its individual elements using short, non-prescriptive descriptions, for example, 'rivet together part A and part B',

Identification of alternatives

At this stage, alternative ways of achieving the necessary functions are considered.

- What alternative materials can be used? This may include considerations about the grade, dimensions or quantity of the materials used.
- What other processes or technology can be employed? Can processes be wholly or partly removed? Can processes be modified or enhanced?

- How can the mix of skills be changed? Can the number of people be reduced? Can the grade of staff be reduced? Can different skills be employed? Can staff be organized in a more effective way?

An open mind should be maintained during this phase and engineers should avoid focusing too closely on previous designs or pet projects.

Assessment of alternatives

The various alternatives are assessed in terms of their effect on functionality of the product and the potential savings or additional costs involved. It is important that costs and benefits are represented in a single comparable measure, usually money. The best alternatives should be prioritized.

Decision making

The best options identified, should normally be presented to the customer for approval. In some circumstances, the company may choose not to advise the customer for a variety of reasons. Indeed, as a buyer, I have known suppliers who implemented VE changes to products without consultation. In some instances, the quality of the product was poorer and the supplier's position was undermined by their lack of consultation.

Financial assessment of projects

"Only when the tide goes out do you discover who's been swimming naked". Warren Buffet

Cost benefit analysis (CBA)

CBA can be used in a variety of different situations to assess the likely financial success of planned actions. In a purchasing context, it is most likely to be employed to evaluate 'make or buy' decisions, or with reference to purchasing capital equipment.

To be providing the best chance of an accurate assessment, there are several principles that should be applied:

- Costs and benefits must be expressed in terms of a common measure to aid comparison, usually money.
- Costs and benefits, not normally given a value, are assessed and given a monetary value. Even if it is an aesthetic improvement, this may increase its marketability and given a value.
- Costs and benefits are expressed in terms of money value at a particular point in time, again to aid comparison. Future costs or benefits must be corrected according to some discount rate to take account of inflation.
- Add all the positives values together and subtract all the negatives to give a net benefit or cost.

There are a number of methods you can use to financially analyse the information you have collected, some of which are detailed below:

Payback method

This method is simply how long it will take for the project to pay for itself. The payback period, is the time taken for the cost of a project to be recouped from the additional revenue generated by the project. Take the example a 5 year project detailed below:

Cost	-£100,000	
	Revenue	Cumulative
Year 1	+£10,000	£10,000
Year 2	+£15,000	£25,000
Year 3	+£50,000	£75,000
Year 4	+£50,000	£125,000
Year 5	+£70,000	£195,000

So in the above example, the simple payback period would be 3.5 years. A drawback is that the simple payback method doesn't take into account the revenues generated over the projects whole lifetime. A variation of this method may be to discount future cash flows as mentioned below.

Accounting rate of return method

This method takes account of the overall project profitability.

Total net cash inflow	£195,000	
Average over 5 years	£ 39,000	i.e. £195,000/5
Related to original cost	£100,000	
Average annual return	39%	

Discounted rates of return

Cash generally reduces in value as time passes. It is better to have £10,000 today because in 1 or 2 years' time the effect of price inflation will reduce the total quantity of goods it will purchase. Discounting future cash flows to take account of this effect is necessary when returns accrue many years in the future, diminishing the value of their future earnings. There are 2 principle methods of discounting the value of future cash flows, the first being 'net present value' method and the second the 'internal rate of return' method.

NPV method (discounted cast flow)

Cash flows are discounted back to their present values using a minimum acceptable rate of return (cost of borrowing). The present value of the cash inflows are offset against the discounted cash outflows. A positive net present value means the project is viable.

$$\text{Net Present Value} = \frac{A}{(1+r)^n}$$

Where:
A = amount accruing
n= the number of years forward
r = rate of interest

Applying a rate of discount of 8% to the project detailed above would give the following result:

Year	Discount factor 8%	Net cash flow	Present value
0	1.000	-£100,000	-£100,000
1	0.9259	+ £10,000	+£9259
2	0.8573	+ £15,000	+£12,860
3	0.7938	+ £50,000	+£39,690
4	0.7351	+ £50,000	+£36,755
5	0.6806	+ £70,000	+£47,642
			+£46,206

Internal rate of return (IRR)

Instead of using a specified rate of discount to assess the financial viability of the project, this method seeks to establish the discount rate which will reduce the net present value of cash flows to zero. This is essentially a matter of trial and error to determine, so:

Year	IRR at15%		IRR at 20%	
0	1.000	-£100,000	1.000	-£100,000
1	0.870	+£8,700	0.833	£8,333
2	0.756	+£11,340	0.694	£10,410
3	0.657	+£32,850	0.579	£28,950
4	0.572	+£28,600	0.541	£27,050
5	0.498	+£34,860	0.370	£25,900
		+£16,350		**+£643**

In this case the IRR is just a little over 20% this should be compared with the company's target rate of return. Attractive projects will have a higher rate of return than the company's target rate of return.

Qualitative decisions

"What is a cynic? A man who knows the price of everything and the value of nothing." Oscar Wilde

Not all things are easily quantified and sometimes it is not simply a question of money. When considering whether to go ahead with a project, you may want to consider the following:

- The long term effect on supplier relations. Failure to proceed with a project may harm relations with a supplier. Alternatively, using a supplier on a major project may tie your company into long term dependence on the supplier.
- The effect on morale within your own company. Failure to proceed with a capital project may be read as a signal by employees that the facility doesn't have a long term future.
- The long term effect on customer relations. Failure to invest in new facilities or products may convince customers that you are not a progressive company and they look for alternatives.
- The effect on competitor behaviour. For example, the failure to invest may signal to your competitors that you are not serious about continuing in a particular market segment.
- The effect on community relations. Investment decisions may result in 'externalities' that is costs to the wider community such as pollution or congestion.
- Unpredictable income streams, for example increasing capacity may drive down the price and hence income streams. In the 1990's several new glass plants were built along the M62 corridor by competing companies. The increase in capacity had the effect of driving down the price of glass and the return on the companies' investments.
- The effect of sunk costs on your marketing strategy. Large investments in new facilities or plant may create perverse marketing strategies.
- Personalities. Sometimes projects and investment are driven not by commercial judgements but by personal egos.

Accounts Payable

Invoice payment terms

No one would remember the Good Samaritan if he'd only had good intentions; he had money as well. Margaret Thatcher

It is important to negotiate the best payment terms possible, as they directly affect the cash flow of your company. If you can extend the number of days credit a supplier will extend to you, your company will save money and you will keep your finance director happy.

Think about it this way, at an interest rate of 10%, every additional 36.5 days of credit you secure, amounts to an approximate reduction in finance costs equivalent to 1% of the invoice value. To put this in monetary terms, if you achieve an extension of terms by 36.5 days on £1,000,000 of spend, then you are potentially saving your company £10,000 per annum and at 5% interest rate it would be £5,000.

As with any agreement, you need to get some basics in place. With payment terms these may be:

- Understanding your own standard payment terms.
- Reaching a clear agreement with the supplier.
- Knowing what variations in terms of payment your finance department can accommodate.
- If you agree non-standard terms, your finance department need to be made aware of what has been agreed; otherwise they will proceed as usual.

If you fail to agree credit terms in the contract, there is no legal presumption of credit in a sale agreement. Consequently, you will be bound to pay when the payment is due, which is normally on delivery of the goods.

There must be close co-operation and understanding between the purchasing department and the finance department. If there are misunderstandings and your company fails to pay on time, the supplier may put you on account stop. If your company is put on stop by the supplier, this will usually result in:

- A refusal to accept any further orders.
- A refusal to despatch finished goods.
- Work being stopped on your outstanding orders.

Perhaps one of the most dispiriting jobs of a buyer is to be expediting goods only to discover that the delivery has not been made because of non-payment of invoices. If the supplier cannot be persuaded to release the goods then a lot of running around has to be done. A special cheque or payment instruction needs to be raised, signed off by directors and sent to the supplier.

To reduce this wasted effort, try to persuade your supplier to give you prior notice of any change in status on your account. Secondly, keep your finance department aware of trigger happy suppliers, so they can be more closely monitored. This also puts the onus on your finance department to get payments out on time.

When negotiating payment terms, always be aware that finance directors may stretch the number of credit days without discussing the matter first with you or the supplier (they do that sort of thing). One finance director I worked for, as a matter of routine would stretch net monthly payment terms to 90 days. Needless to say that a good deal of purchasing time was unnecessarily spent getting goods released from suppliers. One cure for this is by using settlement discounts because the credit for these is often taken by the finance department.

Common payment terms (shortest first)

Pro forma	Payment in advance
Cash Account	No credit given
CWO	Cash with order
CIA	Cash in advance
CBS	Cash before shipment

COD	Cash on delivery
Net 7	Payment 7 days after the invoice date
EOM	End of month in the month invoiced.
Net 30	Payment 30 days after the invoice date.
1MD	Monthly payment of entire month's supply
NMA	Net monthly account. Payment is due at the end of the month following the month of delivery. Ave 45 days.
21 MFI	21st of the month following the month of invoice.
Net 60	Payment 60 days after the invoice date.
Net 90	Payment 90 days after the invoice date.
CND	Cash next delivery.
Contra	Payment from the customer offset by goods supplied by customer.
Staged	Payments dates for payment agreed against delivery milestones.

Settlement discounts

Payment terms can be used in combinations with discounts for early payment, so we could have: 2% 10 Net 60 meaning a 2% settlement discount would be allowed if paid within 10 days otherwise payment would be 60 days from date of invoice. In practice, many companies take the settlement discount and take the credit days as well.

Late payment

"A promise made is a debt unpaid, and the trail has its own stern code". William Service

If your company delays payment from what was agreed, it may be in breach of contract. Normally, breach of contract allows remedies for the injured party including possible termination and damages.

However, suppliers suffering delays in payment do not often commence legal action. It simply is not practical or wise to start legal proceedings against customers unless absolutely necessary. Instead, suppliers faced with slow payments the supplier may take one or more of the following actions.

- Pester you and your purchase ledger clerks repeatedly for payment, causing distraction and wasting time
- Put your account stop, which usually means your orders are not dispatched and in some cases work on your orders is also stopped or put back.
- Claim a lien on your property until payment is made. A lien is a seller's legal right to retain goods until the whole of the purchase price is paid.
- Rely on express provisions in the contract to charge interest on overdue amounts.
- Rely upon statutory provisions to charge interest on overdue amounts.
- Stop dealing with your company.

Slow payment can be a frustrating problem for buyers wishing to maintain good relations with suppliers. If you work for a large company, it will typically take about 80 days for your suppliers to be paid. It is not uncommon for finance department to completely ignore the company's stated terms and conditions of payment.

The problem caused by late payment is particularly bad for small businesses. This was recognised by the UK government who enacted the Late Payment of Commercial Debts (Interest) Act 1998. This Act applies to contracts relating to the sale of goods or the supply of services and allows suppliers to charge interest on overdue accounts and obtain compensation. Interest can accrue from whichever is the latest:

- 30 days after the goods have been delivered or the service completed
- 30 days after receipt of invoice or advice payment is due
- The contractual date of payment

The 'statutory interest' rate applied is set at 8% above the Bank of England base rate. In addition to the statutory interest rate, suppliers are entitle to claim a fixed amount of compensation (presumably to cover their administration costs), the rates are £40 for debts less than £1000, £70 for debts between £1000 and £10,000 and £100 for debts more than £10,000. The courts can exclude or vary the act if the actions of the supplier are unreasonable in the circumstances.

Buyer's cannot opt out of the Act, as such but can render the statutory provisions unnecessary if the contract allows for substantial ways of remedying late payment.

The Act was originally envisaged as a way of helping smaller businesses (less than 50 people) obtain payment from larger business and public sector organisations. The Act was amended by the Late Payment of Commercial Debts Regulations 2002. This amendment removed the distinction of small business. Now, all business can use the Act against any other business whatever the size. There is some evidence to suggest that since the introduction of the Act, the problem with late payments has not improved and for larger companies it has got slightly worse.

In reality, few small companies appear to be using the act or are likely to use this act against valued customers. Indeed, most terms and condition of sale make express provision for charging interest on overdue amounts but I have never known of an instance were a supplier actually carried it through (although some did try to use it as a bargaining tool).

In practice, what suppliers do is identify customers who have a bad payment record, then either:

- They seek to agree settlement discounts for prompt payment.
- They load the price allow for the delay in payment.
- They factor the debt to a third party for collection and load the price to cover the cost.
- They withdraw your credit facilities and insist on pro forma or cash with order.
- They refuse to deal with your company.

What can end up happening is the finance department take credit for increasing the number of creditor days but the buying department end up paying more for the company's goods and services.

Invoicing problems

"No complaint... is more common than that of a scarcity of money". Adam Smith

It is not uncommon for buyers to be called upon to help the company's purchase ledger clerks in resolving invoice queries and disputes. In some cases, holding supplier invoices can be an effective buying tool for securing commercial objectives but in most cases, invoice problems simply waste everyone's time and effort and risk damaging supplier relations.

Invoicing problems can arise for a variety of reasons but in general they can either be categorised as administrative problems or commercial disagreements. The most common administrative errors are:

Un-matched invoiced line items

These are goods that have been invoiced but do not have a corresponding record of receipt. The first step is to request a proof of delivery (pod) from the supplier. If they cannot produce a pod then you will have reasonable grounds to withhold payment until a credit note has been issued by the supplier for the value of the missing goods.

The quality of proofs of delivery can be variable. Ideally it should be a copy of the original delivery note signed by your warehouse staff. Unfortunately, when the supplier is using a third party carrier, all you may get is a signature and date on the carrier's schedule of deliveries. This proves that the supplier has delivered something but not what, and in my opinion is inadequate as a proof of delivery.

It is of course possible that the supplier has delivered the goods and that your goods inwards have not booked them into stock. If this is the case, all you can do is present the carrier's note to the store man who has signed it and ask him to check his work. Failing this you could perform a physically stock check of the parts not booked in and compare this with the physical stock shown on your stock system. If the supplier has made a delivery that hasn't been booked in, you should have a positive stock discrepancy.

If you are having regular problems with matching invoices to deliveries, either something is going wrong with your supplier's carrier, someone in your warehouse is not doing their job correctly, or the supplier's invoicing system is defective.

The best system to prevent goods receipts notes (GRNs), delivery notes and invoices becoming mixed up is to cross reference all of these documents relating to the same delivery. Most computerised stock control systems generate a unique GRN and have a field for the delivery note number. The hard copy of the delivery note should be marked up with the GRN number and passed to the purchase ledger department for physically matching with the invoice and for future reference if necessary.

Premature invoices

Normally invoices are raised at the same time advice and delivery notes are generated. In general, this means that the goods and the invoice should arrive at about the same time. However, sometimes suppliers will either: raise invoices in advance of delivery or date an invoice earlier than it should be. Both are bad practices and are usually driven by the desire to bring despatches into an earlier reporting month than should be the case. This problem is more likely to happen toward the end of a month, a quarter or the financial year.

If a supplier shows a pattern of doing either of these practices they should be advised to stop. Warnings could include de-listing them or delays in processing the invoice.

Duplicate invoices

Sometimes whole or part invoices can be duplicated. In my experience, this is normally due to poor procedures rather than any intent on the part of the seller to double charge.

Commercial disagreements

The principle reasons for commercial disagreements regarding invoices tend to relate to the price, the quality or the timing of a delivery.

By far the most frequent commercial disputes occur because prices do not match. This typically occurs when:

- Either, suppliers try to impose a general price increase or buyers try to impose price reductions on goods that have not agreed or recognised by the other party.
- Suppliers add items like carriage, packing or certificate of conformity charges that are not recognised by the buyer.
- Either the buyer or sellers have not kept their pricing data up to date.
- A typographical error occurs, usually a decimal point in the wrong place or a unit of measure error.

In the latter two cases resolving the problems is usually quick and easy but in the first two cases, invoices become the battle ground for company's trying to change commercial terms.

The most likely scenario a buyer will face is when a supplier imposes a price increase. By disputing an invoice with higher prices and withholding payment the buyer puts pressure back onto the seller. In some instances, this will result in the supplier removing or moderating the increase. Sometimes the supplier will credit the difference in the current order but insist that the new prices apply for future orders. Such a tactic should be weighed up against the risk of the supplier putting you on stop or damaging your long term relationship.

Perhaps the next most common reason to dispute an invoice is to object to additional charges that have not been agreed. These may include items such as: small order charges, carriage costs, packing costs, and charges for documents like certificates of conformity and test certificates. These additional charges are sometimes an attempt to increase margins by stealth, but not always. Sometimes they reflect genuine costs or disbursements made by the supplier. The best way to deal with these charges is to either insist on an inclusive price at the start of negotiations or to insist on paying only genuine costs. For example, insist that you will only pay carriage at cost.

Another genuine reason to dispute an invoice is when the goods are delivered either damaged or defective. For costly items, it is advisable to request that the supplier send a field salesman or engineer to inspect in situ and agree a course of action. For lower cost items, contact the supplier for a returns note number and return as quickly as possible. Part of your procedures should ensure that the purchase ledger clerk is made aware of any returns so the original invoice can be held pending the supplier raising a credit note.

Disputing / querying invoices

A disputed invoice is one that has had its validity or accuracy challenged. In most circumstances, the buyer will have the right to dispute an invoice either if the invoice itself contains material errors, if there was a failure to deliver the goods or a fault with the goods supplied.

If an invoice is incorrect, the supplier should be advised promptly, in writing, that you are disputing the invoice. More specifically, a letter disputing an invoice should include:

- The details of the disputed invoice including the supplier's invoice reference number and date.
- The buyer's order number and date.
- The details of why the buyer believes the invoice is incorrect and the reason why the buyer believes it shouldn't be paid.

By disputing an invoice, the buyer effectively tells the seller that the invoice is put into abeyance pending resolution. Of course, the period that the invoice remains in dispute will depend upon reaching an agreement with the supplier about a course of action.

If you want to be particularly aggressive on this matter, you may consider asking your finance department to raise a debit note on the suppliers account. A debit note is used to reduce the amount payable from the supplier's account.

Stock Management

Stock control

"The first rule of business is: do other men for they would do for you". Charles Dickens

Costs of holding stock

A reasonable estimate of the cost of holding stock would be about 20% per annum of the average stock value. This cost arises from a number of sources:

- Cost of storage, buildings, stores staff, equipment, racking and stock control systems.
- Obsolescence when parts are superseded.
- Deterioration and damage because parts have a shelf life and perish or lose some of their pristine value.
- Finance costs of the money tied up in stock.
- Insurance of materials.
- Theft.

There is therefore a need to minimise stock wherever possible. Some traditional methods of stock control are detailed below.

Re-order point (ROP) control

The re-order point is the level at which purchase action must be taken to avoid running out of stock. It is normally determined by reference to the usage, the lead time and the level of safety stock of an item.

Q = average use rate x lead time + safety stock, where Q is the re-order point level. So if average daily use is 50, lead time is 7 days and safety stock is 350

$Q = 700$

Alternatively, Q can be determined by maximum usage x maximum delivery period + safety stock.

The economic order quantity (EOQ)

There is a trade-off between the administration costs of ordering small quantities frequently and higher stock holding costs from ordering larger quantities less often.

The EOQ is an attempt to quantify this trade off and can be calculated using the following formula:

$$Q = \sqrt{2DS/H}$$

S = Order Costs (fixed)
D = Annual Demand
H = Unit stockholding costs (assume 20% of unit cost)
I = Inventory costs
C = Unit cost
If S = £50 D=2000 I=20% C=£200 H=C x I = £40
Q = 71 (to the nearest part)

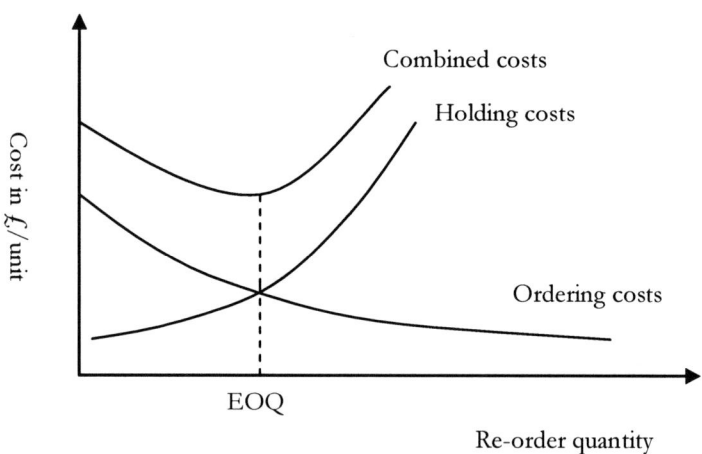

The EOQ is the point where the combined costs of holding materials and ordering materials are at a minimum.

Safety stock

This is material held in addition to what is required by normal cyclical replenishment of materials. It is essentially a buffer against stocking out. There are many methods to determine safety stock but no definitive one, however, most rely upon statistical probability tables, average lead times and either actual or forecast demand data.

- Assume that the probability of events such as demand fluctuations or lead time delays can be estimated by using the standard deviations from normal distribution tables.
- Decide and set the desired level of 'service performance', for example a 95% service level.
- By reference to normal distribution tables this will give a 'service level factor' or in other words the number of standard deviations required to meet the service level percentage. For example a 50% service level = 0, a 95% service level = 1.64 and a 99% service level = 2.33 standard deviations.
- Using actual or forecast demand data, work out the standard deviation.

For the forecast demand data 5, 9, 4, 6, 5, 6, 8, 3, 8, the standard deviation is worked out as follows:

1   Work out the mean 5+9+4+6+5+6+8+3+8 / 9 = 6
2   Calculate the differences of each value from the mean. Then square each difference. $(5-6)^2+(9-6)^2+(4-6)^2+(6-6)^2+(5-6)^2+(6-6)^2+(8-6)^2+(3-6)^2+(8-6)^2$
3   Calculate the average of the squares 1+9+4+0+1+0+4+9+4 / 9 = 3.55
4   Find the square root of the average. $\sqrt{3.55} = 1.886$

The simplest of calculations would be:

Safety Stock = *(standard deviation)*(service factor)*
So a 95% service level on the above data would be calculated as:
Safety stock = 1.886 x 1.64 = 3 (3.09 to be precise).

The calculation can be amended to take into account other factors such as lead time differences (lead time factor), order cycle periods (order cycle factor) and other factors which may be specific to the particular company. Using complex formulas like these are only practical if they can be modelled into software.

A simple way of including a safety stock into the re-order point calculation is to calculate the safety stock level as a flat value across all products, for example 100 units. Alternatively the safety stock value could be made a function of the ROP value. For example, safety stock could be set at ROP x 0.5, giving an additional 50% safety margin.

Materials requirement planning (MRP)

"To err is human but to really foul things up you need a computer". Paul Ehrlich

Materials requirements planning (MRP) is a planning and control system for coordinating the procurement and allocation of raw materials and stock to meet production and customer requirements. The initial development of MRP has been ascribed to Joseph Orlicky in the 1960s.

MRP is almost exclusively used in manufacturing industries and is ideally suited to batch production, where the finished product or sub-assemblies are made up of a number of material components. MRP can be executed manually but except for very limited applications it is really only practical to operate it through computer software. It can also be used in conjunction with other materials planning systems like JIT and vendor managed stocks.

MRP systems are designed to answer two basic questions what parts are required when they are required. By time bucketing require-ments it is then able to demand resources as they are required which has the benefit of minimising stock and resources employed.

MRP works by taking a sales requirement (independent demand), breaking it down into its component parts and operations through the bill of materials, and then re-assembling the information into a series of time phased instructions for production and purchasing (dependent demand). The basic elements of an MRP system are:

- A sales plan.
- A master production schedule (MPS). This is the means of translating the sales plan into demand for manufactured products. The MPS takes all sources of net demand for finished product (mainly customer orders), and sorts it into a time-phased schedule of production requirements that can be processed by the MRP system.
- A part numbering system is a basic pre-requisite for operating an MRP system. The part number system must allow differentiation between different types (manufactured, bought-out, manufactured sub-contract or phantom) and levels of parts (allows structuring of parts and routing).
- A bill of materials (BOM). This is structured list of parts and sub-assemblies that make up the finished product. Key features of a bill of materials are: distinctions between bought-out, manufactured and manufactured sub-contract items; a hierarchy of parts which effectively links finished parts, assemblies, sub-assemblies and individual parts.
- Inventory records. These detail the number and location of parts already available to the manufacturing process. To make inventory records more useful, rules (part modifiers) are set up which govern the management of parts. Typically these rules will include matters such as minimum order quantities, lot sizes, routings, safety stock levels, order policies etc.

A typical sequence of events for an MRP system would be:

- Contracts and sales orders are loaded onto the system.
- Rough cut capacity planning. This is checking that the sales plan is achievable given the available resources; it also serves to identify potential production bottlenecks. With MRP this is largely a manually controlled affair, relying upon the experience of staff and systems outside of the MRP program.

- The reviewed sales plan is adopted into the master production schedule (MPS).
- MRP takes the MPS and converts this into scheduled materials requirements. It does this by 'exploding' the MPS through the bills of materials (BOMs). It then aggregates these materials requirements and allocates (assigns) existing free stock from the inventory record and outstanding free orders.
- MRP creates recommendations to put into effect the plan. These recommendations are normally printed off by the business function responsible for each element of the plan. For example, recommended order reports are printed by the purchasing department, recommended works orders by the production planners and picking lists by the stores function.

Requirements for successful MRP

Data must be very accurate. In particular, sales order input of part numbers and quantities must be accurate. Wrong part numbers or quantities at this stage will cascade through the system generating instructions which can be very costly and difficult to reverse.

Stock records must be very accurate for MRP to run effectively. A reasonable guide would be a 95% accuracy rate but some would say at least 99%. In a minimum stock environment, the late discovery of stock discrepancies can have serious knock on consequences for the delivery schedule. Good stores procedures and systems like perpetual inventory checking can reduce the risk. Access to stores and stocks must be strictly controlled. Open stores and MRP don't mix well.

The supplier parts file must be regularly maintained and reflect reality. Prices, lead times and supplier links must be current and accurate. The old adage about computer systems 'garbage in, garbage out' (GIGO) couldn't be more appropriate. Without accurate supplier part file records, suggested orders and the roll up of costs will be wrong and misleading.

Manufacturing Resources Planning (MRP2)

"I would not say that the future is necessarily less predictable than the past. I think the past was not predictable when it started." Donald Rumsfeld

The problem with MRP was that it did not satisfactorily address capacity or integrate other business functions. Manufacturing Resources Planning (MRP2), sought to correct these weaknesses by extending the principles of integrated computerised control to other business functions. Over time, the use of the term MRP2 has declined and has been superseded by the term Enterprise Resource Planning (ERP), although it is arguable that they are essentially a development of the same thing.

Most modern ERP systems are modular in nature, offering core business solutions and bolt on modules covering a wide range of organisational needs including: finance, sales order processing (SOP), purchase order processing (POP), inventory control , manufacturing control, engineering control and HR.

The principle aim of ERP systems is to integrate all of a company's business systems using a common database. Whereas earlier systems were manufacturing specific, later ERP systems can be applied to a much wider range of applications and organizations. Another distinction is that MRP systems process information on a time bucketed basis whereas ERP systems operate on a real time basis.

The supply market for ERP systems is still very fragmented, largely due to the high level of customisation that most organisations require. As a result there is very little inter-compatibility between different systems making automated data transfers between trading partners difficult resulting in the growth of B2B facilitator companies.

Part numbering systems

"Lies, damn lies and statistics". Benjamin Disraeli

Part numbering systems are important because they are the building blocks and language of materials planning systems. Since they are used by computers and people alike it is important to develop a part numbering system that is both efficient for modern IT systems and yet intelligible enough for people to recognise, input and interpret effectively. Generally parts fall into 2 broad categories, descriptive or intelligent part numbers that are people friendly and pure number sequences that are more suitable for processing.

Intelligent part numbers

These tend to be alpha numeric parts which embody certain aspects of the part. Parts can include details such as pattern numbers, die references, the type of material, the size or length. For example, an intelligent part number for an extrusion may be A3067588350001, which breaks down as follows:

A3 067588 3500 01

A	= material aluminium
3	= grade of aluminium
067588	= die number
3500	= length (mm)
01	= finish

Another example would be a piece of glass:

G03781275410

G	= Glass
0378	= width
1275	= length
4	= thickness
10	= type of glass or pattern

Intelligent part numbers tend to intuitively help people identify parts and are useful when conducting information searches. On the downside, it is argued that the ideal length of a part number should be about 7 characters longer numbers tend to lose intelligibility. Unfortunately, intelligent part numbers are generally much longer than 7 characters long, however, most people find them much simpler to recognise and remember than shorter numbers that have no relation to the part.

Descriptive part numbers

Part numbers may be described in an abbreviated form of the full description for example:

STABZPAN35019ZC

Would be an abbreviated part number of a self-tapping screw, AB point, poZi, PAN head, 3.5mm x 19mm Zinc Cr3

Numerical sequenced numbers

Part number systems based on sequential number, are usually shorter than intelligent part numbers, are simple to key and are less likely to duplicate. Often purely numerical part numbers are give pre-fixes that make them semi-significant such as the Brisch system. For example parts in the sequence 10000 may relate to metals, 20000 series parts electrical etc. All part numbers should avoid using embedded dots, spaces or other symbols in part numbers.

Creation and maintenance of part numbers

In any organization, there should only be one source of part numbers. Normally this will be the technical / engineering department. However convenient it may seem, the purchasing department should avoid becoming the source of part numbers. It is not good practice to have the department responsible for committing the company to expenditure being able to independently create the items being bought.

ABC stock analysis

"Dealing with complexity is an inefficient and unnecessary waste of time, attention and mental energy. There is never any justification for things being more complex when they could be simple". Edward de Bono

ABC analysis, sometimes called selective inventory control, is a way of classifying the importance of parts, normally by value or some other factor. Categorisation of parts, allows the buyer or stock controller to organize and concentrate their efforts on the parts which are most important to the company.

The first step is to decide on the ranking criterion, which should be based on one or more relevant criterion. Possible criterion could include: regularity of usage, length of lead time, location of suppliers, highest cost items, highest sales margin, product type etc. However, in most instances, companies rank parts by annual value (cost x quantity).

Parts are then typically split into 3 groups for example 'A', 'B' and 'C'. The theoretical basis for this split is the 80:20 rule (Pareto principle), which states that in the majority of cases, 80% of the effects derive from 20% of the causes. In the case of stock:

- Category 'A' items are the top 20% of items accounting for 80% of the stock value.
- Category 'B' items are the next 30% of items amounting to on average 15% of the stock value.
- Category 'C' items typically constitute 50% of the items and about 5% of the stock value.

Although splitting parts into 3 groups is common practice, it doesn't mean that parts cannot be split into however many groups you want to, so long as a workable criterion can be found and the split is relevant and can be organised.

Category 'A' items

These items should receive 80% of the effort. Stock should be closely controlled and ordered frequently and in small quantities on an EOQ basis. Ideally they should be ordered to meet specific customer demand. Suppliers of category 'A' items should be closely managed and will form the pool of companies that may be partnered in the development of new products.

Category 'B' items

These tend to be low volume items that have relatively high price tags. Often they are too expensive to bulk issue but too low volumes to actively manage. Sometimes they are important parts which are complimentary to category 'A' items, maybe they are supplied by the same vendor. More often than not, they are parts found on bills of materials of older products, which are still listed and bought occasionally by customers. As such they need to be regularly reviewed but not to the same degree of category 'A' items.

Category 'C' items

These will be parts with very low individual value that may be used or issued in bulk, for example fasteners or drill bits. As little time as possible should be spent on these items by buying staff. Methods should be used to group these items together as a package and switched to vendor managed stocks.

Once parts have been categorised, stock reports can be programmed to discriminate between the different groups. Potential uses for this sorting could be:

- Frequency of requirements reports.
- Perpetual stock counting can be set to pick higher numbers of particular categories.
- Planning commodity buyer groups.
- Selective reporting and hence avoid reams of unnecessary output.

Forecasting

"Americans are apt to be unduly interested in discovering what average opinion believes average opinion to be". John Maynard Keynes

A forecast is a prediction of outcomes for future unknown events. Forecast information is valuable because it allows us to plan and make educated decisions about matters such as stock levels, order quantities and budgets. In most circumstances, buyers will be trying to predict what demand for a product is likely to be.

Most forecasting methods are heavily reliant upon having raw data to work with. It is therefore vital that purchasing staff create systems for collecting, sorting and recording data for future use. The most valuable pieces of information that buyers can collect are: the usage rates of parts, prices paid, supplier spend and raw material prices. If we can understand these basic blocks of data we are better able to predict the future movements of these key factors. The 2 principle types of forecasts are quantitative and qualitative methods.

Quantitative methods

There are some very complex quantitative ways of forecasting but for most purchasing needs the simplest are often the quickest are the best.

- Simple average. Add you numbers together and divide by the number of observations.
- Simple moving average (SMA). This method calculates the average over a specified number of time periods. Every time an additional period is added the oldest data falls out of the calculation. For example a 6 month moving average would look like:

	Jan	Feb	Mar	Apr	May	Jun	Jul	Aug	Sep	Oct	Nov	Dec
Demand	10	30	40	30	60	70	50	60	40	80	70	90
Moving av.							40	47	52	52	60	62	65

The benefit of moving averages is that they smooth out data to make it easier to spot trends. However, SMA suffers from time lags. In the above example, any safety stock is going to be eroded pretty quickly. To overcome the problem of time lags exponential moving averages can be used. This method gives the most recent observations a greater weight in the calculation.

Other methods of quantitative forecasting could include single and multiple regression but these are generally out of scope of a buyer with a pen and paper.

Qualitative or judgmental methods

- Consensus. Ask a sample of people to predict an event. The basis of consensus prediction is that a large group will average out the likely result. Just like polling, the larger the sample size the greater the accuracy you will achieve. In effect you are mirroring a normal distribution curve.
- Consensus of expert opinion. If you don't have the time or access to a large sample group then a consensus of experts may be an alternative. Since experts can often have very diverse views, the Delphi technique can be used to narrow the range of predictions toward a consensus. The essence of this technique is to record all the predictions and feed the results back (anonymously) to the experts to justify outlying results. This method tends to quickly narrow down the range of predictions and is particularly effective in picking up factors that are not readily identified by quantitative methods for example, the emergence of new technologies or products. Beware of experts with an agenda, many of us remember the misguided panic over Y2K.
- Genius predictions. In the days of Shakespeare, they were called soothsayers. These predictions have no scientific basis but sometimes they have been uncannily correct. A historic cases being Michel de Nostradamus and Mother Shipton.

The blood of the just will be demanded of London,
Burnt by the fire in the year 66 (Century 2; Quatrain 51). The great
fire of London, 1566.

The ancient work will be accomplished,
And from the roof evil ruin will fall on the great man:
They will accuse an innocent, being dead, of the deed:
The guilty one is hidden in the misty copse.
(Century 6, Quatrain 37). The assassination of John F. Kennedy.

Around the world men's thoughts will fly, quick as the twinkling of an
eye. Mother Shipton c.1488 – 1561.

- The bush telegraph. This is the rumour mill that pervades most
  organizations. For scientific credibility, this is on a par with genius predictions but despite deriving its power from dark forces
  within an organization, it can be remarkably accurate.

Some simple rules and basic truths about forecasting:
- The further out you try to forecast the less accurate the forecast
  will be.
- The wider the range of sources and the larger the number of
  observations the greater the accuracy of the forecast will be.
- Forecasts for ranges of items tend to be more accurate.
- Always expect the unexpected. "To expect the unexpected
  shows a thoroughly modern intellect". Oscar Wilde
- Sales Managers avoid forecasting.

A final note, when forecasting consider the phenomenon known as
the 'S' curve. The basic principle of the S curve is that change often
starts slowly until a point is reached when there is a dramatic take-off
(normally linked to mass adoption). The period of rapid increase is
typically followed by a tail off as the market becomes saturated. Of
course many products never actually reach the stage of mass adoption.

Warehouse management

"An army marches on its stomach" Napoleon I

Functions of a warehouse

Receiving goods:

- Physical goods should be checked against delivery paperwork. Any discrepancies between the paperwork and the actual goods should be recorded on both the customer's copy and the supplier's copy.
- Receipt of supporting quality documentation such as test certificates, certificates of conformity, manuals etc., should be checked. Missing documents should be noted on delivery paperwork (goods can be worthless without backup paperwork).
- Any obvious physical damage to packaging or the goods should be brought to the attention of the carrier and recorded on paperwork. If possible, take a digital photograph for future reference.
- The supplier's copy of the delivery note should be marked up 'received unchecked' on 'the buyer's conditions of purchase'. It is a good idea to have a stamp with the details on for your stores staff.
- Stores staff or the buyer should immediately advise the supplier in writing of any discrepancies, damages or faults with the delivery. Photographs of any visible problems should be included.
- If there are serious problems with the goods delivered, the supplier's area sales representative should be invited to inspect the goods in situ.
- Goods should be input onto your computer system as quickly as possible, at the very latest by the end of the day of receipt. This is important both for stock accuracy and for later audit trails if required.

Goods inwards inspection

Many companies have done away with goods inwards inspection for all receipts, on the basis that deliveries should be 100% acceptable and therefore inspection is an unacceptable expense. This means that if goods are wrong or defective, the first time anybody finds out they are unusable is when production departments try to use them. In a JIT environment this can be disastrous.

My own view is that some goods should always be inspected on receipt or shortly afterwards. Goods flagged up for inspection will typically be; samples, PPAPs, items being supplied for the first time, high value items, operational critical items and items with a history of defective deliveries.

Another reason to inspect certain goods on receipt is because trying to claim redress from a supplier of defective goods, weeks or months after delivery, is more difficult. In addition, unless advised the goods are unacceptable, a supplier may continue to supply similarly defective goods.

Typical goods inward inspection procedures may require:

- Goods flagged for inspection should be placed in a designated area until passed.
- Goods requiring certification such as certificates of conformity or test certificates should have these details checked on arrival.
- Goods that are rejected should be placed in quarantine, tagged and entered as quarantine items on the stock control system.
- A non-conformance note (NCN) or similar failure report should be raised by the quality authority and passed to the buyer for resolution with the supplier.

Locating stock

Following receipt of stock the goods must be locating. There are 2 main types of goods location system:

i.   Fixed storage location. The same space is assigned to particular stocks or part number. Advantages: parts are easy to find even if the computer system crashes. Location or racking can be made to suit particular stock type. Regularly used items can be placed in convenient locations.

ii.   Random space allocation. This is ideal for use with standard pallet loads. Often this system is used in high bay type warehouses. Advantages: Optimal use of space. Disadvantages: If the system crashes it is difficult to find stock. Stock of a similar type may be kept at several different locations.

Both these systems of locating stocks can be combined with a policy of zoning stock. This is achieved by categorizing your stock by factors such as frequency of picking, or size / weight of load. Items that are picked frequently will be located close to picking locations. Heavy items are located on floor spaces rather than high up in racking.

Closed or open warehouse?

A closed store is one which has restricted access to personnel. This is usually achieved by making the warehouse a caged, or walled off area. Essentially, it is physically closed off to all but authorized staff, which is sometimes why it is unflatteringly called a 'monkey in a cage' system.

Receipts and issues into and out of the warehouse are controlled by authorized documentation. Either a delivery note in the case of a receipt, or picking lists and stores requisitions in the case of issues. Stock movements are generally recorded on the company's ERP system.

The main benefit of a closed warehouse is that stock records tend to be more accurate than other systems. This may be particularly important when operating an MRP type system. A secondary benefit is that stock loss due to theft or otherwise is minimized.

On the negative side, closed stores are expensive and they require specialist warehouse staff. They also tend to increase the amount of stock handling and stock handling.

Planning and control systems that are heavily dependent on stock accuracy will usually operate a system of perpetual inventory counting. This is a system whereby a certain number of stock items are picked daily for stock checking. The frequency that parts are stock checked will usually be controlled by an ABC type categorization of parts.

By contrast, open stores tend to locate stock at the point of use within the factory. Methods of control are often visual or a kanban type control systems. Open stores lend themselves to vendor managed inventory (VMI).

The benefit of an open store is that a tier of management is effectively removed from the organization. Stock is immediately available at the point of use and the amount of handling is reduced. Levels of inventory are generally lower with this system.

On the downside, this system relies on a high degree of supply chain co-ordination between suppliers, buyers and production staff. Without doubt this system is the most cost effective system if it works efficiently. However, it can easily fail, if: suppliers are not flexible, production demand is erratic or the range and scale of components is simply too great to keep on the shop floor.

Measuring stock control performance

Key performance indicators for warehouse operations

- Stock accuracy, as measured by perpetual inventory and by full stock checks.
- Kitting / picking lists in full.
- Processing time for booking in goods.
- Stock location, picking and retrieval times.
- Warehouse operating costs.
- The overall cost of store operations.
- Deterioration of stock.

Scrap and surplus material

"How much?" Traditional Yorkshire saying

Scrap is the waste created during the production process, surplus material is that which not suitable for or in excess of what is required for production or sale. Scrap and surplus have of course a negative effect on the company's balance sheet, when it is ultimately written off.

Identifying scrap and surplus

Typical sources of scrap and surplus material are:

- Normal production off cuts, usually small metal pieces or turnings.
- Stock that has been superseded and is now obsolescent or redundant i.e. surplus to requirements. Typically, unused parts or raw materials that are still in the condition they were originally bought and maybe still in the original packaging.
- Bi-products of the production process. Some chemical processes have bi-products that can be sold in their own right, for example gypsum is a bi-product of power station's scrubbing process that takes place in smoke stacks.
- Other company property. The most common items for disposal are used company cars and used equipment.

Methods of disposal

Mainly because it is dealing with third parties who are not customers, it routinely falls upon the purchasing manager to dispose of waste or surplus materials. There are three financial outcomes when dealing with disposal of scrap and surplus items these are:

- The materials can be sold at market prices. This is clearly the preferred option.
- The materials are collected by a third party at no additional cost.
- You have to pay someone to take the materials away.

There are a variety of routes for disposing of waste and scrap, in commercially preferred order these are:

- Selling back to the original supplier. You are more likely to have success with this method if you are an on-going customer. Suppliers will normally charge a re-stocking fee, which may be in the region of 20 or 30% but is usually negotiable depending upon the condition of the stock and the strength of your relationship.
- Send parts back to the supplier for modification or upgrading.
- Auctions, used for disposal of equipment.
- Selling to recognised scrap dealers. Typically this is the usual way of disposing of waste metals although some non-metals may have a scrap value such as pvcu extrusions and some paper products.
- Selling direct to re-processors or recycling companies who re-work materials. Some materials may not have a positive scrap value but may be collected by specialist recycling companies free of charge.
- Skip the material and send to landfill, add to the cost of any skip removal costs the costs of the landfill tax currently landfill costs are From April 2008 £32 / tonne, 2009, £40 / tonne and 2010 £48 / tonne and rising at a rate of £8 / tonne per year.

Selling the company's assets is clearly an area which could be open to abuse by the company's employees. It is therefore important that the purchasing manager records what the material is, the original cost, its book value and the reason why it is considered as scrap or surplus. Most companies will incorporate these requirements in a procedure. Normally, this procedure will have to be signed off by a senior financial manager or director.

Public Sector Procurement

*"Any change is resisted because bureaucrats have a vested
interest in the chaos in which they exist".*
Richard M. Nixon

The public sector amounts for approximately 45% of UK gross
domestic product or about £650 billion, at least £100 billion of this is
government spending on goods and services. By any measure, public
procurement policy has a massive effect on the rest of the economy.

The goals and constraints on public sector procurement are
somewhat different to those found in the private sector. Public
spending is guided more by principle than necessarily by commercial
considerations. These principles would include:

- A higher requirement for transparency.
- A degree of accountability to the public through the political system.
- Demonstrable consistency and equal treatment of suppliers.
- Compliance with EU directives and government regulations.

Sometimes there are bound to be tensions between the administrative
principles and commercial pressures. In particular, public sector
procurement has been criticised for being:

- Bureaucratic and slow, stemming from the need to demonstrate that a system (not wholly commercial) has been followed.
- Uncompetitive. Consider the number of cost overruns on government spending programs.
- Subject to political interference.

There is without doubt a recognition of these weaknesses within the
public sector and there have been and continue to be concerted
efforts to make public procurement more commercially effective.

'Managing Public Sector Procurement' produced by The Office of
Government Commerce (OGC) sets out a number of ways for
maximizing value. These are common sense suggestions that could

equally apply to the private sector buyer as well as those working in the public sector.

- Commercial issues should be considered at the design and specification stage rather than be an afterthought.
- Use standard products whenever possible, avoid using specials.
- Find out if other public bodies are using similar products and services and group together your requirements.
- Use standard procedures and systems.
- Avoid ad-hoc purchasing, plan your requirements to take advantage of economies of scale.
- Use e-auctions to create competitive pressure.
- Be open and receptive to suppliers.
- Perform a spend analysis on your activities. Who are your top 50 suppliers? Where do you spend most of your effort?
- Minimize risk by using long term contracts.
- Employ suitably qualified staff and continue their training to keep them up-to-date.

EU public sector procurement rules

"There seems to be some perverse human characteristic that likes to make easy things difficult". Warren Buffet

One of the more recent considerations for those employed in UK public sector procurement is the need to be compliant with EU rules on public procurement.

The EU rules are intended to promote fair and open competition within the single market. The fundamental requirements for public bodies when awarding contracts are:

- Non-discrimination.
- Equal treatment of bidders.
- Transparency.
- Free movement of goods and services.

The detailed requirements are contained in The Contracts for Supplies, Services and Directive 2004/18/EC also known as the Consolidated Directive (as it brings together 3 previous directives on this area of policy). It is given effect in England and Wales by the Public Contracts Regulations 2006 (SI 2006/5).

The directive applies to public bodies. This includes: central government, local government, the police and the fire services, the NHS, universities, government agencies and other bodies governed by public law. Other bodies governed by public would include any organisation which is financed or supervised in the most part by the government departments detailed above.

Thresholds and aggregation

The directive applies to contracts that exceed a financial threshold which is set by the EU every 2 years. Public bodies are required to estimate the value of the contract to the best of their ability. The value of the contract should be estimated over its entire life, if the contract has no apparent duration then the estimated monthly spend x 48 will be used to estimate the value. Individual contracts may have to be aggregate if they are considered part of the whole. Underestimates may be judged to be in breach of the rules and result in the competition being re-run.

With respect to 'services', when valuing a contract for services account must be taken of insurance premiums, financial fees, commissions, interest and design fees. If services are broken down into several packages of work, these must be aggregated when determining the value of the contract. Some services such as surveying or architects can be excluded from the calculation as long as they individual do not exceed the threshold.

Similarly for 'works' projects, the directive requires that individual but linked work packages are aggregated when determining the contract value. For individual work packages less than €80k euro, the directive may be waived so long as the package does not exceed 20% of the total value of the combined lot.

Where the contract is one of a series of similar contracts, the value of each must be aggregated to determine the estimated value. The directives expressly prohibit the splitting of requirements into smaller units or orders in an attempt to avoid the application of the directives.

Some contracts are potentially excluded from the operation of the directive either by general exclusion or special exclusion. General exclusions can exist for contracts:

- Classified as 'secret' in the interests of national security.
- War-like stores.

Special exclusions may include:

- Contracts of employment.
- Acquiring or renting land.
- Research and development with shared rights in the intellectual property.
- Part B services, service contracts relating to technical specification and post-award information.

The exemptions are very narrowly interpreted by the European Commission and the European Court of Justice.

Publication

Contracts that are covered by the directive must be published in the prescribed way.

- An advert, using standard forms, must be sent to the Official Journal of the European Union (OJEU).
- Contracts must not advertise the work in any other publication before the OJEU forms have been submitted but you don't have to wait until the advert is published in the OJEU.
- The detail provided in any other publication must be the same as the detail in the OJEU advert.
- Voluntary publication of a contract in OJEU (contracts falling below the threshold) do not have to follow the requirements of the Directives but must follow the 4 principles of, non-discrimination,

equality, transparency and free movement of goods and services. This latter point was decided in the Telaustria case.

Contract award procedure

There are 4 award procedures; the open procedure, the restricted procedure, the negotiated procedure and the competitive dialogue procedure.

The Open procedure

The main requirements:

- Invitation to Tender documents must be issued to all companies requesting one within 6 days of being requested (may be reduced to 4 days if accelerated procedures are allowed).
- The minimum closing date for bids is 52 days following the day after the advert was posted to the OJEU.
- If there has been a prior information notice (PIN) published not less than 52 days previously and no longer than 1 year ago, then the 52 day period that must elapse before bids can be received is reduced to 36 days (or 22 days in exceptionally justified cases).
- The electronic issue of documents can reduce the timescales.

Restricted procedure

This is a 2 stage process, the first part is to shortlist the candidates and the second part is to invite a selected group of candidates to submit proposals.

Stage 1

- Send the advert to the OJEU.
- Potential suppliers are given 37 days following the despatch of the advert to the OJEU to register their interest in being short listed (timescale can be reduced to 15 days if 'accelerated procedures' are allowed).

- Suppliers registering interest are short listed on the basis of the company's capacity and past experience.
- A minimum of 5 companies must be short listed, when 5 suitably qualified companies have registered an interest.
- Electronic issue of documents can reduce the timescales.

Stage 2

- Invitations to tender are issued to short listed companies.
- Tender documents should allow bidders a minimum of 40 days to submit their tenders. (40 days can be reduced to 10 days if 'accelerated procedure' is allowed)
- If there has been a prior information notice (PIN) published not less than 52 days previously and no longer than 1 year ago, then the 40 day period can be reduced to 26 days. Note: the 37 day requirement remains.
- Electronic issue of documents can reduce the timescales.

Negotiated procedure

The 'negotiated procedure' is used in exceptional circumstances when both the 'open' and 'restricted' procedures have proved unsuitable because the lack of information or complexity that makes drawing up detailed specifications and hence accurate pricing problematic.

There are two forms of negotiated procedure; negotiated procedure with a call for competition and negotiated procedure without a call for competition.

Negotiated procedure with a call for competition

This is a 2 stage procedure.

Stage 1

- Advert is sent to the OJEU.
- Potential suppliers are given 37 days following the despatch of the advert to the OJEU to register their interest in being short

listed (timescale may be reduced to 15 days if Accelerated Procedure is allowed).

- Suppliers registering interest are short listed on the basis of the company's capacity and past experience.
- A minimum of 3 companies must be short listed when 3 suitably qualified companies have registered an interest.

Stage 2

- Enter negotiations with short listed companies with a view to agreeing the terms of the contract.
- There are no time limits laid down for this stage.

Negotiated procedure without a call for competition

This procedure is used when seeking competition has not been successful, or is in response to an emergency, or where competition is not practical or commercial. Examples may include: emergency relief contracts, additional works or services (not greater than 50% of the original contract), repeat works or research and development. In this case, no advert is placed with the OJEU.

Competitive Dialogue Procedure

This procedure is used in exceptional circumstances for supply, services or works contracts that are particularly complex and where it is not practical to specify technical or commercial terms of the project. It is a 2 stage process:

Stage 1

- Publication in the OJEU of 'needs and requirements' further defined by a 'descriptive document'.
- Potential suppliers are given 37 days following the despatch of the advert to the OJEU to register their interest in being short listed.
- Pre-qualification of bidders.
- Short listing of potential bidders.

- A minimum of 3 companies must be short listed when 3 suitably qualified companies have registered an interest.
- Electronic issue of documents can reduce the timescales.

Stage 2

- Dialogue is entered into with the potential bidders with a view to agreeing the details the contract.
- Criteria may be introduced to successively reduce the number of bidders.
- If and when the contracting authority has identified solutions, it declares the dialogue phase closed and calls for final tenders based on all the elements identified as necessary to meet the objective of the contract.
- Tenders may be subject to requests for clarification and further details but this should not change the core features of the contract
- Bids are assessed on the most economically advantageous award criterion.
- There are no time limits

In addition to the 4 award procedures described above, the directive now recognises and authorises specified procurement arrangements which can be categorized as:

- Framework agreements. These agreements govern the terms by which a number of contracts can be entered into. The establishment of a framework agreement must be set up using one of the established award procedures and is limited to 4 years duration. Call off orders would fall under framework agreements.
- Dynamic purchasing system (DPS), which is a completely electronic system of procurement. The establishment of this system must be by the open method of award and is time limited to 4 years duration.
- Electronic auctions. Normally set up using the open or restricted award procedure and can be used in conjunction with DPS.

Post tender negotiations when using open or restricted award procedures

The opportunities for post tender negotiations is restricted by Council Directive 90/531/EEC which states, "in open and restricted procedures, all negotiation with candidates or tenderers on fundamental aspects of contracts, variations in which are likely to distort competition, and in particular on prices, shall be ruled out; however, discussions with candidates or tenderers may be held but only for the purpose of clarifying or supplementing the content of their tenders or the requirements of the contracting authorities and provided that this does not involve discrimination."

Award Criterion

An evaluation criterion must be set prior to the ITT. The evaluation criteria should be based on either, the lowest price or the most economically advantageous bid.

The use of the most economically advantageous criterion allows the contracting authority to include criterion other than just price, when evaluating a project. Assessment criteria could include an assessment of a wide variety of measures including: quality, technical specification, after sales services, even aesthetic value. However, all the criteria used must be linked to the subject of the contract.

The weighting of each of the criteria must be set out in the OJEU notice and contractual tender documents. Criteria may be weighted as appropriate. Normally, price is the most heavily weighted item in any criteria. The actual balance of price to other criteria may be subject to official review prior to issue. Where it is not practical to give weightings, the criteria should be placed in order of importance.

Post award of contract

- Notice of the award must be published by the contracting authority within 48 days of the award.
- Following the award of contract there is a 10 day mandatory standstill period before the contract commencement. The pe-

riod runs 10 calendar days from the written notice of the award to all tendering parties.

Unsuccessful tendering parties must be advised in writing of:

- The award criterion
- If appropriate, the score the tender received against the criterion
- If appropriate, the winning tender's score.
- The name of the winning tender.

The contracting authority is obliged to provide an additional debrief, if an unsuccessful tender requests it by the end of the second day following the commencement of the standstill period.

- The contracting authority will be advised why the bid was unsuccessful.
- If the tendering party submitted an admissible tender, then the contracting authority is obliged to inform them of the relative advantages of the successful bid.
- If the tendering party misses the 2 day deadline, then the contracting party is obliged to provide details within 15 days of receiving a written request.

Accelerated procedure

Can be used with 'restricted' or 'negotiated with call for competition' procedures where the normal timescales are impractical.

Framework agreements

"More than 50% of significant new regulations that impact on business in the UK now emanate from the EU"
John Hutton

Framework agreements are blanket type orders, where the main terms and conditions of contract are decided at the outset but certain details such as the supplier, the quantities and the delivery dates are only decided when requirements are called off.

The principle benefits of using framework agreements are speed, flexibility and reduced administration. Framework agreements facilitate easier transactions because the buyer does not have to re-apply the full selection and award procedures called for by the directives.

Setting up framework agreements

The framework agreement itself must be set up according to the directives and the usual rules regarding procedures, thresholds, publication, award etc. will apply as detailed below:

- When considering whether the contract meets the thresholds, it is the expected value over the lifetime of the agreement that is considered.
- The tendering procedure will be the 'open' or 'restricted' procedures, although the use of negotiated and competitive dialogue procedures cannot be ruled out if the conditions are met.
- If the correct procedures and rules regarding threshold are not applied correctly, then it may be necessary for subsequent call-offs to be advertised in the OJEU, which defeats the object of increasing flexibility and reducing the administration costs.
- Both the framework and the individual call-off must comply with treaty obligations seeking transparency and should not seek to distort or restrict competition or be discriminatory.
- Generally, obligations are not created by the award of framework agreements but only when actual call offs are made.
- The maximum duration of a framework agreement is 4 years.
- Mandatory standstill rules apply to framework agreements.
- Framework agreements can be placed with 1 supplier or multiple suppliers.

Single supplier

Single supplier framework agreements are often chosen where the product supplied is complex or requires close liaison between the buyer and the supplier. Call-offs should be on the same basis as the original terms of the framework agreement. If the original agreement is not sufficiently clear, then the contracting authority should make further enquiries of the supplier.

Multiple suppliers

The award of call-offs will depend upon whether the original agreement is sufficiently precise.

1. Where the terms of the framework agreement are sufficiently precise to cover the particular goods or services required, apply the terms of the framework agreement. Call-offs should be placed on the basis of the most economically advantageous value for money supplier.
2. Where the framework agreement is not sufficiently precise regarding the call-off of particular goods or services it may be necessary to hold a mini-competition amongst the holders of framework agreements.

Mini-competitions

The terms of the mini-competition should be essentially those of the framework and no substantive changes should be made. Award should be made according to the criteria set out in the framework. New criteria should not be added but weighting can be changed.

Call-offs

Individual obligations are created only when goods and services are called off under the agreement. The directives are silent on the maximum duration of a call-off order. The mandatory standstill rules do not apply to call-offs.

Authors note. This section relies heavily upon the excellent, Scottish Public Procurement Toolkit. www.scotland.gov.uk. Other useful guidance can be found at Office of Government and Commerce, www.ogc.gov.uk

Lean Manufacturing

*"What's the aim of the school of business for example? They
teach students how business is conducted today and how to
perpetuate it. Any wonder we're in trouble? They ought to be
preparing students for the future, not for the past".*
W Edwards Deming

History

Lean Manufacturing is a management philosophy and culture that has
been adopted by many companies in the UK as a route to business
improvement, competitive advantage and in some cases business survival.

Lean manufacturing can trace its roots back to Henry Ford. Some of
Ford's early writings spelt out many of the concepts that we would now
recognise as lean concepts including: continuous production flow,
standardization and elimination of waste ('Today and Tomorrow' (1926).

In the post war era, it was Japanese industry with support from
Americans like Dr W E Deming, who took Henry Ford's ideas to the
next level. At the forefront of developing these ideas into a fuller
manufacturing philosophy was Toyota. A delegation from Toyota had
visited Ford's manufacturing facilities in the 1930s, it is said that the
Toyota team were more impressed by the layout and organisation of
American supermarkets than the car plants.

The manufacturing philosophies and practices became the Toyota
Production System (TPS). The Toyota system was adopted and copied
by many western companies, but it wasn't until the late 1980's that the
term 'Lean' was coined by John Krafcik in his article, "Triumph of the
Lean Production System".

The main elements of lean manufacturing

- Removal of waste
- Smoothing demand and production
- Develop a culture of continuous improvement

Removal of waste (mura)

"I am looking for a lot of men who have an infinite capacity to not know what can't be done" Henry Ford

A key principle of lean manufacturing is that a customer will only pay for what he values and will not pay for mistakes or waste. Manufacturing effort must be focused on delivering customer value and eliminating non-value adding activities. To achieve this, the manufacturing process is broken down into its component steps and analysed to identify which activities add value and those that don't. The goal is to remove non-value activities and waste from all manufacturing processes. Activities are characterised as:

- Value adding (VA). Something the customer will pay for.
- Non-value adding (NVA). These activities may not add value directly but are necessary to the successful running of the business. In effect they are necessary non-value adding (NNVA).
- Pure waste.

When we are looking to reduce waste in a lean manufacturing environment we are specifically targeting the pure waste. Pure waste is something unnecessary in the realization of final customer value. It occurs when more resources are used to produce goods than are actually necessary. Another way of thinking about waste is what slows the process down or what roadblocks cause the process to deviate from the quickest route. Taiichi Ohno, Toyota's chief engineer identified seven categories of waste:

1 Over-production. No immediate customers for products.
2 Unnecessary transportation or handling of the product.
3 Stock in all forms.
4 Unnecessary movement of staff or equipment.
5 Defective products and returns.
6 Over-processing or over design.
7 Waiting or queuing time.

Over-production

This is making more than the customer wants. This waste is most commonly found in production driven companies, which aim to reduce unit costs through large and long batch runs. It is likely to occur because the costs of breaking down production may be perceived to be high and the cost of holding stock underestimated.

In a lean manufacturing environment over-production is often considered the worse type of waste because it can easily lead to other wastes. Every item of unnecessary production diverts raw materials, labour, machine time and demands additional handling and storage.

The lean solution to overproduction would be to develop a more flexible production system. By reducing the cost of breaking down equipment and releasing works orders in smaller quantities.

Of course, in certain circumstances long production runs are entirely appropriate. When low unit costs are paramount and products are relatively homogenous, such as commodities. Large scale processing industries, like oil, chemical and flour milling production spring to mind.

Unnecessary transportation and handling

An unnecessary movement of raw materials around your factory diverts resources and increases the risk of damage and deterioration. At the same time, handling goods does not add any recognizable value for your customers.

Unnecessary movement of staff or equipment

Time spent moving from or around the workstation is less time performing the task. Factory layout and organisation of work stations need to be planned to minimise unnecessary movement. All equipment should have a station.

Stock

Stock may take a number of forms including: raw materials, work in progress and finished stock, all share the same characteristics, they tie up cash, they occupy space and they need protecting. Furthermore, high levels of intermediate stock tend to be symptomatic of long queuing times for the next process. High levels of finished stock indicate over-production and high levels of raw material stock indicate poor materials management.

In a lean manufacturing environment, large stocks tend to hide problems which should be addressed. In addition high levels of stock can engender a culture of comfort rather than a culture of removing waste and improvement. Finally, the higher the level of stock the higher the risk some of it will be superseded and become obsolete.

Defects and returns

Defects and returns necessitate remakes, re-shipping and re-invoicing not to mention loss of customer goodwill. Lean aims at eliminate this waste by making things right first time, using tools like poka yoke and root cause analysis. A war cry of lean advocates is "if you can't find time to make it right then you will not have time to remake it".

Over-processing and over-design

This is incorporating features or processes that are superfluous to the customer's requirements. A simple question that should be asked, "Is it good enough?" There is no point in diverting resources on something that the customer doesn't value or is not paying for.

Waiting or queuing time

This is anything which interrupts the flow of work and causes delay is a waste. Typically sources of waste are caused by interruptions are:

- Machine set-ups. Ways of improving set up times need to be considered.
- Poor staff skills and training.
- Poor instructions, no instructions or waiting for instructions.
- Equipment breakdowns and repairing equipment.
- Waiting for labour, materials or equipment.
- Searching for resources.
- Using the wrong materials, equipment or labour.
- Inspection.

Smoothing out work flow

"It is better to travel well than to arrive." Buddha

Another key element of creating a lean manufacturing system is removing (production) unevenness and ensuring that work flows through the production processes as quickly and smoothly as possible. In lean management this is achieved by:

- Levelling (smoothing) production.
- Levelling (smoothing) demand.

Level production processes

In traditional manufacturing systems, production tends to be uneven and batch sizes large. This is partly because changeover times are long and expensive driving up the economic batch size. In lean manufacturing, smoothness is achieved by minimising batch sizes, by reducing the time and cost of changeover. The overall goal is to make the production process as flexible as possible, with the ultimate goal of single piece flow of work.

More specifically, flexible production is achieved by the systematic elimination of impediments, such as bottlenecks and uncoordinated work flows. To do this, it employs methods such as:

- Single minute exchange of dies (SMED), to reduce the cost and time of switching production.
- Poka Yoke, to fool proof systems.
- Andons and Jidoka, to focus effort on resolving production line problems.
- The use of Heijunka boxes to balance and visually schedule work.
- Pull systems and the use of kanbans.
- Takt time planning to set the pace of production.

Levelling demand

Efforts are made to manage demand to avoid fluctuations. This may be achieved by setting the pace of production at the long term level of demand. For example, if demand is 400, 600, 800 over a period, production will be set at 600. To allow for variations in demand, stock is put in place at the final product stage or the stage just prior to customization. This is perhaps one of the few exceptions were stock is tolerated in a lean manufacturing environment.

Developing a culture of continuous improvement

Lean manufacturing is as much about the creation of a culture of continuous improvement as it is about systems or methods. This philosophy can be summed up by the Japanese word kaizen, meaning improvement or change for the better. The culture needs to be adopted company wide, from bottom to top and extend to the wider supply chain. In particular, all staff must be committed to:

- The continuous improvement of the production process through continuous incremental changes, evaluation and re-evaluation.
- The continuous improvement of the product through elimination of defects in the product.
- The continuous improvement of the workforce through self-improvement and training.

To successfully develop a culture of continuous improvement all staff must accept if not embrace:

- An acceptance of change within the organisation. Successful companies are those which are able to identify and adapt to changing circumstances.
- The removal of blame culture from the organisation and the acceptance of openness. This helps to expose problems and weaknesses which can then be solved.
- Teamwork, with empowerment at the operator level realized in decision making from the bottom up.

Lean Tools

5S

"Enjoy failure and learn from it. You can never learn from success". James Dyson

During a visit to the Ford plants in the 1950s, the Toyota delegation was not inspired by the car factories but by the organisational methods of US supermarkets. They were apparently impressed that stock was only ordered to replace goods purchased by customers (what developed into kanbans) but also the cleanliness and orderliness of the supermarket layout and organization. Toyota took this model of orderliness and cleanliness and developed it for their factories, the result was 5S.

The aim of 5S is to create a working environment which will enable manufacturing excellence through structured workplace organisation and housekeeping methods. 5S refers to the 5 disciplines required to achieve a suitable working environment. The 5 disciplines are detailed below:

Preliminary audit

The first practical step when introducing 5S is to perform an initial audit. The purpose of the initial audit is to record the starting point of the process. Take photographs, as these can be used to great effect when assessing the success of a project.

Sort

Physical stock is sorted with the aim of removing clutter and unnecessary objects from the shop floor. This is achieved by deciding what is needed and what is not. When deciding what to keep and what to remove, prioritise by frequency of use. Items identified for removal are red tagged and placed in a holding area to be assessed.

Stabilize

Assess what parts to keep, how many to keep and where to keep them. Make it easy to identify the parts by signposting. Parts should be made readily accessible and easy to return them. The motto is "A place for everything and everything in its place." For example, location of tools may be indicated by silhouette boards, floor markings may identify designated areas for parts, and signposts will indicate directions and locations.

Responsibility for maintaining the system of organization is taken by the workplace team. Faulty items are identified with duplicate yellow tags. Yellow tags are marked up with details of the fault, the location of the item, the date and the name of the person who has identified the fault. One part of the tag is passed to maintenance for action.

Shine

Clean the work area to the extent that anything out of place is immediately recognizable. Put in placed routine cleaning schedules.

Standardise

The aim of standardization is to adopt consistent, uniform and repeatable methods. Information on standard methods is recorded and shared often by way of work point information boards.

Sustain

Disciplines are put into place to audit the methods, identify possible improvements and provide training. The aim is to make the correct procedures second nature.

To aid the establishing of 5S

- 5S needs to be implemented on a company wide basis.
- The principles of 5S need to be understood by the workforce and their importance to company success recognised.
- Senior managers need to lead the initiative.
- Procedures must be codified and formally approved.

Andons

"The first rule of any technology used in a business is that automation applied to an efficient operation will magnify the efficiency. The second is that automation applied to an inefficient operation will magnify the inefficiency". Bill Gates

Andons are a system of signals, usually lights, used on machines and processes to indicate operational status. Typically, green lights indicate normal operation; amber lights routine action required, for example, planned restocking; red lights indicate operation interrupted and immediate action required. To be effective the signals need to be supported with routines and a plan(s) of action linked to each andon state.

When considering the introduction of an andon scheme, the following questions should be considered:

- Is a signal really necessary? (Too many signals can become counter-productive consider the clutter of signs on some British roads).
- What does each signal mean? Too complex a system of signals would create confusion and apathy.
- Who monitors the status of andons and who takes action?
- What action is taking in each circumstance?
- Preventative action to stop recurrence. Typically red lights should instigate a root cause analysis to prevent recurrence.

Brainstorming

"Great minds discuss ideas; average minds discuss events; small minds discuss people". Eleanor Roosevelt

Normally brainstorming sessions are convened by management either to address a particular problem, or as a general management tool to gain acceptance and input on a wider business issue. In the first case, teams may be relatively small and focused groups for example a team to address a problem with a component may consist of the design team and sales.

In the second case, management's goal maybe wider, for example, changing methods of operation. In this instance, the purpose of the meeting may not really be to get new ideas at all but only to motivate and engage the workforce, possibly in changes to working practices.

As an employee it will normally be obvious what type of brainstorming event you are in. In the second case, the team will generally be larger and made up of 'influencers' within the company. There will normally be a 'facilitator', who is either an external consultant or a member of the senior management team, whose job is to guide the meeting along the right path.

The usual method of brainstorming is structured in the following way:

- The team is brought together but away from everyday work distractions.
- The objective of the meeting or the issue to be discussed is agreed.
- The main headings are agreed and placed on a flip chart, dry wipe board or better still on large pieces of paper stuck to the walls of the room you are in.
- Ideas generated are listed under these main headings. The basic premise of a brainstorming session is that all ideas however lateral should be considered.
- Ideas are then sifted to remove duplications, categorized into major headings and condensed into key propositions.
- Review your results. Identify ideas that are inconsistent prevent or cancel out each other. Identify factors which are consistent and support each other.
- Take the list of categories along with their strengths and weaknesses and prioritize them in terms of validity and importance. Prioritize the ideas within each list.
- Use your priority to start to formulate a plan of action. Gain a consensus on a timescale and appoint people to manage various aspects of the plan.
- The team should meet periodically to review progress and if necessary agree changes to plan.

Cellular manufacturing

"A goal without a plan is just a wish" Antoine de St Exupery

This is the organization of manufacturing processes into modular areas of production. Each cell is configured to produce a particular family of parts or assemblies. Each family of parts may have a high level of differentiation but the basic manufacturing process will be standardized. Machinery is grouped to service these families of parts.

The layout of the cell will aim to minimize the amount of unnecessary movement of operators and materials. For this reason cells are often 'U' shaped but the actual layout will often depend on the nature of the product and equipment needs. Individual cells may be staffed by 1 person or a team.

The aim of cellular manufacture is to achieve a high degree of flexibility into the production and so the system is ideally suited to batch manufacture.

Deming cycle

"A circle is the reflection of eternity. It has no beginning and it has no end - and if you put several circles over each other, then you get a spiral". Maynard James Keenan

The Deming cycle or sometimes referred to as the Deming wheel or Shewhart cycle is one of the most well-known of all manufacturing problem solving processes. It is summed up by the acronym, PDCA (Plan Do Check Act) and as its name suggests it is process based on hypothesis, experiment and evaluation.

Plan	Set objectives and process to achieve a particular result.
Do	Implement the process.
Check	Measure the new processes and compare results against expected.

Act   Analyse any difference and determine the cause. Implement changes to rectify shortfalls. Then start the process again.

Heijunka box

"Control your own destiny or someone else will." Jack Welch

A heijunka box is a matrix of pigeon holes which serves to control the production of a group of products or components. Normally, horizontal rows will indicate different products or components and vertical columns will represent a series time slots. Production control kanban cards are placed in the holes indicating the number of items or components to be produced during that time slot. At regular intervals the kanban cards are distributed to production areas for processing.

Jidoka

"A person with a new idea is a crank until the idea succeeds." Mark Twain

This is the practice of shutting down a line or process when a defect or abnormality is detected. Of course stopping a production line when something is not right requires that both the support of the organization for the person stopping the line and a system to rapidly correct any abnormalities. The concept of jidoka is quite radical but does serve to focus attention on continuous improvement, since problems are ironed out quickly rather than tolerated.

Just in time (JIT)

"Three o'clock is always either too late or too early for anything one might want to do". Jean Paul Sartre

Just in time, is a widely used term that has come to have several different meanings in supply management theory. As far as a purchasing manager is concerned, it is simply a word to describe a method of inventory control with the object of reducing stock.

JIT probably has its origins in the philosophy of lean manufacturing and in particular the concept of eliminating waste from the manufacturing process. In its fullest sense, JIT should seek to eliminate stock throughout the supply chain, from the supplier through to the end customers.

The essence of JIT is to ensure that the exact quantity of materials arrive at the point of use at exactly the time they are required. The theory is that in doing so the amount of material in the supply chain will be minimized. If stock is minimize, there will less risk of stock deterioration, damage or obsolescence and less need for warehousing and finance.

JIT in operation

To operate an effective JIT system requires a very effective demand forecasting system or extremely flexible suppliers, or both.

Effective demand forecasting means that buyers can determine in advance the exact quantities required, when they are required and with sufficient time to use the information effectively. Most buyers know that this is a virtually impossible task when dealing with a large number of parts with independent demand which has no relationship to the demand for any other item). This is one of the reasons why JIT acquired the reputation of being 'just too late'. For this reason JIT tends to work best in continuous production environments or where production demands are 'smoothed' by cutting out the peaks and troughs.

The other way of achieving JIT is to develop extremely flexible suppliers who have an extremely reliable and consistent quality of product. The quality of the supplies is important because with a JIT system there is no slack time to replace defective goods. Similarly there is no goods inwards inspection, deliveries of goods go straight to the point of use. If supplies are defective there are no standby materials to keep production going, so JIT relies upon a zero defect rate. It is said that quality must be built into products.

Minimisation of stock throughout the supply chain requires suppliers to produce products only against customer demand and to make frequent small deliveries of product to the customer. In reality, suppliers only achieve this level of service by either holding stocks of finished product or putting consignment stock into the customer. Furthermore, to achieve this level of service, a close understanding and excellent communications are needed between the supplier and the customer. Consequently, it is usual for parts to be sourced from a single supplier with 'partnership' type arrangements with suppliers. Indeed many of the Japanese companies, who pioneered JIT, developed a policy of sourcing materials from suppliers located very close to their factories. Often these suppliers only supplied the one customer and in some cases where owned wholly or in part by the customer.

JIT supplies have also been closely related to the development of lean manufacturing and the spread in the use of kanbans and pull type production systems. Sometimes these systems are managed externally by suppliers through vendor managed inventories (VMI). The use of long duration open and blanket orders is typical with JIT supply arrangements.

The use of JIT inventory systems is not without risks. Due to the lack of safety stock within the system, a failure in one part of the chain can have serious consequences for the whole chain. In 1997, one of Toyota's suppliers, Aisin Seiki Co, suffered a fire which destroyed its ability to supply brake valves. Unfortunately, the company was the sole supplier of a component and the loss of the supplier's factory resulted in production delays for Toyota and large losses.

A common criticism of JIT systems is that stocks are just pushed onto suppliers. It has been suggested that suppliers providing JIT supplies simply create stocks of goods and financing them by charging the customer a premium price.

Kanbans

"A person buying ordinary products in a supermarket is in touch with his deepest emotions." John Kenneth Galbraith

The principal tools of pull systems are kanbans (Japanese for signboard or instruction card) and heijunka boxes. Kanbans are manual pull devices, usually visual, by which downstream operations signal to upstream operations the need to supply more product. Kanbans come in a variety of forms but the most common ones use cards and containers.

One bin systems are perhaps the most basic form of kanban. With this system, consequential production processes are paired up in a closed loop system. A kanban card is attached to the container and is sent to the upstream consuming department. When the first part in that bin is started the card is sent back downstream to signal the need to supply another container. Supply quantities are usually fixed. Sometimes signal cards and bins can accumulate at the production area awaiting a sufficient quantity to make a production batch. Upstream production processes can be paired up with external suppliers and the return of the card is the signal to the supplier to send more supplies.

Another form of kanban is a top up at point of use. In this case a buffer stock at the point of use is checked at a fixed frequency and top up to a predetermined maximum level (variable quantity). This is perhaps the most common method for vendor managed stock systems. With this system, cards are often replaced by barcode and scanner inventory control.

The challenge with this system is to confirm the delivery quantities made by the supplier because the system is open to abuse, there must be a high degree of confidence and trust in the supplier and your own staff. When designing a kanban system, the following issues may be considered.

- Where to locate buffers. Options typically include: at the point of use, at a parts supermarket or at the point of production. Often this will depend upon the factors such as the number of supplying or receiving work stations and the availability of space.

- The quantity of parts held in an individual bin. The number of bins held at the location. The trigger point for sending a replenishment signal. When considering the trigger point consideration would need to be given to the time required to send the signal, the time for the supplying department to respond, the travelling time to restock the buffer and potential delays in the supplying department due to other production priorities.

- The design of the signal and the information it would contain. Typically the signal to upstream operations is performed by the kanban card. This would normally include the key information about the process including: details of the part, the refill quantity, the part location and the priority level.

- Other signals may be required such as are coloured lamps, email, faxes, empty containers, marked floor locations (Kanban squares), EDI, trolleys, cards or a variety of other signals.

- Single or multi card systems. Multiple card systems are more appropriate when the supplying operation produces several products, or supplies several downstream operations, or the production lot size is different from the kanban bin size.

- Kanban squares or shelf reserves are normally used when the producer and consumer are adjacent. The size of the space is normally used to indicate the desired buffer quantity.

- The capacity of the bins, number of bins and the re-supply quantities may be estimated using the takt time of the production processes. Fine tuning the right levels may be a matter of trial and error. If stock repeatedly builds up in one part of the chain then it may be necessary to reduce the bin capacity or take out some the bins to avoid overstocking.

Potential problems with kanbans:

- Cards or containers can go missing.
- High fluctuations in demand can cause stock outs. Kanban relies on relatively stable and repetitive demand.
- The number of cards and the supply details need to be continually reviewed to meet changes in the system.
- Kanbans are best suited to continuous production situation with relatively small ranges of variations. They are probably not best suited to the supply of custom made products, supplied in low quantities on extended lead times. However, even in industries like shipbuilding, kanbans have been set up on individually paired processes even when it cannot be rolled out across the whole production process.

Poka yoke (mistake proofing)

"A person who never made a mistake never tried anything new". Albert Einstein

The poka yoke method is credited to Shigeo Shingo, who worked at Toyota in the 1960s. Its aim is to eliminate potential areas for failure before a process is performed in anger. The motto of poka yoke could be 'right first time'. It follows a similar methodology to root cause analysis but uses hypothetical problems rather than actual failures. The poka yoke method normally has the following stages:

- Define the process or product that you want to scrutinize.
- Identify the steps in the process and consider all potential reasons for failure. Use the '5 whys' method to get to the root of the problem or think of Murphy's Law, 'what can go wrong will go wrong', to identify all potential problems. Consider potential design failings using Design Failure Mode Effects Analysis (DFMEA) and Process Failure Modes Effects Analysis (PFMEA).

- Develop methods or design products that avoid the hazards and risks identified. The use of 'foul tabs' and bar code checking of components are typical steps to avoid the wrong parts or parts fitted incorrectly.
- Use hypothesis testing and trials to dry run systems.
- Formulate procedures and train staff.
- Regularly review procedures and update.

Pareto analysis (80:20 rule)

"Give me a fruitful error anytime, full of seeds, bursting with its own corrections."
Vilfredo Pareto

The essence of the pareto principle is that 20% of the possible causes result in 80% of the effects. This is useful information when you have limited resources and you want to concentrate your efforts on the most important factors.

It is not uncommon for your top 20% of suppliers by spend when added together will amount to about 80% of your total spend, try it!

Pull systems

"Consumption is the sole end and purpose of all production". Adam Smith

Pull systems work on the basis that downstream operations send signals back to the upstream operations to produce product. Typically, the receipt of a customer order is the trigger for the last process in the chain to draw materials from upstream operations signalling the need to produce components. These processes in turn draw materials from the proceeding process and in this way each upstream process receives a signal from the downstream process to make product, all the way to the suppliers of raw materials. Each operation just makes what is needed for the next upstream operation. This is of course the opposite way around to the traditional method.

Quality circles

"Circles create soothing space, where even reticent people can realize that their voice is welcome". Margaret J. Wheatley

Quality circles or kaizen groups are teams of people brought together to identify improvements to a process. Within a lean manufacturing environment, these teams are likely to be drawn from cellular teams or groups of people responsible for a particular area of manufacture.

Single minute exchange of dies (SMED)

"Being busy does not always mean real work. The object of all work is production or accomplishment and to either of these ends there must be forethought, system, planning, intelligence, and honest purpose, as well as perspiration. Seeming to do is not doing". Thomas A. Edison

One of the core aims of lean manufacturing is to increase the flexibility of the manufacturing system by reducing the costs associated with switching production. Single minute exchange of dies is one such way of reducing the cost of changeovers.

In reducing change-over times there are 2 main elements to consider:

- The internal set-up activities. These are activities that can only be performed when the process is stopped such as removing or attaching tools to a machine. These activities directly affect the change over time.
- The external set-up activities. These are activities that can be performed whilst the process is still running and so are less critical.

One of the challenges of reducing change over times is converting internal activities into external activities. Examples could include:

- The movement or preparation of tools required prior to fitting. For example pre-heating dies.

- The collection and return of tools/dies.
- Cleaning down.
- Preparing materials.
- Changing feed hoppers.
- Recording information.
- Routine maintenance of equipment.

After converting as many internal to external activities take the remaining internal activities and break them down into detailed steps, with a view to identifying and removing unnecessary operations or improving the ones that remain. Some methods may include:

- Making jobs parallel activities rather than sequential. If two or more tasks can be worked on at the same time this will generally reduce the time needed.
- Consider steps to simplify fixing operations like quarter turn locking and using quick release fasteners.
- Create and use teams of specialist staff (Like formula one pit teams).
- Map the movement of parts and shorten routes.

After identifying possible sources of improvement, trial test them and record the improvements or otherwise. When new activities work, set up a new standard procedure, train staff and roll-out to similar processes.

Takt time planning

"Determine never to be idle. No person will have occasion to complain of the want of time who never loses any. It is wonderful how much may be done if we are always doing". Thomas Jefferson

In order for material to flow smoothly through the manufacturing processes, there needs to be a common pacing mechanism, this is the takt time. In its simplest terms, it is the targeted pace of production and can be defined as the total production time / the total customer demand during that period. For example, if production time is an 8 hour shift and daily customer demand is 2400 units then the takt time would be 8 x 60 x 60 /2400 = 12 seconds.

This is the pace which all processes should try to synchronise with. Of course some processes will have different cycle times to the takt time, this is not a disaster but it is not ideal. Running faster than takt time will either mean there is spare capacity or stock will build up. Running slower than takt time indicates a bottleneck requiring additional resources or re-organisation.

Value process mapping

"If you can't describe what you are doing as a process, you don't know what you're doing". W. Edwards Deming

This is an end to end analysis of the flows of materials and information within the business, from the receipt of orders through to the despatch of finished goods to the customer. The technique works best for systems that are reasonably routine and standardised. There are several stages in the process:

Mapping the current state of the process

- Define the process you want to analyse.
- Identify the start and end points.
- Pick a team of people who together, know the process from start to finish. The team must include the people who actually perform the current process.
- Using brainstorming, the team should aim to detail all the steps in the process. The analysis must be detailed including costs, times (including delays), quantities, information and material flows.
- Diagrammatically represent the sequence(s) of events using a process map.

Analyse the current state map

The overall aim is to find the shortest and most effective way to produce the end product. This is achieved by identifying blocks to the smooth flow of work from process to process and identifying waste within the system. In performing this task you may want to consider some of the following questions and steps:

- Identify the operations that add value and those that don't.
- Identify the information flows. How effective are they? Is all the information relevant or necessary? Is too little or too much information provided?
- Does the customer value all operations? Can some operations be removed?
- Is there duplication of operations? Can operations be consolidated?
- Is there over or under manning? Are people used effectively? Is there scope for multi-tasking? Do operators have downtime when they can perform other tasks?
- Can the number of movements of materials, labour or equipment be reduced? Can the distances be reduced? Can handling equipment be employed to speed up the process?
- Is the flow of raw materials at an optimum? Are their queues of products building up at any point in the process, indicative of bottlenecks?
- Are all quality checks necessary? Can they be rationalized?

The future value stream map

Redraw the future state map with identified imperfections removed and the improvements added. Whilst doing this:

- Keep an open mind on what can be achieved.
- Consider what you would do with a blank canvas.
- What would someone do if there were no resource limitations.

Formulate an implementation plan

To implement the future value stream map

- Use members of the team to act as change leaders.
- Measure performance of the new system against the old.
- Continuing with the original team, identify what has improved and what hasn't.
- And the process starts all over again.

Toyota Production System - 14 principles

1 Base your management decisions on a long-term philosophy, even at the expense of short-term financial goals.

2 Create a continuous process flow to bring problems to the surface.

3 Use "pull" type systems to avoid overproduction.

4 Level out the workload.

5 Build a culture of stopping to fix problems, to get quality right the first time.

6 Standardised tasks and processes are the foundation for continuous improvement and employee empowerment.

7 Use visual control so no problems are hidden.

8 Use only reliable, thoroughly tested technology that serves your people and processes.

9 Grow leaders who thoroughly understand the work, live the philosophy, and teach it to others.

10 Develop exceptional people and teams who follow your company's philosophy.

11 Respect your extended network of partners and suppliers by challenging them and helping them improve.

12 To thoroughly understand the situation, go and see for yourself.

13 Make decisions slowly by consensus, thoroughly considering all options; implement decisions rapidly.

14 Become a learning organization through relentless reflection and continuous improvement.

The SCOR model

"Beginning reform is beginning revolution." Duke of
Wellington

This is a supply chain process improvement methodology developed by the Supply Chain Council and its members from 1996 onwards.

The model seeks to improve individual company competitiveness by methodically examining the elements of its supply chain. It does this by using in-house teams, guided by mentors, to disassemble and compare its procedures and performance with its business comparators. The model follows a staged or phased approach, comprehensively addressing supply chain processes from the supplier's supplier through to the customer's customer. Typical sequences of activities involved with a SCOR project are outlined below:

Establishing the need and preparatory steps:

- The recognition of the need for supply chain improvement within a company.
- Creating company wide support for supply chain improvement but in particular senior management support.
- Building a core team to drive the process: an evangelist to guide the process, an executive sponsor to support the project at board level, a steering committee and a design committee.
- Create a project charter, which outlines the scope and objectives of the project.

Create a business context summary (the company's current state); this would include:

- Perform a strategic appraisal. This would look at the company's goals and mission. How and where the company positions itself

in its markets. How it compares with its competitors and identifies issues that are critical to the company's success.

- Perform a financial appraisal. This will include reviewing the
balance sheet and profit and loss accounts.
- Consider the organisational structure of the company. Is the
business organised by products, by geography or some other
method.
- Appraise the markets that are serviced and the types of product
that are demanded.

Establish your performance gap

- Select measures (metrics) by which to assess your company's
performance. Choose measures that have relevance to: customer value, internal performance measures like profit, and
measures that relate to shareholders e.g. dividends. Measures
are set-out on scorecards (analysis sheets).
- Collect data on performance measures chosen for both the
company and competitors.
- Using the data, benchmark the company against its comparators.
- Assess the importance of each benchmark in relation to the
markets and their relative importance (rank them).
- Using the data collected identify where the company's performance falls below par and estimate the potential value of
matching or meeting industry standard and best performers.

Work out why you have the performance gaps

- Map out the 'AS IS' supply chain, in terms of geography of
operations, planning processes and material flows.
- Map out the work, material and information flows between the
various individuals and companies in the supply chain using
flow charts. Analyse transactions using methods like 'staple
your-self to…' exercises.

- Identify weaknesses, duplications or misalignments in the information, work and materials flows using methods like root cause analysis and brainstorming.
- Assess the process efficiency of existing transactions and identify weaknesses, like duplication, missing links, unclear responsibility, poor documents etc.

Define improvement projects

- Rationalise the results of brainstorming and root cause analysis into a manageable number of improvement projects.
- Define the projects and prioritise by their costs and estimated net benefit.
- Set up project teams to run with the projects.
- Identify 'best practice' methods to inform project teams.

Implementation and reporting

- Implement the improvements identified using a project implementation method such as Define, Measure, Analyse, Improve and Control (DMAIC).
- Results are compared on the scorecards.
- Performance gaps are re-assessed.
- Provide feedback to project teams and the company in general.
- Redefine projects to tackle performance gaps that still exist.

Purchasing Terms

Lean terms and acronyms

Activity ratio	The sum of individual process times divided by the lead time. This measure indicates process efficiency.
Andons	Visual signals to indicate the status of a process or a machine. Red = Process stopped requiring attention, Yellow = Routine maintenance or changeover required, Green = normal operation.
As-Is	The existing processes and systems.
Autonomation	Machine or process programmed to stop when a defective product is produced.
Bump-back	Helping the next person upstream or downstream in the process cell.
C&A	Complete an accurate, normally given as a percentage.
CS	Current state is the steps used to complete the process at the present moment in time. Sometimes called the As-Is state.
CT	Cycle time - The time it takes to do one repetition of a task, from start to start.
Empowerment	Giving staff responsibility, authority and accountability for a task or process. Leads to 'self-directing' teams.
FMEA	Failure Modes and Effect Analysis. Method for identifying potential sources of failure and likely effect of their occurrence. Ideally used in product development.

FSM	Future state map or 'To Be' state. The ideal way of manufacturing identified by the company.
Gemba	Literally meaning 'real place', is the place were value is added.
Genchi genbutsu	Solving problems at the source not from behind desks.
Hansei	Relentless reflection.
Heijunka	Sometimes called level loading or mixed level loading. This is the smoothing of production to meet customer requirements.
Ishikawa diagram	Sometimes called a fishbone diagram. Used to identify cause and effect particularly with reference to defects.
Jidoka	Human intervention in an automated process, for example a machine or process is stopped when a defect is identified.
Jishu kanri	voluntary participation
Kaikaku	Radical change
Kaizen	A philosophy of continuous incremental improvement.
Kaizen event	A cross-functional team problem solving activity.
Kanban.	Meaning signboard. A production system which relies upon downstream process to signal the need to replenish resources. Systems tend to rely upon bin and tickets.
Karoshi	Death from overwork.
MBPM	Metrics based process mapping.
Muda	Waste
Mura	Unevenness
NNVA	Necessary Non Value Added.
NVA	Non Value Added.
PDCA	Plan Do Check Act (Deming cycle)

Pitch	The time it take to produce 1 kanban pack / takt time
Poka yoke	An error proofing system for eliminating defects
Seiketsu	Standardize
Seiri	Sort
Seiso	Shine
Seiton	Put in place order.
Shitsuke	Sustain
Set up	Changeover. The time it takes to change equipment or staff onto a new operation.
Single piece flow	Workers only work on one unit at a time and only single units move from process to process.
Standardised	Standardizing work procedures or instructions
Taylorism	Term used for scientific management practices named after Frederick Taylor.
To-Be	The desired state of processes and systems.
TT	Takt Time - The speed at which work must be processed to achieve the customer delivery or a pace process
VS	Value Stream - Activities necessary to get the product to the supplier
VNM	Value Network Mapping
VSM	Value Stream Map - A diagram of all the processes steps required to transform a customer order into a successful customer delivery.

Commonly used acronyms

3PL	Third Party Logistics
ABC	Activity Based Costing
ABCM	Activity Based Cost Management
ADD	Anti-Dumping Duty
ALAP	As Late As Possible
APS	Advanced Production Scheduling
ASL	Approved Supplier List
ATO	Assemble To Order
ATP	Available To Promise
BACS	Bankers Automated Clearing Service
BATNA	Best Alternative To Negotiated Agreement
BOM	Bill Of Materials
BPR	Business Process Re-engineering
CAPEX	CAPital Expenditure
CBA	Cost Benefit Analysis
CCOR	Customer Chain Operations Reference model
CFM	Continuous Flow Manufacturing
CIP	Continuous Improvement Programme
CIPS	Chartered Institute of Purchasing and Supply
CLM	Career Limiting Move
COB	Close Of Business
CPA	Contract Price Adjustment
CPB	Conducting Personal Business
CPC	Customs Procedure Code
CPEoD	Cross Price Elasticity of Demand
CPFR	Collaborative Planning Forecasting Replenishment
CPM	Critical Path Method
CPOF	Capacity Planning using Overall Factors
CRM	Customer Relationship Management
CRP	Capacity Requirements Planning
CSO	Central Statistics Office
DCOR	Design Chain Operations Reference model
DFM	Design For Manufacture

DRP	Distribution Requirements Planning
EBQ	Economic Batch Quantity
EDI	Electronic Data Interchange
EIC	European Information Centre
EoI	Expression of Interest
EMAS	Eco Management and Audit System
EMS	Environmental Management System
EORI	Economic Operator Registration Identification
ERP	Enterprise Resource Planning
FAS	Final Assembly Schedule
FCL	Full Container Load
FIFO	First In First Out
FM	Facilities Management
FPO	Firm Planned Order
GIGO	Garbage in Garbage out
GRN	Goods Received Note
GSP	General System of Preferences
HID	High Initial Demand
IPR	Intellectual Property Rights
IRR	Internal Rate of Return
ITT	Invitation To Tender
JIT	Just in Time
KPI	Key performance indicator
LC	Letter of Credit
LCL	Less than Container Load
LDs	Liquidated damages
LIFO	Last In First Out
LL	Less (savings) Later
LoL	Limit of Liability
MEAT	Most Economically Advantageous Tender
MF	More (savings) Faster
MPC	Manufacturing Planning and Control
MPL	Materials, Purchasing and Logistics
MPandL	Materials Planning and Logistics
MPS	Master Production Schedule

MRO	Maintenance, Repairs and Operating
MRP	Materials Requirements Planning
MRP2	Manufacturing Requirements Planning
MTO	Make To Order
MTS	Make To Stock
MPV	Material Price Variance
NPV	Net Present Value
NVE	Non Variable Element
OEM	Original Equipment Manufacturer
OJEU	Official Journal of the European Union
OGC	Office of Government Commerce
OPEX	OPerational EXpenditure
OTIF	On Time In Full
PAC	Production Activity Control
PED	Price Elasticity of Demand
PEST	Political Economic Social Technological
PI	Perpetual Inventory
PIN	Prior Information Notice
PMO	Project Management Organisation
PO	Purchase Order
POD	Proof Of Delivery
POQ	Periodic Order Quantities
PPB	Part Period Balancing
PPM	Parts Per Million
PQQ	Pre-Qualification Questionnaire
PTN	Post Tender Negotiations
QCDSM	Quality, Cost, Delivery, Safety, Moral
RBWA	Routing By Walk About
RCCP	Rough Cut Capacity Plan
RFI	Request For information
RFQ	Request For Quotation
RFT	Request For Tender
ROP	Re-Order Point
SAMI	Supplier Assistance in Managing Inventory
SCAN	Strategic Creative Analysis

SCE	Supply Chain Excellence
SCM	Supply Chain Management
SGandA	Selling, General and Administrative expenses
SKU	Stock Keeping Unit
SLA	Service Level Agreement
SME	Small to Medium Enterprise
SMED	Single Minute Exchange of Die
SMI	Supplier Managed Inventory
SOP	Start Of Production
SoR	Statement of Requirements
SoW	Statement (Scope) of Work
SRM	Supply Resource Management
SRM	Supplier Relationship Management
SWAG	Super Wild Ass Guess
SWOT	Strengths Weakness Opportunities Threats
TAC	Total Annual Cost
TDABC	Time Driven Activity Based Costing
TCO	Total Cost of Ownership
TOC	Theory Of Constraints
TPM	Total Preventative Maintenance
TPOP	Time-Phased Order Point
TQM	Total Quality Management
UPC	Universal Product Code
VA	Value Analysis
VE	Value Engineering
VFM	Value For Money
VOP	Variation Of Price
VMI	Vendor Managed Inventory
VSM	Value Stream Mapping
WIP	Work In Progress

Quality acronyms

Anova	Analysis Of Variance
AOQL	Average Output Quality Level / Limit
APQP	Advance Product Quality Planning
AQL	Acceptable Quality Level
CAR	Corrective Action Report
CE	Conformite Europeenne
CPI	Continuous Process Improvement
CoC	Certificate of Conformity
CoQ	Cost of Quality
CSP	Continuous Sampling Plan
DFMEA	Design Failure Mode Effects Analysis
ECN	Engineering Change Note
ECO	Engineering Change Order
ECR	Engineering Change Request
ELF	Early Life Failure
FMA	Failure Mode Analysis
FMEA	Failure Mode Effects Analysis
FTA	Fault Tree Analysis
HALT	Highly Accelerated Life Test
HASA	Highly Accelerated Stress Analysis
HASS	Highly Accelerated Stress Screening
ISR	Initial Sample Report
KPC	Key Product Characteristic
KQI	Key Quality Indicators
LSL	Lower Specification Limit
MDS	Material Data Sheets
MTBF	Mean Time Before Failure
NCR	Non-Conformance Report
NCN	Non-Conformance Note
NDT	Non-Destructive Testing
PCAN	Problem Corrective Action Notice
PCR	Process Change Request
PEI	Product Engineering Instruction

PFMEA	Process Failure Mode Effects Analysis
PPAP	Production Part Approval Process
PPM	Parts Per Million
PTR	Performance Test Report
PSW	Product Sample Warrant
PSW	Part Submission Warrant
QA	Quality Assurance
QADF	Quality Assurance Document File
QC	Quality Control
QM	Quality Management
QMS	Quality Management System
RCA	Root Cause Analysis
SCAR	Supplier Corrective Action Report
SPC	Statistical Process Control
SQAM	Supplier Quality Assurance Manual
SQFN	Supplier Quality Failure Note
SQI	Supplier Quality Improvement
TPM	Total Productive Maintenance
TQM	Total Quality Management
TS	Technical Specification
Test Certs	Chemical and mechanical certificates
UCL	Upper Control Limit
WI	Work Instructions
ZD	Zero Defects

Purchasing and office speak

Above board	Legal, honest and open.
Acluistic	Clueless.
Action	A task to be completed.
Allocation	A process of reserving on hand stock to jobs or customer orders.
Alpha geek	Head of IT.
Assmosis	Absorbtion of success by sucking up.
Audit trail	A process of following system or paper evidence showing what processes and functions were carried out and by whom.
B2B	Business To Business
Backdoor	Devious or unethical.
Backflush	Stock automatically subtracted from stock records based upon theoretical usage.
Back of a fag packet	Informal, off the cuff planning.
Back to back	A deal where the customers terms and conditions are passed onto your supplier.
Bait and switch	Offering low price items that turn out to be unavailable.
Ball park figure	A rough or approximate figure given as guidance to the final price / cost.
Bandwidth	somebodies physical and mental capability.
Bangalored	Offshored.
Bells and whistles	Non-essential additions.
Bench marking	Comparing your business performance with that of other similar companies.
Best practice	Rather nebulous management consultant speak meaning the most effective method based on experience rather than theory but often taken as the latest management fad.
Blamestorming	A meeting to find a scapegoat.
Boiler plate	A standard clause used on all contracts.

Boiler room	A sales organization with dubious practices.
Brainstorming	A group exercise to generate ideas.
Betamaxed	An inferior product but better marketed.
Bring to the table	What offers are brought to a negotiation.
Bucket	A period of time used to groups demands for processing purposes.
Change management	A process of guiding a company through internal or external changes.
Chinese wall	Procedures to guard information.
Competitive dialogue procedure	preliminary discussions held to establish whether a supplier is suitable to proceed to formal tendering procedure.
Concession	A controlled deviation from the specified quality.
Consignment stock	Stock under the control of the buyer but still owned by the seller. The stock is only paid for when used.
Cost down	Price reduction
Critical path	A sequence of events where a delay at any point will cause a delay in the whole program.
Cyberslacking	Wasting company time surfing the internet. I knew an quality manager who was king cyberslacker, he used to play solitaire for about 2 or 3 hours a day. Hi John.
Deceptionist	A reception who stalls or blocks incoming calls with a sweet smile.
Delegatorship	A department where the manager cannot make a decision.
Duck shuffler	Someone who disrupts your work when you have got all your ducks in a row.
Due diligence	Thoroughness required to ensure correct business decisions are made. Usually applied to business acquisitions.

Dunnage	Waste material used as protective packaging.
Enail	An email sent for the purpose of putting something in writing generally to pass the blame onto someone else and copied to senior staff.
Evaluation Criteria	EU requirement that selection criteria are transparent and are known in advance by bidders.
Exploding offer	A time limited offer.
Fishing expedition	Searching for information to support your position without any clear leads.
Free stock	Stock on hand, not allocated to a job or sales order.
Framework agreement	Term used in EU procurement directive for 'agreements with providers which set out terms and conditions under which specific purchases (call-offs) can be made throughout the term of the agreement'. O.G.C.
Gatekeeper	Someone, usually a PA or reception who controls access to decision makers.
Gazump	To increase the price of something after an agreement has been made.
GL code	A general ledger code is a way of recording costs.
Goldbricker	Someone who works hard at looking valuable.
Heads of agreement	A document, which often precedes formal legal agreements, which outlines the main issues, goals and intentions of the parties.
Heads-up	An early warning of something.
Kitting	Picking and grouping items from stock to meet a released works or customer order.

Lead time	The time it takes for the supplier to deliver from receipt of order.
Leverage	To use a resource or power to get a better deal.
Low ball	A very low quote, sometimes used to remove competitors.
Malicious obedience	Following a boss's instructions to the letter knowing failure is likely.
Mark your card	An early warning of something.
Matrix management	Staff are assigned to work on multiple projects and report multiple managers.
Method Statement	Questions submitted to a supplier seeking clarification of how they intend to complete the contract.
Metric	A standard for measuring performance.
On cost	Additional costs.
Open tenders	Tenders that aren't restricted and open to all.
Paradigm	Management consultant speak for model.
Pay cycle	All the steps from raising a purchasing requisition through to the payment to the supplier.
Pegging	A method of tracing the demand for a part back to the source of the demand.
Prime (Main) contractor	The party who has contract with the buyer and who is responsible for its completion of the entire job or project.
Putting to bed	To close a deal.
Revenue case	Business justification for spending money on tooling or other non-direct material.
Routing	A sequence of operations needed to manufacture a part.
Seagull manager	A manager who flies in, makes a lot of noise, craps on everything and then leaves.
Screamer	Very urgent requirement.

Service level agreement	A document that sets out the agreed requirements and standards to be provided by the supplier.
Specification	Details of the quality, performance and service that the buyer expects or the seller is offering.
Stress puppy	An over-anxious person. Often seeks sympathy.
Terms and Conditions	Legally binding rules that govern the contract along with the rights and responsibilities of the parties.
Tender	Essentially a quote, but usually provides much more information than just the price. Tenders usually include details of how the supplier intends to execute a complex work, services or supply.
Traceability	The ability to follow a product or information through every step in a chain of processes. The usual methodology of auditors.
Type 1 error	Decision to reject a something when it is acceptable.
Type 2 error	Decision to accept something when it is unacceptable.
Wiggle room	The amount of flexibility in a price.
Win-Win	An outcome where both parties gain or at least think they do.
World Class	Normally used to describe a company with the best business practices, both Enron and IBM where probably described as World Class at some point.
Zero sum game	A situation where if one person wins

Economics terms for buyers

Adverse selection	The making of bad choices due to poor information. Sellers may choose to withhold relevant information from buyers.
Amortization	Often used when buying tooling. Costs are spread over a period of time.
Appreciation	Rise in the value of an asset or currency.
Arbitrage	Buying in one market and simultaneously selling an identical asset in another.
Asymmetric information	One of the transacting parties has better information than the other, can lead to adverse selection.
Backwardation	Spot prices for an asset are higher than the futures market. May occur when there is an immediate bottleneck in supply.
Barriers to entry	Factors restricting new competitors entering a market including: economies of scale, patents or control of key resources.
Bear market	A market characterised by falling pricing.
Bull market	A market characterised by rising prices.
Cartel	An agreement by two or more companies in the same industry to co-operate in the fixing prices.
Commoditisation	The process by which a product becomes accepted as a standard and widely traded.
Commodity	A product with a degree of homogeneity or standardisation.
Complimentary goods	The demand for 2 or more goods is positively related eg TVs and DVD players.
Contango	Spot prices for a commodity are lower than futures prices (this is the normal state because of the interest costs).
Deflation	Falls in the general price level.
Depreciation	The fall in the price of an asset or currency.

Disintermediation	Cutting out intermediate sellers.
Dumping	Selling at below the average cost usually a target export market.
Economies of scale	Average costs fall as output increases. The rationale for bulk buying and quantity price breaks.
Effective demand	The quantity of goods a buyer is both willing and able to buy at a particular price.
Externality	An economic consequence not reflected in the price for example pollution.
Inflation	Increases in the general price level.
Non-price competition	Companies compete through methods such as product differentiation and advertising rather than by reducing prices.
Opportunity cost	All the costs sacrificed in acquiring something not just the money spent on it, typically the foregone opportunities of acquiring something else.
Price discrimination	Charging different customers different prices for the same product.
Price elasticity	The responsiveness of demand to changes in price.
Public goods	Things that must be consumed by everybody in society or nobody at all. For example clean air.
Queuing	Customers forced to wait for supplies when demand exceeds supply. Some suppliers are able to create queuing by restricting supply, usually as a tool to increase prices.
Substitute goods	Goods that are essentially interchangeable.
Sunk costs	Costs that cannot be reversed or recovered

Legal Terms

Ab initio	From the start. For example an agreement may be invalid ab initio if the parties do not have the right status to contract.
Ad valorem	According to value.
Bona fide	Good faith. Someone who is genuine for example a bona fide seller would not hide any known defect in their title to the property.
Caveat emptor	Let the buyer beware. A common law rule that places the responsibility for verifying the quality of goods on the buyer.
Ceteris paribus	all other things being remaining constant.
Consensus ad idem	Agreement on an idea. Parties need to be in agreement to form a valid contract.
De facto	By deed.
De minimis non curat lex	The law does not concern itself with trifles. It is a common law rule that the law will not concern itself with minor matters.
Ergo	Therefore.
Escrow	Money or documents delivered to a neutral third party to be delivered to the other party upon performance of a condition.
Et cetera	And the rest.
Ex gratia	Out of grace. Something given without obligation on the part of the giver or receiver.
Ex parte	On behalf of. An action taken on behalf of another.
Facta, non verba	Actions, not words.
Inter alia	Among other things.
Ipso factor	By the fact itself.
Lien	This is a non-consensual form of security recognised in the common law e.g. an un-

	paid seller main retain the buyer's property as security for payment.
Mala fides	Bad faith.
Modus operendi	Method of operating.
Nemo dat quod non habet	You cannot give what you haven't got.
Non compos mentis	Not of sound mind.
Non est factum	Not my act. For example a forged signature.
Pacta sunt servanda	Contracts must be honoured.
Per annum	Per year.
Per capita	By heads.
Per se	Through itself.
Prima facie	At first sight.
Pro forma	As a matter of form.
Pro rata	For the rate. The same proportion applies.
Quantum meruit	What it merits.
Quid pro quo	Something for something. For example, consideration in a contract.
Re	In the matter of
Res ipsa loquitur	The matter speaks for itself.
Res perit domino	The owner of property bears the risk of its damage.
Sic	Thus.
Uberrima fides	Utmost good faith. Usually applies to insurance contracts.
Ultra vires	Beyond the legal authority.

References

Bibliography

"From the moment I picked your book up until I laid it down, I was convulsed with laughter. Someday I intend reading it." Groucho Marx

Allright, A.D., Oliver, R.W. Buying Goods and Services. The Chartered Institute of Purchasing and Supply (1993).

Baily, P.J.H. Purchasing and Supply Management, Fifth Edition, Chapman and Hall (1987).

Bolstorff, Peter and Rosenbaum, Robert. Supply Chain Excellence, 2nd Edition, Amacom (2007)

Bradgate, Robert, White, Fidelma and Fennell Steven. Commercial Law

Brainyquote www.brainyquote.com

Cheshire, Fifoot and Furmston's - Law of Contract, Twelth Edition. Butterworth and Co (Publishers) Ltd. (1991).

Deming, W. Edwards. Out of the Crisis

Dobler, Donald W. , Lee, Lamarr, Jr. Burt, David N. Purchasing and Materials Management, Fourth Edition. McGraw Hill (1984).

Farmer, David and van Weele, Arjan J. Gower Handbook of Purchasing Management. Second Edition. Gower Publishing Limited (1995).

Galford, Robert M. and Drapeau, Anne Seibold - The Trusted Leader. Free Press; 1 edition (2002)

Goldratt, Eliyahu M. : Critical Chain, North River Press (1997)

Giles, R.S., Capel, J.W., Finance and Accounting. 3rd Edition. MacMillan 1994.

Herzberg, F., Mausner, B., Snyderman, B.B.The Motivation to Work (1959)

Harvey P. Modern Economics, 4th Edition (1983).

Hiroyuki Hirano -JIT Implementation Manual: v. 3: The Complete Guide to Just-in-time Manufacturing. Productivity Press; 2 edition (30 April 2009)

Johnson Spencer - Who Moved My Cheese: An Amazing Way to Deal with Change in Your Work and in Your Life. Vermilion; Reprinted Ed edition (4 Mar 1999)

Kaplan, Robert S. and Anderson, Steven R. Activity-Based Costing

Karrass, Chester L. Give and Take. Harper Business (1993)

Kennedy, Gavin. Profitable Negotiation. Orion Business Books (1999).
    www.greenprocurementcode.co.uk]

Krafcik, John. "Triumph of the Lean Production System," Sloan Management
    Review (1988)

Kraljic, Peter. Purchasing must become Supply Management, HBR Sept-Oct 1983

Liker, J.. The Toyota Way: 14 Management Principles from the World's Greatest
    Manufacturer. McGraw-Hill. (2004)

Maslow, A. H. Motivation and Personality (1970)

Onken, William and Wass, Donald - 'Management Time: Who's got the monkey',
    Harvard Business Review (1974).

Pease, Allan. Body Language. Sheldon Press 1984.

Porter, Michael E. Competitive Advantage: Creating and Sustaining Superior
    Performance. Free Press; 1 edition (June 1, 1998)

Production and Inventory Control Handbook – Greene Time-Driven
    www.greenprocurementcode.co.uk

Rose, F.D. – Statutes on contract and tort. 3rd Edition. Blackstone Press Ltd (1991).

Saunders, Malcolm - Strategic Purchasing and Supply Chain Management. Pitman
    (1994)

Scottish Public Procurement Toolkit. www.scotland.gov.uk

Thornton, Paul B. - Be The Leader, Make The Difference – Griffin Publishing
    Group (2001).

Thomas E. Vollman, William L.Berry, D. Clay Whybark, F.Robert Jacobs. Manufac-
    turing Planning and Control Systems for Supply Chain Management. Fifth
    Edition. McGraw Hill (2007).

Transparency International - http://www.transpare

Table of Cases

"The secret of creativity is knowing how to hide your sources".
Albert Einstein

Lightning Source UK Ltd.
Milton Keynes UK
UKOW031253080212

186888UK00001B/44/P